Managing Technology Entrepreneurship and Innovation

Managing Technology Entrepreneurship and Innovation is the first textbook for non-business-based entrepreneurship courses, focused on students with a background in science and technology. Its comprehensive, rigorous and yet accessible approach originates from the authors' considerable experience mentoring students as they turn their technological ideas into real-life business ventures.

The text is separated into three parts, providing a roadmap for successful entrepreneurial projects:

- Part I focuses on how to create your venture, turning technology into businesses and how to link together entrepreneurship and innovation.
- Part II shows you how to grow your venture and make it profitable, looking at the early development of academic spin-outs and how to adapt your technology to the customers' needs.
- Part III takes you through the day-to-day running of your business: whether to adopt a contingency or contextual approach; how to develop new products and services; and alternative options for growth.

With a wide range of practical steps, lists of things to consider and guidelines on how to turn your technology-based ideas into a successful business, this text will be essential for all non-business students who need to understand entrepreneurship, management and innovation. It will also prove a useful introduction to all Masters-level students taking these subjects in business schools.

Paul Trott is Professor of Innovation Management at the University of Portsmouth, UK.

Dap Hartmann is Associate Professor of Innovation Management and Entrepreneurship at Delft University of Technology, The Netherlands.

Patrick van der Duin is Assistant Professor of Innovation Management and Foresight at Delft University of Technology, The Netherlands.

Victor Scholten is Assistant Professor of Technology-based Entrepreneurship at Delft University of Technology, The Netherlands.

Roland Ortt is Associate Professor of Technology Management at Delft University of Technology, The Netherlands.

Managing Technology Entrepreneurship and Innovation

Paul Trott, Dap Hartmann,
Patrick van der Duin,
Victor Scholten and Roland Ortt

Routledge
Taylor & Francis Group

LONDON AND NEW YORK

First published 2016
by Routledge
2 Park Square, Milton Park, Abingdon, Oxon OX14 4RN

and by Routledge
711 Third Avenue, New York, NY 10017

Routledge is an imprint of the Taylor & Francis Group, an informa business

© 2016 Paul Trott, Dap Hartmann, Patrick van der Duin, Victor Scholten and Roland Ortt

British Library Cataloguing in Publication Data
A catalogue record for this book is available from the British Library

Library of Congress Cataloging in Publication Data
Trott, Paul.
  Managing technology entrepreneurship and innovation/Paul Trott, Dap Hartmann,
  Patrick van der Duin, Victor Scholten and Roland Ortt.
  pages cm
  Includes bibliographical references and index.
  1. Technological innovations – Economic aspects. 2. High technology industries –
  Management. 3. Entrepreneurship. 4. Intellectual property. 5. New business
  enterprises – Management. I. Title.
  HC79.T4T76 2016
  658 – dc23
  2015021495

ISBN: 978-0-415-67721-9 (hbk)
ISBN: 978-0-415-67722-6 (pbk)
ISBN: 978-1-315-71350-2 (ebk)

Typeset in Bembo
by Florence Production Ltd, Stoodleigh, Devon, UK
Printed and bound in Great Britain by
Ashford Colour Press Ltd, Gosport, Hampshire

Contents

Figures

Images

Tables

Preface

The purpose of this book is to provide students with a text that can help them improve their entrepreneurial skills and enable them to be more successful at turning their technology into a business venture.

After many years of helping students start their own business and teaching many more aspects of entrepreneurship and innovation management, we felt we should combine our thoughts, ideas and experience into a single volume. For us, entrepreneurship is more than simply starting up a new business. It is a process that involves a combination of different skills. Many of those skills are teachable, and we have taught them and seen students develop their own business ideas into sizeable businesses at Delft University of Technology (TU Delft). Moreover, many of the skills required in entrepreneurship and innovation management are useful within the wider sphere of corporate life. Indeed, Howard Stevenson from Harvard Business School views entrepreneurship as a mode of management that differs from traditional management; we too subscribe to this view.

Our experience is with technology-based ideas and ventures, and these are what we focus on within this book. This is not to say that the ideas presented will not be applicable to those buying and running a corner store or for someone contemplating setting up a kite-surfing retail business. They will almost certainly be equally relevant to all business start-ups. But, to those of you studying science-, technology-, engineering- and mathematics-based courses, this book is targeted at you. We offer here a wide range of practical steps, lists of things to consider and guidelines on how to turn your technology-based ideas into a business.

Part I

Creating the venture

The purpose of creating a start-up business is the intent of profiting financially. Although there are many laudable organizations established for other reasons, this book deals with turning technology into businesses. Chapter 1 sets the scene for this book and links together entrepreneurship and innovation. The cyclic model of innovation provides a useful framework for viewing technology-based small businesses. The second chapter examines how we can develop useful knowledge about the future to help improve the chances of success for our start-up. We can predict, analyse and explore the future by applying methods of futures research and taking into account certain principles and concepts. Chapter 3 illustrates how the starting place for many technology-based businesses is the development of a solution. So this chapter looks at problem-solving techniques. The final chapter in Part I of this book shows how start-ups need to frame their opportunity in terms of a venture that will make money.

Part I

Creating the venture

1 How entrepreneurship and technological innovation are bound together

Entrepreneurship is all about stepping into the unknown and breaking away from the familiar. For some people, this is less of a challenge than for others. This can be for a wide variety of reasons, including background and parental influence. Across Europe, unlike in the USA, it remains true that more graduates would sooner work for Siemens, Shell or Nokia than start their own business. This picture, however, is changing, and the number of people interested in starting their own business is rising rapidly. Furthermore, an injection of entrepreneurship, by which creative people are encouraged to strike out and develop new products or services, is important to the financial health of all organizations. Yet, fundamental questions appear as major obstacles: Where is the opportunity? How do I capitalize on it? What resources do I need? How do I gain control over them?

For many, the entrepreneur and entrepreneurship are best captured by George Bernard Shaw's famous quote (today, 'man' would be replaced with 'person' to include men and women): 'The reasonable man adapts himself to the world. The unreasonable one persists in trying to adapt the world to himself. Therefore, all progress depends on unreasonable men' (1903).[1] This captures the essence of entrepreneurship – that it is about change, about doing something different. Often, this change will be met with resistance, and it is the entrepreneur who will persist and get things done. Without such people, improvements are less likely.

But what does *entrepreneurial* mean? Managers describe entrepreneurship using such terms as innovative, flexible, dynamic, risk-taking, creative, and growth oriented. The popular press, on the other hand, often defines the term as starting and operating new ventures. That view is reinforced by the alluring success of such upstarts as SAP, Dyson and TomTom.

Neither approach to a definition of entrepreneurship is precise or prescriptive enough for managers who wish to be more entrepreneurial. Everybody wants to be innovative, flexible and creative. But, for every SAP, Dyson and TomTom, there are thousands of new restaurants, clothing stores, and consulting firms that presumably have tried to be innovative, to grow, and to show other characteristics that are entrepreneurial – but have failed.

In this book, we want to reinforce the idea that entrepreneurship is not just about starting a new business. Our focus on innovation management underscores this point. We are all aware of many medium and small businesses that consistently develop new products and markets and also grow at rates far exceeding national averages. For example, Subocean Group grew an incredible 237 per cent in 2009, increasing its turnover from €1.9 million to €77 million. Subocean runs power cables along the sea floor, from offshore wind farms to substations on land (Fast Track 100, 2010). Moreover, we're all aware of many of the largest corporations – BMW, AstraZeneca and Ericsson are just a few of the best known – that make a practice of innovating, taking risks and showing creativity. And they continue to expand.

Entrepreneurship and innovation

In the US, the subject of entrepreneurship has been taught in business schools for more than 50 years. The content of these courses clearly varies, but many of them study growing a small business into a large one. When it comes to innovation management, this has not been generally studied, and, until recently, there were far fewer courses available. This is changing. Yet, in Europe, we have a long history of teaching innovation management but not entrepreneurship (Tidd *et al.*, 1997; Trott, 1998). This is changing, and entrepreneurship is a rapidly growing subject in universities across Europe. As an academic field, entrepreneurship has flourished. In 1983, Babson held the first research conference on entrepreneurship, with thirty-seven papers presented. In 2014, there were over 1,000 papers presented. Entrepreneurship now has its own division within the academy of management.

In Europe, there is recognition of the need, and a considerable emphasis, especially within the technical universities, on trying, to understand how entrepreneurship and innovation can help create the new technology-intensive businesses of tomorrow. Moreover, it is the recognition of the entrepreneur's desire to change things that is so important within innovation. We will see later that the role of an entrepreneur is central to innovation management.

Trying to uncover separate definitions for innovation and entrepreneurship is increasingly a purely academic exercise. The main traits associated with entrepreneurship such as growth, flexibility and creativity are also desirable traits for innovation. Theorists and practioners alike recognize that these constructs are close relatives, or two sides of the same coin. We will now briefly outline the roots of these terms and their linkage.

Traditionally, it is Jean-Baptiste Say who is credited for having coined the word and advanced the concept of the entrepreneur, but in fact it was Richard Cantillon who first introduced the term in *Essai*, written in 1730. Cantillon divided society into two principal classes – fixed-income wage earners and non-fixed-income earners. Entrepreneurs, according to Cantillon, are non-fixed-income earners who pay known costs of production, but earn uncertain incomes; hence, it was Cantillon who saw the entrepreneur as a risk-taker, whereas Say predominately considered the entrepreneur to be a planner (1730/1952).

A few years later, in the 1776 thought-provoking book *The Wealth of Nations*, Adam Smith explained clearly that it was not the benevolence of the baker but self-interest that motivated him to provide bread (1776/2005). From Smith's standpoint, entrepreneurs were the economic agents who transformed demand into supply for profits. In 1848, the famous philosopher and economist John Stuart Mill described entrepreneurship as the founding of a private enterprise. This encompassed the risk-takers, the decision-makers and the individuals who desire wealth by managing limited resources to create new business ventures.

Although entrepreneurship may have a long history, the term entrepreneur continued to be used to define a businessman until the arrival of Joseph Schumpeter. It was his work in the 1930s that made the clear linkage between the terms innovation and entrepreneurship. He considered entrepreneurship as influencing growth in the economy. It is something that disrupts the market equilibrium, or 'circular flow'. Its essence is 'innovation'. He writes that: 'the carrying out of new combinations we call enterprise; the individuals whose function is to carry them out we call entrepreneurs' (1934, p. 74). After Schumpter's work, most economists (and many others) have accepted his identification of entrepreneurship with innovation (see Kilby, 1971 for a summary of the term 'entrepreneur').

According to Schumpeter, economic development is the result of three types of factor (Schumpeter, 1939/1964, p. 61):

1 external factors, such as demand by government (changes in legislation, defence orders);
2 factors of growth or gradual changes in economic life that are accomplished through day-to-day activities and adjustments;
3 'the outstanding fact in the economic history of capitalist society', innovation.

For Schumpeter, entrepreneurs are galvanized into action under the following conditions (Schumpeter, 1961, p. 214):

1 the existence of new possibilities more advantageous from the private standpoint – a necessary condition;
2 limited access to these possibilities because of personal qualifications and external circumstances;
3 an economic situation that allows tolerably reliable calculations.

For Schumpeter and his direct disciples (Duijn, 1977; Mandel, 1978, 1980, 1981; Freeman, 1979; Mensch and West Internationales Institut für Management und Verwaltung, 1979; Kleinknecht, 1981), innovation is the chief force in what he calls 'economic evolution'. It is worthy of note that, for Schumpeter, his concept of innovation is broader than some innovation theorists have since argued. For Schumpeter, innovation is not simply the patenting of new inventions; it includes new combinations in organizations, commerce and the market, as well as the creation of new business organizations (Schumpeter, 1961, p. 66, 1939/1964, p. 59). This then may be helpful as we try to consider together the concepts of entrepreneurship and innovation. We also need to recognize a wider definition of innovation that includes more than the hard physical outputs from a traditional science-led institution, such as a technical university (TU), and consider new 'service offerings' as well.

Defining entrepreneurship

For many people, Box 1.1 captures what it is to be an entrepreneur.

Entrepreneurship can be described as a process of action that an entrepreneur undertakes to establish an enterprise. Entrepreneurship is a creative activity. It is the ability to create and build something from practically nothing. It is an ability to see an opportunity where

---

Box 1.1 Penny apples – selling them thrice over

In his autobiography, the Irish entrepreneur Billy Cullen (2003) tells the story of how, as an 8-year-old boy, he demonstrated sharp entrepreneurial skills. In a poverty-stricken area of Dublin, young Billy would buy wooden crates of apples for a shilling and then sell the apples on a Saturday afternoon to the hundreds of local people who would flock to watch their local football team play. This provided Billy with a healthy profit of a shilling if he could sell all the apples. But, his entrepreneurial skills did not stop there. He would then take the wooden apple boxes to the football ground and sell them for a penny to people at the back of the crowds, so that they could stand on the box for a better view. Finally, when the match had finished, Billy would collect up the wooden boxes, break them up and sell them in bundles for firewood.

---

others see chaos, contradiction and confusion. Entrepreneurship is an attitude of mind to seek opportunities, take calculated risks and derive benefits by setting up a venture. It comprises the numerous activities involved in the conception, creation and running of an enterprise. Similarly, an entrepreneur is a person who starts such an enterprise. He searches for change and responds to it. There are a wide variety of definitions for an entrepreneur: Economists view him as a fourth factor of production, along with land, labour and capital. Sociologists feel that certain communities and cultures promote entrepreneurship. The US is often cited as having a culture that supports entrepreneurs. Still others feel that entrepreneurs are innovators who come up with new ideas for products and markets. To put it very simply, an entrepreneur is someone who perceives opportunity, organizes resources needed for exploiting that opportunity and exploits it.

Peter Drucker's classic book *Innovation and Entrepreneurship* was first published in 1985, and it was the first book to present innovation and entrepreneurship as a purposeful and systematic activity. According to Drucker, 'Innovation is the specific function of entrepreneurship', and entrepreneurship, 'is the means by which the entrepreneur either creates new wealth-producing resources or endows existing resources with enhanced potential for creating wealth'.

In this classic book, Drucker focuses on large-scale entrepreneurship, rather than small-business management. Drucker's recurring theme is that good entrepreneurship is usually market-focused and market-driven. Contrary to the belief of many, Drucker says that innovation isn't inspired by a bright idea; rather it 'is organised, systematic, rational work'. Innovation can be mastered and integrated into a company or non-profit organization.

In a study of past and future research on the subject of entrepreneurship, Low and MacMillan (1988) define it as 'the process of planning, organising, operating, and assuming the risk of a business venture'. Risk, particularly willingness to take a risk with one's time and money, is surely a key feature of entrepreneurship. It is the analysis of the role of the individual entrepreneur that distinguishes the study of entrepreneurship from that of innovation management. Howard Stevenson, who developed entrepreneurship teaching at Harvard Business School, defines entrepreneurship as follows: 'Entrepreneurship is the pursuit of opportunity beyond the resources you currently control' (Stevenson, 1983; Stevenson and Gumpert, 1985; Stevenson Jarillo, 1990).

Table 1.1 A process definition of entrepreneurship

Key business dimension	Entrepreneur	Administrator
Strategic orientation	Driven by perception of opportunity	Driven by resources currently controlled
Commitment to opportunity	Quick commitment	Evolutionary with long duration
Commitment process	Multistage with minimal exposure at each stage	Single-stage, with complete commitment upon decision
Control of resources	Episodic use of rent of required resources	Ownership or employment of required resources
Management structure	Flat, with multiple informal networks	Formalized hierarchy
Reward system	Value based & team based	Resource-based individual & promotion oriented

Source: Stevenson (2000)

This definition takes into account both the individual and the society in which the individual is embedded. The individual identifies an opportunity to be pursued, then, as an entrepreneur, must seek the resources from the broader society. Stevenson argues that entrepreneurship activities can be identified as distinct from those of the administrator (see Table 1.1). This is significant, for it recognizes that entrepreneurship can be viewed as a mode of management within a corporation.

Overview of studies of entrepreneurship

The literature on entrepreneurship can be divided into two broad schools focusing on individuals and structure, respectively (e.g. Martinelli, 1994; Thornton 1999). The first seeks to explain the prevalence of entrepreneurs in terms of inborn psychological traits or how special characteristics are formed in certain social groups. The second highlights how social and cultural structures create opportunities for entrepreneurship. Management researchers often emphasize the special influence of organizations and especially prior employment in established firms (Freeman, 1986). This is not surprising; for example, if John has spent 10 years working in an industry where he has learnt about its business model, developed many contacts and friends and uncovered industry secrets, this would seem to be an excellent position from which to start his own new venture. Prior employment within organizations is said to serve three critical functions:

1   it provides opportunities to build confidence, especially in the ability to create new organizations;
2   it provides general industry knowledge and specific information about entrepreneurial opportunities; and
3   it provides social networks and access to critical resources (Audia and Rider, 2005).

A review of the entrepreneurship literature suggests huge differences exist between entrepreneurs and the ventures themselves (Gartner, 1985; Wortman, 1987). Nonetheless, four main perspectives dominate within the field:

1   characteristcs of the individual;
2   the venture they create;
3   the environment in which it is created;
4   the process by which the venture is created.

A generally accepted conceptual framework for describing the creation of new ventures is shown in Figure 1.1. In a wide review of the literature on entrepreneurship, Shane and Venkataraman (2000) argue that entrepreneurship is dependent on the existence, discovery and exploitation of entrepreneurial opportunities. Therefore, the key areas that need to be addressed are as follows:

• How are opportunities created?
• By whom are they created?
• What affects the discovery and creation of opportunities?

The field of entrepreneurship has grown rapidly over the past few decades, and there is now a burgeoning mass of articles and books on the subject. Howard Stevenson and Carlos Jarillo usefully divide this into three main categories: what happens when entrepreneurs act, why they act, and how they act (Stevenson and Jarillo, 1990). This remains a useful overview of the main different streams of research (Figure 1.2).

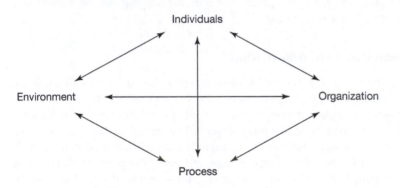

Figure 1.1 A framework for describing new venture creation

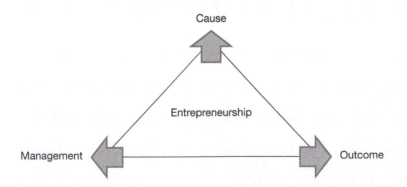

Figure 1.2 The three dimensions of entrepreneurship

The outcomes of entrepreneurship

Within economics, there are two main interpretations of the effects of entrepreneurship. The first, represented by Cole (1968), views entrepreneurship as disrupting the equilibrium and advancing the economy to higher levels and further economic growth. The second, represented by Kirzner (1979), argues that the entrepreneur has superior knowledge of market imperfections that he uses to his advantage to help restore the theoretical equilibrium. The key point here, however, is that, within economics, there is recognition that entrepreneurship is a process distinct from the individual, and it is the activities within the process that lead to change in the economic environment.

In *neoclassical economics*, individuals are assumed to act rationally and maximize their expected utility within an equilibrium framework. Both preferences and action alternatives are therefore seen as given. Action thus becomes choice, and choice merely calculation. It has therefore been argued that neoclassical economics has no real place for entrepreneurs (Baumol, 1968; Bianchi and Henrekson, 2005). Entrepreneurial action will only occur when the economic system is at disequilibrium. This typically happens as a result of exogenous forces such as public research and development (R&D) (Schultz, 1980). The result is a novel framework in which individuals may optimize their utility. As all individuals have access to the same information, entrepreneurs are often characterized as extraordinarily capable or fast at optimizing given problem frameworks (e.g. Caplan, 1999) or extreme in terms of risk-taking propensity (e.g. Kihlstrom and Laffont, 1979). Others use the opportunity cost of time to differentiate individuals in terms of human capital (Becker, 1965; Schultz, 1980). The argument is that the way people have historically allocated their time (i.e. built up entrepreneurial 'human capital') will affect the opportunity cost and, hence, value of entrepreneurship. This affects both the decision to pursue existing opportunities and the decision to search for yet unknown opportunities (Fiet, 1996; Gifford, 2003). Entrepreneurs are still completely rational but make different choices based on extraordinary capacities or acquired human capital.

The causes of entrepreneurship

It is not surprising that there has been a lot of research and many studies within this area. Understanding why some people decide to act would clearly be of interest to all economies wishing to grow. Famous entrepreneurs of the past, including Henry Ford, and more recent entrepreneurs such as Bill Gates provide appealing subjects for study. What is it about such people that makes them successful? Do they have special talents? How are they different to others? These are the questions, and many more like them, that have driven this area of research that has sought to identify personal characteristics of entrepreneurs (see Marcin and Cockrum, 1984, for details of the characteristics of entrepreneurs compared with non-entrepreneurial fellow workers).

Another key stream of enquiry in this area is the personal motivations of entrepreneurs and whether they are linked to environmental characteristics. Sociologist David McClelland's best-selling *The Achieving Society* (1961) pioneered this field. He attributed growth to the need for achievement (n-achievement, sometimes shortened to n-ach) present in the psychological make-up of large parts of the population in those societies. Since this work, many other sociologists have developed this theme. Today, how the environment affects the practice of entrepreneurship has become a large and established body of work. It is clear that environmental factors play a part in developing opportunities for exploitation, and they also provide positive and negative influences on the entrepreneur, such as the availability of finance, legislative framework, etc.

The management of entrepreneurship

This body of work takes a practical view of trying to establish how to be successful and the pitfalls to avoid. It includes, unsurprisingly, many practical guides, as well as many 'how to be successful like me' types of book, especially within the popular literature. In addition, it also has a growing stream that is linked to business strategy, which has focused on how entrepreneurs go about developing and growing their business. This subdivides into two very relevant areas: (1) the different life cycles of a new venture, and (2) the problems encountered by the entrepreneur as the venture matures.

It is on the area of what entrepreneurs do that this book is focused. We wish to provide a useful book for students that can help them improve their entrepreneurial skills and enable them to be more successful at turning their technology into a business venture. Our experience is with technology-based ideas and ventures, and these are what we focus on within this book. For us, entrepreneurship is more than simply starting up a new business. It is a process that involves a combination of different skills. Many of those skills are teachable, and we have taught them and seen students develop their own business ideas into sizeable businesses.

Innovation management

Innovation is one of those words that suddenly seem to be all around us. Firms care about their ability to innovate, on which their future allegedly depends, and many management consultants are busy persuading companies about how they can help them improve their innovation performance. Politicians care about innovation too: how to design policies that stimulate innovation has become a hot topic at various levels of government. The European Commission, for instance, has made innovation policy a central element in its attempt to invigorate the European economy. A large literature has emerged, particularly in recent years, on various aspects of innovation, and many new research units focusing on innovation have been formed (Fagerberg and Verspagen, 2009).

There is extensive scope for examining the way innovation is managed within organizations. Most of us are well aware that good technology can help companies achieve competitive advantage and long-term financial success. However, there is an abundance of exciting new technology in the world, and it is the transformation of this technology into products that is of particular concern to organizations. There are numerous factors to be considered by the organization, but what are these factors and how do they affect the process of innovation? Corporations must be able to adapt and evolve if they wish to survive. Businesses operate with the knowledge that their competitors will inevitably come to the market with a product that changes the basis of competition. The ability to change and adapt is essential to survival. Indeed, Bill Gates reminded us that innovation is the responsibility of firms and their leaders: 'The share price is not something we control. We control innovation, sales and profits' (Rushe and Waples, 2008).

Today, the idea of innovation is widely accepted. It has become part of our culture – so much so, that it verges on becoming a cliché. But even though the term is now embedded in our language, to what extent do we fully understand the concept? Moreover, to what extent is this understanding shared? A scientist's view of innovation may be very different from that of an accountant in the same organization.

There is one organization at present that seems to be able to do no wrong when it comes to innovation and new products. The incredible rise of Apple Inc. (*The Economist*, 2015) puts into context the subject of innovation and new product development. For the past

10 years, Apple has consistently been able to launch new product after new product, each time generating new revenues for the firm and enabling it to grow in new markets. Innovation is at the heart of many companies' activities. But to what extent is this true of all businesses? And how can entrepreneurs ensure that their businesses are innovative and able to develop new products and services? These questions and others will be addressed in this book.

Why the funnel model of innovation is unhelpful

One of the key limitations of current models of innovation is that they still represent variations on the familiar pipeline architecture. In addition, they are not embedded in the strategic issues of company boards and, therefore, remain isolated entities. Equally, the activity of entrepreneurship, although long recognized as a key factor in firm innovation management, is not captured and is inadvertently understated or only implied at best. The approach of this book is to offer a sociotechnical framework that replaces the family of linear concepts by a cyclic alternative: the Cyclic Innovation Model (CIM) (Berkhout *et al.*, 2010). It combines hard and soft sciences, bridges R&D and marketing communities, and helps firms and policymakers to better understand the iterative nature of the innovation process. In a recent article in the *R&D Management* journal, Jeremy Howells (2008) discusses some of the key developments that are currently affecting R&D activity. He identifies the following changing dynamics of R&D:

1   the increasingly distributed and open nature of networked research and innovation;
2   the growth of externally sourced R&D (and, as a consequence, the relative decline in internally generated R&D) within firms;
3   the overcoming of barriers towards the increased productivity and effectiveness of R&D;
4   the continued globalization of R&D, particularly in terms of its spread and reach, associated with R&D offshoring;
5   the relative shift from manufacturing-centred R&D towards more service-oriented R&D.

It would seem that the challenges that lie ahead for R&D will be as significant as those that have been faced in the past. Beyond R&D laboratories, innovation remains poorly understood. The linear model of innovation, from scientific discovery to commercialization in the market, still dominates thinking, not just with the general public, but also within boardrooms and government policy-making departments across our nations. Moreover, this misunderstanding extends beyond the linearity of the process to the characterization of it. For example, there remains a strong belief that innovation is fuelled by serendipity, and that R&D departments are freewheeling places of artistic disorder. Yet, in the large, industrialized firm where R&D is institutionalized, it is fully recognized that invention and creativity emerge from the routine of R&D, and innovation follows under management instruction and control (Pearson, 1983). This is not merely understood but also a requirement. When a firm such as Siemens spends in excess of US$5 billion on R&D annually, its shareholders would rightly expect that this investment is closely managed and its activities monitored. Moreover, a decent return on these R&D investments is expected. R&D must be looked at in the same way as any other investment in the business – the benefits it produces must exceed the costs.

Innovation as a management process

'The fact is coming up with an idea is the least important part of creating something great. The execution and delivery are what's key' (Sergey Brin, co-founder of Google, *The Guardian*, 2009).

The statement by Sergey Brin, co-founder of Google, confirms that we need to view innovation as a management process. The preceding sections have revealed that innovation is not a singular event, but a series of activities that are linked in some way to the others. This may be described as a process and involves:

1   a response to either a need or an opportunity that is context-dependent;
2   a creative effort that, if successful, results in the introduction of novelty;
3   the need for further changes.

Usually, in trying to capture this complex process, the simplification has led to misunderstandings. The simple linear model of innovation can be applied to only a few innovations and is more applicable to certain industries than others. The pharmaceutical industry characterizes much of the technology-push model. Other industries, such as the food industry, are better represented by the market-pull model. For most industries and organizations, innovations are the result of a mixture of the two. Managers working within these organizations have the difficult task of trying to manage this complex process.

The management of innovation requires a new set of skills

Many of the old, traditional approaches to management need to change, and new approaches need to be adopted. Increasingly, managers and those who work for them are no longer in the same location. Gone are the days when managers could supervise the hour-to-hour work of individuals. Often, complex management relationships need to be developed because organizations are trying to produce complex products and services and do so across geographic boundaries. Cross-functional and cross-border task forces often need to be created, and managers have to manage without authority. In these circumstances, individual managers need to work with and influence people who are not their subordinates and over whom they have no formal authority. Frequently, this means leadership must be shared across the team members. An important part of getting work done without authority is having an extensive network of relationships. In today's complex and virtual organizations, managers need information and support from a wide range of individuals (see Box 1.2). To summarize then, new skills are required in the following areas:

* virtual management;
* managing without authority;
* shared leadership;
* building extensive networks.

Technological entrepreneurship: A question of context

Like so many things in life, our perception of something depends upon our vantage point. For us, considering entrepreneurship, this is particularly relevant. Do we wish to consider the individual entrepreneur, the organization, an industry, an economy or even the wider society? Hence, the level of analysis needs to be specified. Also, do we wish to investigate

---

Box 1.2 The young world rising

Three forces are shaping the twenty-first century: youth, entrepreneurship and ICT. Young entrepreneurs around the world are blending new technologies and next-generation thinking, building radically new kinds of organization adapted to a flat and crowded world. Rob Salkowitz illustrates the new centres of entrepreneurial innovation on five continents. He identifies an exciting new trend in global business and introduces us to a fresh young cast of entrepreneurs whose ideas are literally changing the world.

The Boston Consulting Group (BCG) confirms that the information-technology revolution continues apace. It calculates that there are already about 610 million Internet users in the BRICI countries (Brazil, Russia, India, China and Indonesia). BCG predicted that this number would have nearly doubled by 2015. And, in one respect, many consumers in emerging markets are leapfrogging over their Western peers. They are much more likely to access the Internet via mobile devices (which are ubiquitous in the emerging world) rather than PCs. That gives local entrepreneurs an advantage, says Rob Salkowitz, the author of *Young World Rising* (2010). Whereas Western companies are hampered by legacy systems and legacy mindsets, they can build their companies around the coming technology. One of the most popular films in the US in 2011 was *The Social Network*, about a group of young Harvard students who founded one of the world's fastest-growing companies, Facebook. The next Facebook is increasingly likely to be founded in India or Indonesia, rather than middle-aged America or doddery old Europe.

Sources: Salkowitz, 2010; *The Economist*, 2010.

---

the past or the future? There are many studies that have tried to explain why some firms or individuals were successful – for example, the growth (and fall) of Microsoft or Nokia. There are also historical studies of periods of time, such as the growth of the Roman Empire or the demise of the Ottoman Empire. So, the time frame needs to be specified. Finally, do we wish to investigate or study a particular phenomenon or issue? For example, entrepreneurship education has received a great deal of attention from policymakers and politicians, as they have tried to enhance their country's economic growth. Nonetheless, this area of business management is problematic. In his book *High Technology Entrepreneurship*, Professor Ray Oakey provides a comprehensive overview of all aspects of high-technology small-firm (HTSF) formation and growth and illustrates that they have not been attractive assessment vehicles for those with money to invest (Oakey, 2012).

In this book, the context is clear. It is technology development and growing businesses. The evidence is mounting up all over the world that innovation is key to competitiveness and growth, and that entrepreneurial dynamism is key to economic renewal and growth. The focus is therefore provided by a combination of several areas of policy. One of the major weaknesses of the effectiveness of policies to develop technological entrepreneurship is insufficient recognition of the overlaps and linkages between these four areas (see Figure 1.3):

1   science and technology (S&T);
2   small and medium-sized enterprise;
3   innovation;
4   entrepreneurship.

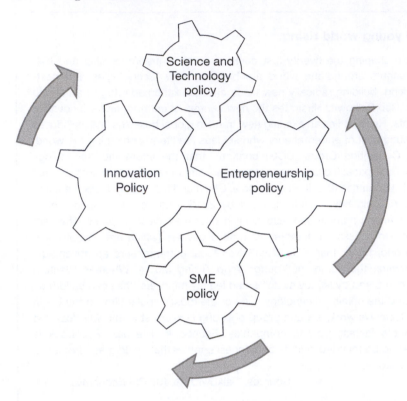

Figure 1.3 Technological entrepreneurship is the integration of policies

Science and technology policy

S&T policy is an area of public policy concerned with the government decisions that affect the conduct of science and research enterprise, including the funding of science, often in pursuance of other national policy goals such as technological innovation to promote commercial product development, weapons development, health care and environmental monitoring. Indeed, innovation policy has evolved from S&T policy.

Small and medium-sized enterprise

There has been recognition for a long time that small firms require support and help if they are to grow into larger firms and help develop and grow the economy. Many economies embraced the concept of 'acorn to oak tree' as they put in place numerous measures to help small and medium-sized enterprises (SMEs) grow. Entrepreneurship policy has evolved from SME policy. However, it has been recognized for many years now that most small businesses are not investment ready. Their owners are unwilling to seek external equity finance, and those who are willing do not understand what equity investors are looking for or how to 'sell' themselves and their businesses to potential investors. These weaknesses, in turn, compromise the effectiveness of supply-side interventions, such as initiatives to stimulate business angels or to create public-sector venture capital (VC) funds (Oakey, 2007b).

Box 1.3 The YES!Delft Incubator

YES!Delft – the Young Entrepreneur Society – inspires, educates, coaches and supports students, professionals and researchers interested in starting a high-tech company or further developing an early-stage high-tech company. A major part of YES!Delft is the YES!Delft Incubation Centre at TU Delft. This is a nurturing environment for successful high-tech entrepreneurship. The centre provides high-tech companies with operational guidance, strategic advice and infrastructure support for product or service development.

YES!Delft BUILDING TOMORROW'S LEADING FIRMS
INSPIRATION | EDUCATION | INCUBATION | GROWTH

Image 1.1 Yes!Delft logo
© YES!Delft

Within this area, we find business incubators. Business incubators can offer start-ups various forms of assistance, from economies related to shared business services, to expert advice and access to venture funding opportunities. Incubator facilities vary widely in size, as measured by the square footage or total start-up costs and the number of tenants resident in the facilities. Technology-oriented incubators are increasingly located near research parks, universities or research labs to offer '*technology entrepreneurs*' access to a wider range of facilities, individuals and opportunities within their field. Tenant firms can have access to the research facilities and personnel of established firms, universities and research institutes. Additionally, they are able to network more easily with experienced and successful entrepreneurs and may even engage in strategic alliances to exploit business opportunities, either as a subcontractor or a supplier (see Box 1.3).

Innovation policy

Within the EU and in other countries too, such as South Korea, innovation policy has generally focused on four key objectives:

- the generation of new knowledge;
- making government investment in innovation more effective;
- enhancing diffusion of knowledge and technology (network interaction effects); and
- establishing the right incentives to stimulate private-sector innovation to transform knowledge into commercial success.

Much of the policy assistance for HTSFs over recent years has been directed at encouraging their R&D collaboration through local networking and technology transfer, such as working with larger partners or universities. Research by Professor Ray Oakey has questioned the value of external collaborative R&D to internal R&D management, inside incubators, science parks or industry clusters. His research suggested that the extent of R&D collaboration with external partners is very limited, and, moreover, much of the collaborative HTSF R&D is highly confidential, competitive and wholly internalized, thereby limiting the benefits to the wider economy (Oakey, 2007a).

Entrepreneurship policy

Entrepreneurship policies have attempted to concentrate on developing an environment and support system to foster the emergence of new entrepreneurs and the start-up and early-stage growth of new firms. However, there has been limited recognition of the full integration of entrepreneurship and innovation. Indeed, there has been a disconnect between entrepreneurship and innovation policies. There needs to be a convergence between the two to ensure optimization of complementarities. Unfortunately, all too often, innovation policies do not incorporate entrepreneurship as a focus. Yet we know that entrepreneurship involves the act of innovation, and that entrepreneurs are essential to convert knowledge into economic and social benefits.

University–business interface and spin-outs

Japanese public authorities are concerned that Japanese industry is losing its competitive advantages in high-technology industries because of the over-reliance on large, science-intensive organizations. There is a strong belief that this innovation model is giving way to innovation via smaller start-up firms that work in partnership with larger firms and, more significantly, are providing the creativity. Furthermore, Japan does not have a tradition for this type of innovation model, and its universities have been slow to adapt. This is despite the fact that more than 50 per cent of the basic research undertaken in Japan is in universities (Kondo, 2004). So far, Japanese professors have not been given the opportunity to acquire the mix of technical and managerial expertise required to create a business venture. Like the Netherlands, Japan is characterized by a low-rate creation of 'Silicon Valley'-type, fast-growing, high-technology, entrepreneurial companies (Kenkyujo, 2006). Since 1995, Japan has been encouraging its universities to form partnerships with industry and create university spin-outs. Indeed, targets for spin-outs were even set (Motohashi, 2005). A closer examination of the literature on university spin-outs reveals surprising evidence:

- The average number of spin-outs from American universities in 2012 was a measly three (AUTM, 2015).[2]
- The income generated from technology transfer as a proportion of research income is insignificant (at MIT, for example, in 2012, it was 2.4 per cent of its research income).
- Most American universities lose money on technology transfer activities, because of their high running costs (the exceptions are the handful of universities that own patents on blockbuster drugs).

Even the high-profile business successes of Yahoo and Google are sometimes used to support the notion of university spin-outs, but even here the evidence cannot be found. Although both Yahoo and Google were founded by Stanford University students, Stanford did not claim intellectual property for the Yahoo technology, because this was developed in the students' own time. In the Google case, Stanford was able to generate income from ownership of the intellectual property, but most of its income comes from its VC investment made through local VC firms, rather than from the licence. The definition of a university spin-out is critical here. In the survey above, a new business venture by university students is not classified as a spin-out. A university spin-out involves staff from the university starting a new business.

The devil is in the detail here, for, although university spin-outs cannot claim significant economic impact, the role of universities in supplying educated and trained personnel who can then exploit opportunities certainly can. What is clear then is that, when we examine the business–university interface, we see university graduates as a driver of economic growth, rather than university technology as the driver.

All surveys on new venture start-ups and university spin-outs mention financing as the highest entry barrier (Motohashi, 2005). In Japan, the VC markets are not developed enough. In addition, unlike in the USA, there are very few people with science and engineering expertise and an MBA. These types of hybrid manager seem to be a key component in university spin-offs. It seems also that for many entrepreneurs, whether you listen to the founders of Google or more local entrepreneurs running their own small businesses, frequently the business started and developed with very little strategic planning or thinking. It was a fascination and belief in the technology and the drive of the individuals involved that seem to be the essential ingredients. In addition, we should not overlook the role of sales and developing orders. It is getting the first order and negotiating the first order that seem to shape the business venture. These skills are captured in Figure 1.4. Towards the top right-

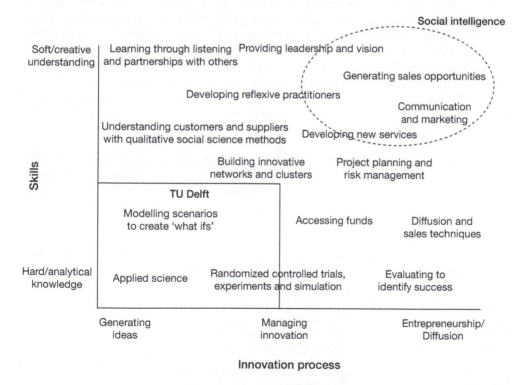

Figure 1.4 Skills required in innovation and entrepreneurship

hand corner, we can group these skills, which are clearly visible within many entrepreneurs, under the concept of social intelligence. When one then places the science and technology skills clearly present in technical universities on this skills map, it raises questions about how to access all the other skills necessary for entrepreneurship.

Later in this book, we discuss the issue of academic spin-outs in more detail; in the meantime, there is an important moral hazard present. Clearly, when entrepreneurs in a free market decide to begin a new firm, the risks that they take are solely attributable to them. However, in academic incubators, where public-funded university staff are trying to encourage students to embark on entrepreneurial ventures, on which their own success depends, there is a lack of incentive to guard against risk where one is protected from its consequences (e.g. possible financial loss, reputational damage, etc). According to Oakey (2012), 'this problem is exacerbated by the rhetoric surrounding university entrepreneurship [where] the likelihood of success is often over-exaggerated, although failure is far more likely than success' (Storey, 1994).

A framework for technological entrepreneurship

Industrial innovation and new product development have evolved considerably from their early beginnings outlined above. We have seen that innovation is extremely complex and involves the effective management of a variety of different activities. It is precisely how the process is managed that needs to be examined. Over the past 50 years, there have been numerous studies of innovation, attempting to understand, not only the ingredients necessary for it to occur, but also what levels of ingredients are required and in what order. Furthermore, a recent study by *Business Week* and BCG (2015) of more than 1,000 senior managers revealed further explanations as to what makes some firms more innovative than others. The key findings from this survey are captured in Table 1.2. Although these headline-grabbing bullet points are interesting, they do not show us what firms have to do to become excellent in design (BMW) or to improve cooperation with suppliers (Toyota). Table 1.3 captures some of the key studies that have influenced our understanding.

This chapter has helped to illustrate the complex nature of innovation management and also identified some of the limitations of the various models and schools of thought. Specifically, these are as follows:

1   Variations on linear thinking continue to dominate models of innovation. Actually, most innovation models show innovation paths, representing a stage-gate type of activity, controlling the progress from idea to market introduction, rather than giving insight in the dynamics of actual innovation processes.

Table 1.2 Explanations for innovative capability

Innovative firm	Explanation for innovative capability
Apple	Innovative chief executive
Google	Scientific freedom for employees
Samsung	Speed of product development
Procter & Gamble	Utilization of external sources of technology
IBM	Sharing patents with collaborators
BMW	Design
Starbucks	In-depth understanding of customers and their cultures
Toyota	Close cooperation with suppliers

Table 1.3 Studies of innovation management

	Study	Date	Focus
1	Carter and Williams	1957	Industry and technical progress
2	Project Hindsight – TRACES (Isenson)	1968	Historical reviews of US government-funded defence industry
3	Wealth from knowledge (Langrish *et al.*)	1972	Queens Awards for technical innovation
4	Project SAPPHO (Rothwell *et al.*)	1974	Success and failure factors in chemical industry
5	Minnesota studies (Van de Ven)	1999	14 case studies of innovations
6	Rothwell	1992	25-year review of studies
7	Sources of innovation (Wheelwright and Clark)	1992	Different levels of user involvement
8	MIT studies (Utterback)	1994	5 major industry-level cases
9	Project NEWPROD (Cooper)	1994	Longitudinal survey of success and failure in new products
10	Radical innovation (Leifer *et al.*)	2000	Review of mature businesses
11	TU Delft study (Van der Panne *et al.*)	2003	Literature review of success and failure factors
12	Ben Martin (Martin 2012)	2012	Review of fifty years of science policy literature

2   Science is viewed primarily as technology-oriented (physical sciences), and R&D is closely linked to manufacturing, causing insufficient attention to the behavioural sciences. As a consequence, service innovation is hardly addressed.

3   The complex interactions between new technological capabilities and emerging societal needs are a vital part of the innovation process, but they are underexposed in current models.

4   The role of the entrepreneur (individual or team) is not captured.

5   Current innovation models are not embedded within the strategic thinking of the firm; they remain isolated entities.

Innovation needs to be viewed as a management process. We need to recognize that change is at the heart of it, and that change is caused by decisions that people make. The framework in Figure 1.5 attempts to capture the iterative nature of the network processes in innovation and represents this in the form of an endless innovation circle with interconnected cycles. This circular concept helps to show how the firm gathers information over time, how it uses technical *and* societal knowledge, and how it develops an attractive proposition. This is achieved through developing linkages and partnerships with those having the necessary capabilities ('open innovation'). In addition, the entrepreneur is positioned at the centre.

The framework in Figure 1.5 is referred to as the the Cyclic Innovation Model (Berkhout *et al.*, 2010), a cross-disciplinary view of change processes (and their interactions) as they take place in an open innovation arena. Behavioural sciences and engineering, as well as natural sciences and markets, are brought together in a coherent system of processes, with four principal nodes that function as roundabouts. The combination of the involved changes leads to a wealth of business opportunities. Here, entrepreneurship plays a central role: making use of those opportunities. The message is that without the drive of entrepreneurs there is no innovation, and without innovation there is no new business. Figure 1.5 shows that the combination of change and entrepreneurship is the basis of new business. Chapter 6 discusses the cyclic framework in detail.

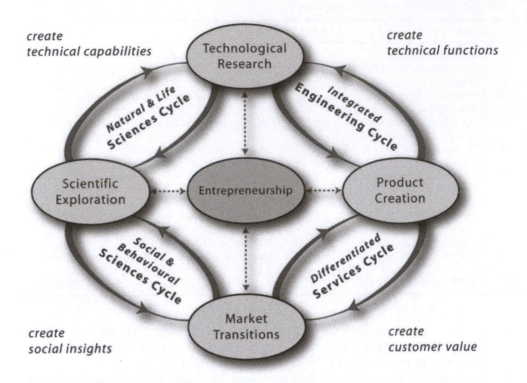

*create
technical capabilities*

*create
technical functions*

*create
social insights*

*create
customer value*

Figure 1.5 Cyclical model of technological entrepreneurship and innovation

Adopting this approach to the management of innovation should help firms, as processes should not be forced into simple one-way pipelines, but should rather be organized by interconnected cycles with feed-forward and feedback connections: from linear to nonlinear thinking. In that way, a dynamic network environment is created in which the social and behavioural sciences are linked to engineering, and where the natural and life sciences connect with market goals (Berkhout *et al.*, 2006). This is what is captured in the proposed innovation framework. Supported by today's powerful communication technology, serial process management along a linear path is replaced by parallel networking in a largely self-organizing circle. Vital decisions in innovation do not occur at the gates of a staged project management pipeline, but do occur on the innovation shop floor itself, or in the nodes of the cyclic networks. In our experience, young people like to work in such an environment. Moreover, according to Salkowitz (2010), young entrepreneurs around the world are blending new technologies and next-generation thinking, building radically new kinds of organization adapted to a flat and crowded world.

Emphasizing the role of entrepreneurship within innovation is at the heart of this book. The remainder of this book will help entrepreneurs consider how their new venture will make money, and there is much room for creativity, as the chapter on business models shows. For example, it may be that the techno-starter believes it has developed a product better than the existing products on the market. It will, therefore, simply offer its product at a competitive price relative to the competition. However, this would overlook other possibilities for the business. Are there opportunities for leasing rather than simply selling?

Box 1.4 Case study: A folding shipping container

This case study tells the story of how three MSc students at TU Delft in the Netherlands had an idea for a folding shipping container and went about building a business. There are many examples of university students starting businesses, but few of these have the potential to revolutionize world trade.

Almost all containers that you see today on ships, trains or trucks are 20 ft or 40 ft in length; the reason for the massive change in both transportation and the global economy is because of this simplicity of size – a small set of standard sizes allowed ships, trucks, receiving bays and all of the related logistical systems to easily adapt to an industry-wide standard. Prior to standardization, there were major inefficiencies in commercial shipping: packaging and crating were inconsistent. But what about empty containers? Are there ships travelling the world with containers that are empty? If so, is this a business opportunity?

Introduction

We are all aware of the anglepoise lamp, which uses springs to enable the movement of its steel arm and lamp. The same principle can be used to move much larger objects, providing one has much larger springs. Initially, the students thought about springs to raise and lower a bridge, but this was soon dismissed. A steel container that could be folded into a small space had many more attractions. What are the benefits of a folding container? Maybe a folding container already exists? A working computer simulation is a long way from a folding 40-ft steel container. Would anyone be interested? And

Image 1.2 Container ship
© Aquarius15

how could they make any money out of the idea? Having interesting technology is a long way from a profitable money-making business.

The TU Delft friends faced a number of difficulties and many uncertainties. They needed advice: after all, they were engineers – very clever engineers, but not experts in developing businesses. Fortunately, the university had a business incubator that helped students develop their ideas and create businesses. It would be able to help them with their patent application, but Jan, Mark and Stephan soon realized they did not know simple answers to questions such as: Who would buy it? Who are the customers? How many containers are there in the Netherlands/Europe/the world? How much does it cost to make a container? How much does it cost to buy one? It was soon clear that many days of research lay ahead.

The port of Rotterdam, which is only 15 km from Delft and is one of the world's busiest container ports, provided an ideal opportunity to gather some information. The commercial director of the port explained to the entrepreneurs that, for their idea to succeed, they would need to receive the necessary certification from agencies such as Lloyd's Register or Bureau Veritas. Their approval is required regarding the seaworthiness of any marine equipment. Without such certification, no shipping company will be interested. There seemed to be many obstacles to their business idea.

Business opportunity: Moving empty containers

Containers are intended to be used constantly, being loaded with a new cargo for a new destination soon after being emptied of the previous cargo. This is not always possible, and, in some cases, the cost of transporting an empty container to a place where it can be used is considered to be higher than the worth of the used container. This can result in large areas in ports and warehouses being occupied by empty, abandoned containers. The shipping industry spends a great deal of time and money repositioning empty containers. If trade were balanced, there would be no empty containers. But trade imbalance, especially between Europe and North America and Asia, has resulted in approximately 2.5 million TEUs[3] of empty containers stored in yards around the world, with empties constituting 20–23 per cent of the movement of containers around the world. According to research conducted by International Asset Systems, the average container is idle or undergoing repositioning for over 50 per cent of its lifespan. It also determined that shipping companies spend US$16 billion repositioning empties. To compensate for these costs, carriers add surcharges to freight rates, ranging from US$100 to US$1,000 per TEU.

Folding containers would provide further advantages. They would relieve congestion at ports. Storing empty containers takes up prime real estate. For example, the storage yards around the port of Jersey, UK, are cluttered with an estimated 100,000 empty containers belonging to leasing companies and an additional 50,000 belonging to ocean carriers. Folding containers would be quicker to load (four at a time), resulting in faster turnaround time for ships. Energy costs would drop as well, as one trailer rather than four would transport empties. Finally, there's also a security feature to the folded container built to ISO standards. Nothing can be smuggled in a collapsed empty. It was estimated that, if 75 per cent of empty containers were folded by 2010, the result would be a yearly saving in shipping of 25 million TEUs, or 50 per cent of the total volume of empty containers shipped.

Concept to product

The background research had been done. There was genuine interest from potential customers. The friends now needed money to build a working scale model of the folding container. They had to prove to everyone that it would work. Moreover, the concept also had to be compatible with existing equipment for intermodal transport. That is, the container would need to be exactly the same size, shape, weight, etc. It would also have to have proper sealing and locking devices and should interlock with other containers. Computer models were fine to a point, but a physical model was now required, especially if they were going to convince people to invest. With the help of the university and the incubator, they set about constructing a fully working steel model. It was to be at one-tenth scale. So it would be 2 ft long and 0.8 ft high. Real working springs would have to be in place. The friends realized immediately that a patent drawing is theory, and it did not resemble reality. Numerous fabrication and manufacturing problems had to be overcome. Eventually, after 2 months of playing around with steel springs and welding equipment in the workshop, a fully working model emerged. It required two people to manoeuvre the steel box. More importantly, it had taken a considerable amount of time and investment in materials and equipment. When they demonstrated the model to senior figures at the port of Rotterdam, the latter were very impressed and immediately wanted to see a full-size version – a prototype. But, who would pay for a full-size prototype? It would be enormous. It would cost thousands of euros to produce.

Questions

1 Would you advise the friends to start this business?
2 Who are their customers going to be?
3 Who can they license the technology to?
4 Can they form any partnerships or alliances?
5 How would you enter this market?
6 What aspects of product diffusion will they need to address?
7 Can you separate innovation activities from entrepreneurship?
8 Is patent protection essential here? If not, why not?
9 How can they help customers adopt the product?
10 Standardization led to growth in container usage; what will be the effect of this non-standard folding container?

Note: This case has been written as a basis for class discussion, rather than to illustrate effective or ineffective managerial or administrative behaviour. It has been prepared from a variety of published sources and from observations.

Can the business adopt a landlord business model? Famous examples abound where new business models have been developed by start-ups that challenge existing dominant business models in an industry. These range from eBay to Facebook.

Chapter summary

This chapter has shown how innovation and entrepreneurship are bound together. This is particularly so when it comes to technological entrepreneurship. The cyclic model of innovation reinforces this view by diagrammatically linking these two concepts. In this framework, successful innovation requires entrepreneurial activities to occur. The cyclic model of innovation will be used throughout this book to help explain how innovation and entrepreneurship are bound together.

Study questions

1   Discuss whether opportunities are created or discovered.
2   To what extent are innovation and entrepreneurship the same, and how are they different?
3   As far back as 1985, Drucker made it clear that innovation is organized, systematic, rational work. Why then do so many believe innovation is due to serendipity?
4   Howard Stevenson argues that entrepreneurship is a style of management. Explain why so many argue that it is an individual pursuit.
5   Discuss whether incubators help or might sometimes hinder the success of entrepreneurs.

Notes

1   George Bernard Shaw (1856–1950) was an Irish playwright and a co-founder of the London School of Economics. He is also the only person to be awarded a Nobel Prize for Literature and an Oscar.
2   In 2012, according to a survey by the Assocation of University Technology Transfer Managers (AUTM), there were 705 spin-out start-ups. This figure is divided into 2,600, as this is the number of significant universities (i.e. universities that operate 4-year degree programmes).
3   The 20-foot equivalent unit (often TEU or teu) is an inexact unit of cargo capacity often used to describe the capacity of container ships. It is based on the volume of a 20-foot-long, standard-sized metal shipping container.

References

Association of University Technology Managers (AUTM). (2015). *AUTM Briefing Book: 2015*. Deerfield, IL: AUTM.

Audia, P. G. and Rider, C. I. (2005). A garage and an idea: What more does an entrepreneur need? *California Management Review*. 48(1): 6.

Baumol, W. J. (1968). Entrepreneurship in economic theory. *The American Economic Review*. 58(2): 64–71.

Becker, G. (1965). A theory of the allocation of time. *Economic Journal*. 75: 493–517.

Berkhout, A. J., Hartmann, D., and Trott, P. (2010). Connecting technological capabilities with market needs using a cyclic innovation model. *R&D Management*. 40(5): 474–90.

Berkhout, A. J., Hartmann, D., Duin, P. van der and Ortt, R. (2006). Innovating the innovation process. *International Journal of Technology Management*. 34(3–4): 390–404.

Bianchi, M. and Henrekson, M. (2005). Is neoclassical economics still entrepreneurless? *Kyklos*. 58(3): 353–77.

Business Week and Boston Consulting Group. (2015). The most innovative companies: An interactive guide. Available at: www.bcgperspectives.com/content/interactive/innovation_growth_most_inno vative_companies_interactive_guide/ (accessed 17 August 2015).

Cantillon, R. (1952). *Essai sur la nature du commerce en général* [abbreviated *Essai*] (ed. H. Higgs). Paris: Ined. (Originally published 1730)

Caplan, R. (1999). The Austrian search for realistic foundations. *Southern Economic Journal.* 65(4): 823–38.

Carter, C. F. and Williams, B. R. (1957). The characteristics of technically progressive firms. *Journal of Industrial Economics.* March: 87–104.

Cole, A. H. (1968). The entrepreneur, introductory remarks. *The American Economic Review.* 58(2): 60–3.

Cooper, R. (1994). Third generation new product processes. *Journal of Product Innovation Management.* 11(1): 3–14.

Cullen, B. (2003). *It's a Long Way From Penny Apples.* London: Macmillan.

Drucker, P. (1985). *Innovation and Entrepreneurship.* New York: Harper & Row.

Duijn, J. J. van (1977). The long wave in economic life. *The Economist.* 125(4): 544–76.

Economist, The (2010). The other demographic dividend. *Schumpeter,* 7 October.

Economist, The (2015). Apple reigns supreme when it comes to making money, but now faces even greater expectations. Business Section, 31 January.

Fagerberg, J. and Verspagen, B. (2009). Innovation studies – The emerging structure of a new scientific field. *Research Policy.* 38(2): 218–33.

Fast Track 100. (2010). Britain's fastest growing private companies, *Sunday Times,* 5 December, p. 3.

Fiet, J. (1996). The informational basis of entrepreneurial discovery. *Small Business Economics.* 8: 419–30.

Freeman, C. (1979). The determinants of innovation: Market demand, technology, and the response to social problems. *Futures.* 11(3): 206–15.

Freeman, J. (1986). 'Entrepreneurs as organizational products: Semiconductor firms and venture capital firms', in G. Libecap (ed.), *Advances in the Study of Entrepreneurship, Innovation, and Economic Growth,* Vol.1. Greenwich, CT: JAI Press, pp. 33–52.

Gartner, W. B. (1985). A conceptual framework for describing the phenomenon of new venture creation. *Academy of Management Review.* 10(4): 696–706.

Gifford, S. (2003). 'Risk and uncertainty', in Z. J. Ács and D. B. Audretsch (eds), *Handbook of Entrepreneurial Research.* New York: Springer, pp. 37–54.

Guardian, The (2009). Interview with technology, 18 June, p. 1.

Howells, J. (2008). New directions in R&D: Current and prospective challenges. *R&D Management.* 38(3): 241–52.

Isenson, R. (1968). 'Technology in retrospect and critical events in science' (Project Traces), Illinois Institute of Technology/National Science Foundation, Chicago, IL.

Kenkyujo, K. S. (2006). *Daigaku hatsu venture ni kansuru kiso chosa jisshi hokokusho* (Basic survey on university spin-offs: Report of the empirical results; in Japanese; Tokyo: Kachi Sogo Kenkyujo).

Kihlstrom, R. E. and Laffont, J. J. (1979). A general equilibrium entrepreneurial theory of firm formation based on risk aversion. *The Journal of Political Economy.* 87(4): 719–48.

Kilby, P. (1971). *Entrepreneurship and Economic Development.* New York: Free Press.

Kirzner, I. M. (1979). *Perception, Opportunity, and Profit: Studies in the theory of entrepreneurship.* Chicago, IL: University of Chicago Press.

Kleinknecht, A. (1981). Observations on the Schumpeterian swarming of innovations. *Futures.* 13(4): 293–307.

Kondo, M. (2004). University spin-offs in Japan. *Asia Pacific Tech Monitor.* (March–April): 37–43.

Langrish, J., Gibbons, M., Evans, W. G. and Jevons, F. R. (1972). *Wealth From Knowledge.* London: Macmillan.

Leifer, R., McDermott, C. M., O'Connor, G. C., Peters, L. S., Rice, M. P. and Veryzer, R. W. (2000). *Radical Innovation: How mature companies can outsmart upstarts.* Boston, MA: Harvard Business School Press.

Low, M. B. and MacMillan, I. C. (1988). Entrepreneurship: Past research and future challenges. *Journal of Management.* 14(2): 139–61.

McClelland, D. (1961). *The Achieving Society.* Princeton, NJ: Van Nostrand.

Mandel, E. (1978). *The Second Slump.* London: NLB.

Mandel, E. (1980). *Long Waves of Capitalist Development: A Marxist interpretation* (based on the Marshall Lectures given at the University of Cambridge). London: Verso.

Mandel, E. (1981). Explaining long waves of capitalist development. *Futures*. 13(4): 332–8.

Marcin, E. R. and Cockrum, D. L. (1984). A psychological comparison of entrepreneurs and small business managers in the United States, West Germany and Mexico in respect to achievement, power, affiliation motivation as well as locus of control. Paper presented at Eleventh International Small Business Conference.

Martinelli, A. (1994). 'Entrepreneurship and management', in N. J. Smelser and R. Swedberg (eds), *The Handbook of Economic Sociology*. Princeton, NJ: Princeton University Press, pp. 476–503.

Mensch, G. and West Internationales Institut für Management und Verwaltung (Berlin). (1979). *Stalemate in Technology: Innovations overcome the depression*. New York: Ballinger.

Motohashi, K. (2005). University–industry collaborations in Japan: The role of new technology-based firms in transforming the National Innovation System. *Research Policy*. 34(5): 583–94.

Oakey, R. P. (2007a). A commentary on gaps in funding for moderate 'non-stellar' growth small businesses in the United Kingdom. *Venture Capital*. 9(3): 223–35.

Oakey, R. P. (2007b). R&D collaboration between high technology small firms (HTSFs) in theory and practice. *R&D Management*. 37(3): 237–48.

Oakey, R. (2012). *High Technology Entrepreneurship*. Abingdon, UK: Routledge.

Pearson, A. W. (1983). Planning and monitoring in research and development – A 12 year review of papers in R&D Management. *R&D Management*. 13(2): 107–16.

Rothwell, R. (1992). Successful industrial innovation: Critical factors for the 1990s. *R&D Management*. 22(3): 221–39.

Rothwell, R., Freeman, C., Horlsey, A., Jervis, V. T. P., Robertson, A. B. and Townsend, J. (1974). SAPPHO updated: Project SAPPHO phase II. *Research Policy*. 3: 258–91.

Rushe, D. and Waples, J. (2008). Interview. Business, *Sunday Times*, 3 February, p. 5.

Salkowitz, R. (2010). *The Young World Rising*. Hoboken, NJ: John Wiley.

Schultz, T. W. (1980). Investment in entrepreneurial ability. *The Scandinavian Journal of Economics*. 82(4): 437–48.

Schumpeter, J. A. (1934). *The Theory of Economic Development: An inquiry into profits, capital, credit, interest, and the business cycle*, Vol. 55. New Brunswick, NJ: Transaction.

Schumpeter, J. (1961). *The Theory of Economic Development*. New York: Oxford University Press.

Schumpeter, J. A. (1964). *Business Cycles*, Vol. I. New York: McGraw-Hill. (Originally published 1939)

Shane, S. and Venkataraman, S. (2000). The promise of entrepreneurship as a field of research. *Academy of Management Review*. 25(1): 217–26.

Shaw, G. B. (1903). *Maxims for Revolutionists*, No. 152. Available at: www.gutenberg.org/cache/epub/26107/pg26107-images.html (accessed 17 August 2015).

Smith, A. (2005). *Wealth of Nations*. Chicago, IL: University of Chicago Bookstore. (Originally published 1776)

Stevenson, H. H. (1983). *A Perspective on Entrepreneurship*, Vol. 13. Cambridge, MA: Harvard Business School.

Stevenson, H. H. (2000). Why entrepreneurship has won. *Coleman White Paper*, pp. 1–8.

Stevenson, H. H. and Gumpert, D. E. (1985). The heart of entrepreneurship. *Harvard Business Review*. March: 184.

Stevenson, H. H. and Jarillo, C. J. (1990). Paradigm of entrepreneurship: Entrepreneurial management. *Strategic Management Journal* (Special Issue: Corporate Entrepreneurship). 11(Summer): 17–27.

Storey, D. (1994). *Understanding the Small Firms Sector*. London: Routledge.

Thornton, P. H. (1999). The sociology of entrepreneurship. *Annual Review of Sociology*. 25: 19–46.

Tidd, J., Pavitt, K. and Bessant, J. (1997). *Innovation Management*. Chichester, UK: Wiley.

Trott, P. (1998). *Innovation Management and New Product Development*. London: Prentice Hall.

Utterback, J. (1994). *Mastering the Dynamics of Innovation*. Boston, MA: Harvard Business School Press.

Van der Panne, G., Beers, C. van and Kleinknecht, A. (2003). Success and failure of innovation: A literature review. *International Journal of Innovation Management*. 7(3): 309–38.

Van de Ven, A. H. (1999). *The Innovation Journey*. New York: Oxford University Press.

Wheelwright, S. and Clark, K. (1992). *Revolutionising Product Development*. New York: Free Press.

Wortman, M. S. (1987). Entrepreneurship: An integrating typology and evaluation of the empirical research in the field. *Journal of Management*. 13(2): 259–79.

Further reading

Aldrich, H. E. (2012). The emergence of entrepreneurship as an academic field: A personal essay on institutional entrepreneurship. *Research Policy*, 41(7), 1240–1248.

Casson, M. (2003). *The Entrepreneur: An economic theory*. Cheltenham, UK: Edward Elgar.

Casson, M., Yeung, B. and Basu, A. (eds) (2008). *Oxford Handbook of Entrepreneurship*. Oxford, UK: Oxford University Press on Demand.

Cope, J. (2005). Researching entrepreneurship through phenomenological inquiry: Philosophical and methodological issues. *International Small Business Journal*. 23(2): 163–89.

Delmar, F. and Shane, S. (2003a). Does business planning facilitate the development of new ventures? *Strategic Management Journal*. 24(12): 1165–85.

Delmar, F. and Shane, S. (2003b). Does the order of organizing activities matter for new venture performance? Paper presented at Babson Kauffman Entrepreneurship Research Conference, Wellesley, June. Available at: www.babson.edu/entrep/fer/BABSON2003/XXV/XXV-P4/xxvP4.htm (accessed 4 August 2015).

Delmar, F. and Shane, S. (2004). Legitimizing first: Organizing activities and the survival of new ventures. *Journal of Business Venturing*. 19(3): 385–410.

Dolfsma, W. and Seo, D. (2013). Government policy and technological innovation—a suggested typology. *Technovation*, 33(6), 173–179.

Ivanova I. A. and Leydesdorff, L. (2014) Rotational symmetry and the transformation of innovation systems in a Triple Helix of university–industry–government relations. *Technological Forecasting & Social Change*, 86(6), 143–156.

Mazzucato, M. (2011). *The Entrepreneurial State*. London: Demos.

Ortín-Ángel, P. and Vendrell-Herrero, F. (2014). University spin-offs vs. other NTBFs: Total factor productivity differences at outset and evolution. *Technovation*, 34(2), 101–112.

Pittaway, L. and Robertson, M. (2004). 'Business to business networking and its impact on innovation: Exploring the UK evidence', Working Paper 2004/032, Lancaster University Management School.

Schumpeter, J. (1975). *Capitalism, Socialism and Democracy*. New York: Harper.

Schütz, A. (1940). 'Parsons' theory of social action: A critical review by Alfred Schütz', in R. Grathoff (ed.) (1978), *The Theory of Social Action: The correspondence of Alfred Schütz and Talcott Parsons*. Bloomington, IN: Indiana University Press, pp. 8–124.

2 Visioning the future for a new venture

How entrepreneurs can become visionary

Entrepreneurship is essentially a forward-looking activity. Setting up a new venture takes time, often a lot of time. Between the first idea for a new venture and its ultimate implementation, many years might pass. Setting up a new venture and looking to the future, therefore, are two sides of the same coin.

Famous entrepreneurs such as Richard Branson and the late Steve Jobs have been celebrated because of their talent for discovering new developments and using them as a source of inspiration to develop new products and services. However, their brilliance is more than being able to see all kinds of change and development; it is about seeing them before anyone else does. Having that ability may mean that people consider you some kind of a lunatic, but many successful entrepreneurs know that those people have a short-term view of the future and do not have the talent and patience to go for long-term developments. For instance, nowadays, everyone considers 'branding' an important asset of any company and its products and services, but Richard Branson was one of the first to notice its business potential. The same is true of the way Steve Jobs used 'design' and 'business models' to build his business empire.

But is it just a talent? Is it a God-given 'core competency' that is reserved only for the likes of Branson and Jobs? Or is looking to the future something that everyone can learn and apply in their business? The Norwegian neurobiologist Ingvar has discovered that some parts of our brain are constantly occupied with looking to the future. We are constantly asking ourselves, 'What if?' If I cross this road now, will the car 50 yards to the left of me accelerate or not? If it does, what can I do to prevent a personal disaster? However, these thinking processes are implicit. The fact that we are continuously thinking about the future means that we are unaware of dealing with the future. Management guru and former Shell employee Arie de Geus has said that, given that every individual has this implicit talent, and that the most important success factor for every company is the ability to learn faster (and better) than its competitors, organizations should create circumstances in which thinking

---

Box 2.1 Techno-starters and the future

A study among forty-three techno-starters in the area of TU Delft in the Netherlands showed that, although almost all techno-starters looked to the future, they did this predominantly in an implicit way, using no specific methods. Furthermore, the study suggested that the larger the techno-starters in terms of start-up costs, turnover and number of employees, the more effort they put in looking to the future. Also, techno-starters that were externally funded looked further ahead than techno-starters who were funded internally, and the same holds for techno-starters who are already established compared with recent techno-starters.

Source: Duin and Hartmann (2007)

---

about the future is made explicit (for instance, by formulating scenarios concerning the future), thereby combining every employee's thoughts and opinions about the future.

So, we argue that looking to the future is not just some talent that only a few people in the world possess. Developing knowledge about the future is possible for everyone, and the crystal ball is not a black box. The future can be predicted, analysed and explored by applying methods of futures research and taking into account certain principles and concepts. Be aware that completely validated knowledge about the future is not possible. However, we do not consider that a problem. As Louis Pasteur once said, 'Chance favours the prepared mind'. Being aware of the future, having an eye for changes, thinking about what the future may look like and assessing what that may mean for your current and future business constitute a learning process in which the use of different methods of futures research can play a vital role. However, also be aware that looking to the future is not an end in itself but a means to making important, often strategic decisions that form the basis of all entrepreneurial activities. That is why we also look at the concept of vision, which is one of the core elements of being an entrepreneur. Vision allows an entrepreneur to envision a future goal based on a study of the future. It is often the most important starting point for becoming an entrepreneur.

Building a vision of the future

Richard Branson and Steve Jobs are often called 'visionaries'. Not only do they (claim to) know what may or will happen in the future, they also know how to combine the developments they identify into a coherent story (vision) that is both consistent and inspiring. A vision can be described as a future goal towards which the entrepreneur wants to work. It is an inspiring image or story of the future that can guide you into the future, or, as the Germans call it, *Leitmotiv*. According to Kuosa (2012, p. 32), 'a vision is a compelling statement of the preferred future that an organization or community wants to create'. He also links vision to entrepreneurship: 'A vision is an entrepreneurial perception which reveals and points to something new and which sees beyond what is already being utilized to what is emerging and becoming invented' (p. 33). So, a vision describes in an inspiring way how an organization sees its favourite future, which is clearly different from the present, and the organization is sufficiently clear about what it wants to achieve, thereby inspiring its employees to act and to decide.

Box 2.2 A vision is not a mission

The terms vision and mission are often mixed up. In short, by a vision, we mean an inspiring goal that a company wants to achieve in the long run. A mission describes the core values that an organization holds in doing business. Examples of these values are that a company wants to be socially responsible and sustainable and/or wants to be a reliable employer for its employees. As such, the mission describes the essence of an organization, what it wants to be. The vision describes what it mainly wants to achieve in business and what it wants (needs) to do strategically to realize the visions. If we take ourselves as an example, your mission describes your nature, your character, what you stand for in life. Your vision describes your personal ambition, what you want to achieve in life. Of course, mission and vision are related. It would be strange (and wrong) if an organization had formulated a mission with a strong emphasis on contributing to the well-being of society, and at the same time had the vision to become the world's number one supplier of small rifles.

Paul J. H. Schoemaker (2002) has defined a set of principles that all good visions should encompass:

1   a statement of what the organization wants to be and how it will get there;
2   concrete goals and milestones (financial and otherwise);
3   core capabilities that need to be developed;
4   a description of how to change the organization;
5   a proposed market and product scope supporting the vision;
6   robustness in the face of multiple scenarios;
7   stretch to reach beyond the organization's current grasp;
8   passion, in order to galvanize the organization;
9   simplicity and clarity of purpose.

This is a comprehensive list that does not seem too difficult to apply. However, appearances can be deceptive. For many companies, both formulating an inspiring and consistent vision and applying it in practice prove harder than they think. Often, employees interpret the vision differently, preventing the company from making the strategic choices that need to be made. As a result, companies are 'stuck in the middle', as Michael Porter (1980) has put it. They develop a strategy that is supposed to enable them to service all customer segments, realize low cost prices, which will allow them to be cheaper than the competition, and produce a constant stream of new products, processes and services, all at the same time. As a result, to put it in athletic terms, they are neither sprinters nor long-distance runners. In our modern, competitive economy, generalists will, however, always lose out to specialists.

Furthermore, in a world where more and more companies specialize, it is hard to maintain a broad strategy. It will never put a company among the top five companies in markets in which it operates. Nor will it be very successful in other markets in which it may operate, which is what a company with a broad strategy will want to do. Any company with such a vague vision, which is open to different interpretations, has a kind of identity crisis and does not really know what to do. As a result, it starts focusing on various different activities.

Box 2.3 Companies with a 'broad' strategy

A company such as Siemens operates in various markets, from telecommunications and medical systems to subway trains. On the other hand, Siemens operates almost exclusively in hi-tech, business-to-business markets. It would appear that Siemens has managed to keep its technological competencies at an acceptably high level, while at the same time making sure that the technologies can be used to make different products. However, it is not easy to operate simultaneously in different markets. Electronics company Philips, for example, has clearly separated its business units: consumer products, medical systems and devices, and light. Of course, the consumer products division is a fairly broad segment, with products ranging from electric razors to light bulbs. Although separating its business units may not be too hard for a company such as Philips, for other, more integrated companies, it can be quite a challenge.

Image 2.1 Philips head office
© Philips

It is this very diversity that makes it hard to match the different activities. As a result, internal cooperation falters, and any chances of achieving synergy are wasted. Companies that have a clear vision and matching strategy are better at cooperating and, as a result, they are more attractive to external parties. Of course, there are exceptions.

For example, formerly state-owned telecommunications companies tend to find it a difficult thing to do. An integrated telecommunications company roughly speaking consists of a network department, a product and service development department and a sales and maintenance department. To provide the best possible service, it is imperative that these three departments cooperate closely. However, because they operate in different markets and industries, that is not an easy thing to do. The network department has a time horizon of at least 10 years and operates in a business-to-business market that focuses primarily on the development of technology. The other two departments have much shorter time horizons, however, and have much closer contact with end-users, who are often consumers. Often, this problem is solved by the company being divided up, and internal coordination being replaced by market mechanisms. The newly independent companies now have a commercial relationship with each other in which coordination needs to take place. Whether or not this will solve the coordination problems remains to be seen, although commercial stimuli can help create a situation in which people are more responsive to each other's needs.

Although any company may have a broad strategy that is based on a vague and less-than-inspiring vision, it is definitely more common among larger companies, which often have a long history in which mergers and take-overs, in addition to (autonomous) market growth, growth of its market share and continuous innovation, have helped the company to reach its current size and market position. As a result, the company has not only become bigger, but, at the same time, has become more diverse, which is reflected in a broad product portfolio, a vague vision and a broad strategy that is used as an excuse to broaden the business activities. Smaller companies are usually less burdened by a strategy that is too broad, because they have a shorter history (although there are also many family businesses that have existed for a long time and that have not diversified). However, a better explanation is that smaller businesses have less capital at their disposal and are not in a financial position to invest in mergers, take-overs or other kinds of activity. In light of the importance of a vision, it is now time to return to the list of conditions for a good vision that Schoemaker has identified. We shall discuss the conditions one by one and apply them in a few instances to a famous vision formulated by former US president John F. Kennedy: 'I believe that this nation should commit itself to achieving the goal, before the decade is out, of landing a man on the moon and returning him safely to earth'.

A statement of what the organization wants to be and how it will get there

In Kennedy's vision, the future goal is very concrete (to the moon and back), as well as challenging. Of course, the vision is too short, and going to the moon is too complicated to be described in one sentence. However, too long a description of how an organization will (or should) fulfil its vision might endanger the inspirational power of a vision. Also, it could provide employees with too much room for interpretation, thereby increasing the inconsistency between their business activities. Going to the moon is different from going to Mars . . .

In a sense, this is the most essential part of a vision. It has to make it clear what the ambitions are and what the company needs to do to realize them. As mentioned earlier, the vision has to be inspiring, concrete and challenging. If a vision is too broad, then so will the strategy be, which will not contribute to the company's success.

Concrete goals and milestones

Realizing a vision takes times, sometimes a lot of time. A vision should not be modified within a short time. A ship that changes course all the time will arrive nowhere. It is important to know how a vision will be realized. Owing to the long-term nature of a vision, it is important to determine from time to time whether or not the company is still on course. That does not mean that the company needs to travel in a straight line, but any major deviations from the 'transition path' need to be explainable, and getting back on track must not take up too many resources.

To make sure the company is still on the right path, intermediate milestones need to be defined, to measure the company's progress along the transition path and to determine the extent of any deviations from that path. Although these milestones can be financial in nature, they do not have to be. Market share, the number of new products and services being implemented and new competences among employees can also be relevant. In particular, in cases where the vision does not emphasize financial objectives, non-financial objectives are important.

With regard to Kennedy's vision, it is good that it is both challenging (man had never set foot on the moon) and feasible (at the time, it was believed a trip to the moon was technologically doable). In addition, the vision is very concrete: it is clear when the vision will or will not be achieved.

Core capabilities that need to be developed

A good vision implies that a company has to change. Any vision that can be realized with existing capabilities is not challenging enough. So, it is important to determine what those existing capabilities are and to identify the capabilities needed to realize the vision. By analysing the difference between the existing capabilities and those that are required to realize the vision, a company can determine which new capabilities need to be improved and which capabilities need to be weakened. This is not an unlimited process. Although a

---

A famous example of a company that has been able to change its core capabilities is telecommunication giant Nokia, which started out as a timber company.

Another example of a company that has redefined its core capabilities is Shell, which has existed for more than 100 years. It has recently ceased all its activities in the area of sustainable energy, stating that it sees itself as an oil and gas company, and that it consequently does not expect to be a big sustainable-energy player.

vision may be aimed at change, often considerable change, that does not mean that a company has unlimited flexibility. In most cases, the company will stay reasonably close to its original core activities.

A description of how to change the organization

In addition to redefining the competences, it is also important to outline what the new company should look like. The question that needs to be answered concerns which new organizational arrangements are needed to shape the 'organization of the future'. This is closely connected to the required core capabilities. To be more exact, the relationship between the future organization and the core capabilities is dialectic in nature. The exact shape of the future organization depends on the core capabilities, because the organization needs to adapt to the tasks and skills of the employees of the future organization. The organizational structure needs to provide the necessary room for that. On the other hand, the future organizational structure places demands on the employees in terms of their tasks and skills. It is important to recognize this dialectic tension and to make sure that the future capabilities and organization develop in parallel as much as possible and create the balance required to realize the vision.

A proposed market and product scope supporting the vision

Ultimately, the question is how the company will earn money in the future. Posing this question can be very illuminating for employees who are still convinced that society and the economy are not in motion. Once people acknowledge that both are changing, they will also realize that the company needs to change and requires a vision that inspires the development of new business. However, this does not go far enough. The new business needs to be translated into the new products and businesses the company intends to develop and the new markets it intends to serve. It is, of course, difficult to provide an accurate description in advance, but a serious attempt has to be made. Future scenarios (see next section) may be helpful here. In addition to new products and markets, having a business model, which can simply be described as 'the way in which a company earns its money and the matching financial flows', is also important.

An example of a different business model is the one low-cost carrier easyJet uses to earn money, not only from its airline tickets, but also from hotel owners at the flight destinations, in the form of a kickback for bringing them customers. This allows easyJet to lower its ticket prices, which in turn attracts more customers. Another example in the aviation sector is Schiphol Airport in the Netherlands, which makes more money exploiting shops than it does from the airline industry proper. An older and more tragic example is Xerox, a company that failed to recognize that companies were no longer interested in buying copying machines, but instead want to rent them and pay per copy. Despite the superior technical quality of Xerox's copiers, the company lost a lot of business because it failed to adapt its business model to changing circumstances. So, in addition to possible new products and services, the new vision must also recognize the potential need to adopt new business models.

Image 2.2 easyJet
© Robert Camp

Robustness in the face of multiple scenarios

As stated earlier, a vision not only needs to be inspiring, but it has to be unequivocal for the entire organization. If every employee interprets the vision differently, the resulting confusion will be detrimental to the company's business success. However, it is not just the employees that can be a source of differences in terms of how a vision is interpreted. It is not easy to capture the future that the vision refers to in a few sentences. The future, especially the distant future, is uncertain and unpredictable. This means that it is, by definition, difficult to formulate a vision for 'the' future. One way of capturing the uncertain future is by thinking in terms of multiple possible images for the future, or scenarios (see, for example, Schwartz, 1991; Van der Heijden, 1996). Scenarios make it possible to connect trends into coherent and inspiring stories about the future. By identifying common elements in those stories of the future, it is possible to detect a number of certainties that the company can anticipate with its vision. However, although an unequivocal vision is very much based on the certainties that have been identified, it is also important to think about the consequences future uncertainties will have for the vision. If the future turns out differently from what was expected, that does not have to be a disaster, provided the company knows in advance what changes have to be made to the vision to make the company robust or future-proof. By using different scenarios (different possible futures), the company will be able to pick up on signals that suggest a different future from the one on which the vision was based, allowing the company to know in time what changes have to be made to the vision.

A future that is uncertain and can be described on the basis of scenarios includes the assumption that the future cannot be 'made' by the company. This assumption may clash with the attitude many entrepreneurs have with regard to the future, an attitude that expresses an ambition to shape the future with the business that is being developed. The future is, as it were, secured by the entrepreneur – at least, that is the ambition. The question is, however, whether a certain future can indeed be created. The future is increasingly dependent on various factors that cannot be controlled by the company, no matter what its size. In the debate concerning the extent to which the future can be predicted and shaped, there are differences between the ideas of Michael Porter (1980) and those of Hamel and Prahalad (1994). Porter argues that the future cannot be predicted, and that the sector in which a company operates cannot be shaped, and, as a result of that, it is wise for a company to position itself as best it can in an environment that to a large extent is a given. Hamel and Prahalad argue that it is better to define ambitious goals and to shape the environment and the future. Instead of scenarios, they see fixed points on the time horizon that a company has to reach as quickly as possible.

The difference between these two opposing opinions is in essence the difference between 'outside–in' thinking (Porter) and 'inside–out' thinking (Hamel and Prahalad). Should the organization position itself as best it can in an environment that it cannot shape, or should it formulate its own ambitions in a bid to change the environment? Both approaches recognize that there is a distinction between the company and its environment. Vision relates to what the company wants to achieve in the future. Whether or not that will happen in a future environment that can be shaped depends on which of the strategic perspectives outlined above one chooses to adopt.

Stretch to reach beyond the organization's current grasp

The Kennedy example shows that a good vision draws a clear distinction between what the organization is currently capable of and what is expected of the organization in the future. We have also stated that a vision has to lead to change. A vision that does not call for any change is merely a continuation of the status quo and, as such, in essence redundant. A good vision benefits the organization by formulating a feasible challenge for which the organization has to fight hard. A good vision helps the organization to walk on its toes without overextending itself.

Passion, in order to galvanize the organization

Those who see a vision as a future goal that has to be reached at all costs are mistaken. A vision is not merely a collection of objectives, but also an important source of inspiration and motivation for the organization's employees. Canon's vision, for example, was 'Beat Xerox'. Not only is this a very simple vision, but one would imagine that it motivated Canon's employees to work harder and better.

Another, more peaceful, vision, although not one that inspired any less passion, is Walt Disney's 'Make people happy'. A disadvantage of this vision is that it has relatively little focus: there are myriad ways to make people happy.

Simplicity and clarity of purpose

As mentioned earlier, a vision that can be interpreted in different ways is not functional. The vision has to be unequivocal to curtail any exotic activities for which a broad vision would leave room. A simple, clear vision expresses where the organization wants to be in the future and is not a starting point for a broad discussion about the organization's possible future.

Let's be honest: there will be few visions that meet all the criteria discussed above. A vision that shows what the organization wants to look like in the future and how it wants to reach that goal, that indicates what the relevant milestones are, that offers insight into the capabilities that are needed, that describes the new products, markets and business models, that offers enough of a challenge for the existing organization, that inspires employees and that is clear to everyone involved will be extremely hard to formulate and may well be utopian. In any case, it is unlikely to meet the criterion of simplicity and clarity of purpose. So, the list of criteria has to be seen predominantly as a checklist, to make sure that the vision at least meets a number of important criteria.

Important principles and concepts for looking to the future

Visions do not fall from the sky, but are formulated by companies that want to pursue a certain future goal, based on an expectation, hope or desire about the future. To define a valid vision, it is therefore important to have an idea what the future will or may look like. A good vision has enough flexibility to match different scenarios, and so we discuss how companies can look to the future as a basis for defining a vision.

We define futures research as follows: 'The ability, the competence and the art of describing, explaining, predicting, exploring and interpreting future developments and their consequences, as a result of actions and decisions in the present' (Duin, 2007). This definition implies different possible approaches to the future, ranging from predictive to exploring. However, looking to the future is not merely a matter of applying a method, but also involves the use of creativity, and looking to the future is not a goal in itself, but is a means to inform decisions that have to be made *in the present*. Considering the last remark, it is precisely the decisions made (for example, on what kind of *vision* to pursue) and actions carried out in the present, based on information and knowledge about the future, that can give entrepreneurs a head start compared with those who are being led by today's problems and worries. An often-used metaphor in this respect is an oil tanker coming from the Atlantic Ocean, heading for the port of Rotterdam (The Netherlands). Because of its

---

Box 2.4 Definitions of looking to the future

In literature, many different terms are used for looking to the future: technology forecasting, forecasting, foresight, futures studies, technology future analysis, and so on. We prefer to use the term 'futures research', because we think it is important to emphasize the plural nature of the future and to consider the future from an exploratory perspective rather than a predictive one (one future, singular). We use the term 'research' because, in our view, that term reflects the right attitude towards the future: it reflects curiosity about the future (without knowing in advance what the future holds) and the possibility to be actively engaged in a process in which one can learn more about the future (thereby preventing the fatalistic standpoint that the future is, in principle, unknowable: '*Que sera sera*, whatever will be, will be', as Doris Day once sang).

enormous size and inflexibility, it has to start braking as it enters the English Channel, if it is to avoid sailing past its destination. In other words, looking to the future is all about deciding and acting in the present.

As there are many methods that can be used to look to the future, and there are also many handbooks available, we shall not discuss the application of the various futures research methods in great detail. Instead, we want to focus on a number of the general principles that apply to any and all methods. We will discuss some important principles and concepts for looking to the future:

- time horizon;
- uncertainty;
- environment;
- creativity.

Time horizon

When we talk about the future, it is important to indicate the period about which we are talking. Do we look at next year, or at 2030? Often, terms such as 'short term' and 'long term' are given fixed values. The short term is between 0 and 5 years, the intermediate term is between 5 and 15 years, and long term is 15 years and more. Although this is in itself a clear division, it is not all that helpful. After all, time is relative, which means that concepts such as short term and long term are as well. What may be the long term for one organization may well be the short term for another. For example, 5 years is a short term for oil companies, but long term for mobile telecommunications companies. Investments in the oil sector have a depreciation period of several decades, whereas the depreciation period in the mobile telecommunications sector is much shorter.

The distinction between the short term, intermediate term and long term is not written in black and white, even within individual companies. An (integrated) mobile telecommunications company not only develops services, but also uses various IT platforms and telecommunications services that have a considerably longer depreciation period than the services that are developed. So, within an individual company, different time horizons may occur. Because services, platforms and networks are connected, the existence of different time horizons is not without problems. The exploitation of mobile telecommunications services often has a short cycle, and the developers do not know which services will be used in, say, 3 years' time. However, decisions have to be made in the present about the type and size of the network, because they determine the kinds of service that can be developed.

The distinction between the short term and the long term also affects the way a company approaches the future. Although it has often been said that it is impossible to predict the future, we are of the opinion that the extent to which the future can be predicted depends on how far we attempt to look into the future. This is illustrated in Figure 2.1.

Figure 2.1 shows that the future can be predicted in the short term, using historical data and information. In the short term, there are fewer variable factors, and the future is more or less a reflection of the recent past. However, in the long(er) term, the reliability of using historical information to predict the future diminishes, and it is harder to predict the future with any level of precision. Rather than thinking in terms of a future, it is better to think in terms of multiple possible futures (scenarios), to capture the diversity of 'the' future. In the long(er) term, companies should not focus on a predicted future, but should instead try

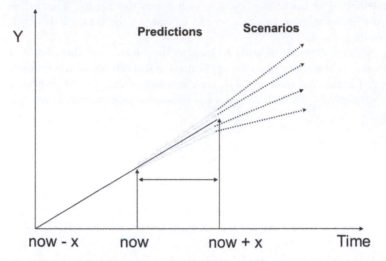

Figure 2.1 Approaches to the future on the basis of the length of the time horizon

to think to what extent they are ready for possible, different futures. The distinction between predicting and exploring the (relative) short term and the (relative) long term is gradual in nature. It is difficult to determine at what point certainty about the future becomes uncertainty.

The environment of an organization

We have argued that the level of uncertainty about the future depends on how far one wants to look into the future and, as such, influences the approach one adopts. In the (relative) short term, uncertainty is limited, and it is to an extent possible to predict the future, whereas in the (relative) long term, there is much more uncertainty, which requires a more exploring attitude. Looking to the future more or less coincides with looking at a company's environment. Entrepreneurs who adopt the approach advocated by Hamel and Prahalad (1994) and believe that the future can be both predicted and shaped will not be very interested in what happens in their environment, because they intend to shape that environment to their strategic needs. More modest entrepreneurs will realize how important the environment is. We are of the opinion that virtually no entrepreneur is able to have a decisive influence over their environment, which means that it is important to map that environment. In the words of Fuller *et al.* (2004, p. 170), 'the future of a particular firm is unlikely to be the result of a single entrepreneurial decision or act. Each firm exists within a context of stakeholder relationships, competitive forces, regulatory frameworks, and other structures'. Figure 2.2 shows a model of a company's environment.

   The environment of an entrepreneur can be divided into two layers:

1   The first and closest layer is the transactional environment, which consists of various *actors*, including suppliers, customers and government, with whom the company has frequent and direct dealings. The relationship with these actors is characterized by lots of feedback: the company's decisions and actions influence the transactional environment, and vice versa. For example, when a competitor lowers its prices, it will influence the

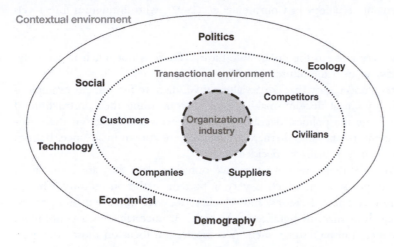

Figure 2.2 The two layers of a company's environment

company's sales and turnover figures. Also, when a company markets a new product, this will affect both its competitors and (potential) customers.

2   The second layer is the contextual environment, which consists of *factors* rather than actors: developments and changes in society, economy, technology, demographics, politics and ecology, which affect the organization, but which the organization in turn cannot influence. Individual companies cannot change the political climate or economic growth. The influence of developments in the contextual environment can be felt via actors in the transactional environment. A demographic development, such as low birth figures, affects the number of consumers and the sales patterns and, consequently, the company.

The difference between the contextual and transactional environments is that the contextual environment consists of factors, whereas the transactional environment consists of actors, and the company can influence the transactional environment but not the contextual environment. Another difference is that changes in the transactional environment affect the short term, whereas changes in the contextual environment affect the long(er) term. In terms of looking to the future, this means that, in mapping short-term developments, changes in the transactional environment have to be leading, whereas mapping long-term developments implies looking at the contextual environment. The assumption is also that it is easier to predict changes in the transactional environment. Although the transactional environment can be complex, owing to the diversity of actors, the assumption is that the behaviour of these actors is reasonably predictable, which gives the company some power to influence their actions. Although changes in the contextual environment will tend to be less dynamic, the interaction between the various trends, their (joint) impact on the actors in the transactional environment and the small influence the company has on that environment make its impact very unpredictable, which in turn makes exploring contextual developments a wise move.

Different types of future uncertainty

It may be clear that predicting the future accurately is rare, because it is almost never possible to be absolutely sure about future developments. There are various kinds of certainty.

We discuss the uncertainty typology of Courtney *et al.* (1997), who distinguish four levels of uncertainty:

1   The first level is very close to the predictable future. There is not much uncertainty, and it is fairly easy to map the future.

2   At Level 2, there is uncertainty that creates alternative, discrete futures. An example is the outcome of a political decision-making process concerning the construction of infrastructure. Because the political decision-making process takes place in the trans-actional environment, the possible alternative outcomes are known in advance, but not the outcome that will eventually be decided.

3   In the case of Level 3, there are also alternative outcomes, but they are continuous. An example is the price of oil, which is very important to the oil industry when it comes to making investment decisions, and which varies over time, with the possible variations ranging from small to significant. At Level 3, uncertainty is a continuum, and certain core areas can be distinguished. A company can focus on those core areas by developing appropriate strategies.

4   In the case of Levels 1–3, the variables to which the uncertainties relate are known. In the case of the fourth level, there is so much uncertainty that the very variables are difficult to determine. The company's environment is chaotic, and it is unclear which actors or factors will have a decisive impact. Applying a strategy in this situation is hard, if not impossible. The best thing to do is to adopt an incremental strategy and look for feedback. A related and more modern strategic approach is to make sure that

Level 4: true uncertainty

Not even a range of possible future outcomes

Level 3: range of futures

Range of possible future outcomes

Level 2: alternative futures

Limited set of possible future outcomes, one of which will occur

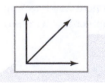

Level 1: clear enough futures

Single view of the future

Figure 2.3 The four levels of uncertainty of Courtney *et al.*, 1997

the company is part of one or more networks, to spread the business risks and improve the information supply (about current as well as future issues) by obtaining information from a variety of different sources.

When we look at the uncertainty levels from a future perspective, Level 1 is very suitable for a predictive approach, although we must realize that this level is less frequent in today's globalized economy. Levels 2 and 3 are suitable for an exploratory approach to the future, in particular the scenario method. The distinction between discrete and continuous uncertainties plays an important role in this regard. Deciding on a strategy on the basis of continuous uncertainties requires a flexible approach, with continuous choices that the company will be able to adjust more easily. If uncertainties change in the future, the company will be able to adapt. Although this is not an easy process by any means, it will be costly, and the company will have to catch up with its competitors, it is possible. In the case of discrete uncertainties, the situation appears to be all or nothing. Because it is virtually impossible to switch from one discrete uncertainty to another, it is difficult to make strategic decisions in time. Under these circumstances, the best way is to adopt a portfolio approach and engage in different activities that are aimed at specific, discrete outcomes. As soon as it becomes clear which future is realistic, the company can expand its activities in that direction, at the expense of the activities aimed at the futures that have turned out to be unrealistic. The problem is that companies always operate in situations of scarcity, which means that there is a limit to the number of possible business activities. In addition, having a vision and strategy that lack the proper focus does not benefit the company's competitive position. In a situation with discrete uncertainties, it is also wise to develop a kind of early-warning system to monitor the company's environment, in an attempt to know as soon as possible which discrete (future) uncertainty is important. In short, in a situation of continuous uncertainty, it is possible to take a strategic position at a relatively early stage, and it is important to be alert so as to change one's strategic position. In a situation of discrete uncertainties, it is best to postpone the final strategic decision, to make strategic investments in different directions of the discrete uncertainty, and to monitor changes in the (contextual and transactional) environment.

Personal aspects of looking to the future

The future, in particular the unpredictable future, is not an algorithm that is easy to apply. Acquiring knowledge about something that may or may not (yet) happen is not an easy job, even though the various approaches and methods of futures research provide valuable support. Personal assessment will always play a role. The following aspects need to be taken into account when looking to the future, regardless of the approach or method one adopts:

1   Do not take yourself as the measure of all things: although we all have the talent to think ahead, making it unnecessary to hire the expensive services of trend watchers and futurologists, that does not mean that the future will play out as you personally expect. We often see this in the case of technology push, when inspired entrepreneurs believe that a certain technology that they have developed will become a commercial success. They only look at the (technology-based) success factors they find important and pay no attention to the factors the market finds important. Many people find it difficult not to mix up their personal hopes for the future and trends that are plausible and probable.

The history of technology and innovation is riddled with examples of technology push, such as the electric car, the picture telephone and the videotape. All these innovations were mainly looked at from a technological perspective and were initially predicted a wonderful future because of technological innovativeness. However, commercial success is much more than having a product with a very high technological performance. Market- and society-related factors should also be taken into account, and these can even be decisive, thereby making new products with a lower technological performance more successful.

2   A dominant discourse: the fact that the future does not develop solely based on one's own preferences (see above) means that it is wise to include many people when studying the future. Although it is tempting to consult experts, research has shown that experts rarely make accurate predictions (Tetlock, 2005). To a large extent, this is because experts are often specialists, which means that they only see a limited part of a complex, integral future and often apply just one method or framework. It is, therefore, wise to include people who move at the edges of the discourse as well, people with different ideas and opinions that may seem incredible now, but that may be commonplace in the future.

3   The future is a social construction: strictly speaking, the future does not exist, by which we mean not only that there are various possible futures, but that the future as a physical entity does not exist. This may be an ontological problem, but not when it comes to studying the future. The future can be seen as a social construction. People have certain ideas and expectations about the future, on the basis of which they act and make

For its strategic thinking processes, the oil company Shell uses what it calls 'remarkable people': people with a special opinion or social position who look at Shell-related issues differently. And, just because they see things differently, they might provide valuable information and will ask questions that people working for Shell will not tend to ask.

Paradoxically, people who are not experts in certain areas may have very valuable things to say. It is their very independence that allows them to maintain the objectivity needed to look to the future. In doing this, they prevent what is called 'groupthink', which means that, in decision-making processes, often a certain opinion given by the most influential person will dominate the discussion. Generalists, as opposed to specialists, are in less danger of developing a form of 'company blindness', which means only looking at the company itself and no longer having eyes for important outside developments. A rather similar concept is 'marketing myopia', meaning that companies only look at their company from a product perspective and do not pay attention to companies that, with their products and services, fulfil the same needs for users. In doing this, they overlook potential competitors. For example, many national train companies did not pay attention to the activities of low-cost airlines, as they considered taking a train and flying as different services, thereby overlooking the fact that they serve the same need (i.e. transportation).

A good example of Aspect 3 is the self-fulfilling prophecy, which means that, when people think something will happen in the future, they act accordingly and, in doing so, make sure their expectations become truth. When people think a bank will collapse, they empty their bank accounts, and the bank will indeed collapse. The reverse is also possible: a self-denying prophecy. When people are presented with the prospect of a grim future, they will do anything to make sure that future does not happen. Figure 2.4 shows a few examples of the relationship between people's expectations regarding the future and their intentions.

decisions in the present. In a sense, the future is 'constructed' in the present. The sociologist W. I. Thomas once said, 'If men consider things as real, they are real in their consequences' (1903).

Some statements about the future are presented as self-fulfilling or self-denying prophecies. The classic doomsday scenario predicting the end of the world is often intended as a wake-up call designed to persuade people, companies and government to behave differently. By contrast, some stock-exchange gurus make predictions about the future course of a certain share and they will convince people to buy (or sell) these stocks, which will then take the future course they predicted. So, sometimes statements about the future are merely designed to inform people, but they end up affecting the behaviour of people, businesses and governments. For instance, it was never the intention of the Club of Rome to change the world, but the unexpected success of its study (i.e. making people aware that, if we go on

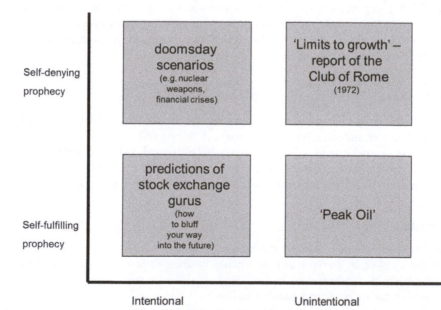

Figure 2.4 The combination of prophecies and intentions

Box 2.5 Ambidexterity and the future

Perhaps looking to the future is not the most difficult thing to do for an entrepreneur. It could be looking to the future to develop new businesses and *at the same time* taking care of daily business. Most companies solve this dilemma, which arises because every company has limited resources, by focusing on the short term, on *business as usual*, as that is the less risky way to earn money. However, successful companies are able to balance both business activities. In business literature, this is called *ambidexterity*. Roughly, there are two ways of realizing ambidexterity: (1) structural ambidexterity: innovative activities are more or less positioned outside the existing organization, and exploration and exploitation are integrated at the top management level; and (2) contextual ambidexterity: every employee needs to balance his or her daily activities with those activities that are focused on the future.

We would like to note that becoming an ambidextrous organization means, for existing companies, that they should care about how to stay innovative and not focus too much on short-term, operational matters, whereas, for entrepreneurs, the challenge is to not only focus on new business but also to earn some money to stay in business in the short term.

Based on: O'Reilly and Tushman (2004), Kauppila (2010)
and Tushman *et al.* (2011).

---

like this, we will destroy the world and ourselves) has urged and inspired many to think about the future of our planet (Beckerman, 1972). In the case of 'peak oil', identifying that possible point increased oil production until that point was reached (although opinions vary on this issue). What is important when it comes to the social construction of the future is that companies need to be aware that the future is not something that lies outside their organization and time, but that it affects what they and their stakeholders (in the transactional environment) decide and do in the present.

Chapter summary

Entrepreneurship is logically and almost naturally related to the future, as it takes time to develop an innovative idea and to set up a new venture. A current innovative idea might not be so innovative and successful later on, when the status quo has changed, and new developments in society, technology and market have emerged. Every entrepreneur, therefore, should have a vision of the future and consider uncertainty as an opportunity and not as a threat per se.

Study questions

1   Why should an entrepreneur look to the future?
2   How can the view of an entrepreneur on his/her business environment be related to how he/she looks to the future?
3   Define a vision that meets Schoemaker's conditions.
4   Which factors decide the (right) time horizon for your business?
5   Which outside influences and which stakeholders could impact your future business?

References

Beckerman, W. (1972). Economists, scientists, and environmental catastrophe. *Oxford Economic Papers*. 24(3): 327–44.

Courtney, H., Kirkland, J. and Viguerie, P. (1997). Strategy under uncertainty. *Harvard Business Review*. Nov–Dec: 67–79.

Duin, P. A. van der (2007). 'Futures research and science: Introduction', in P. van der Duin (ed.), *Knowing Tomorrow? How science deals with the future*. Delft, Netherlands: Eburon Academic Publishers, pp. 9–20.

Duin, P. A. van der and Hartmann, D. (2007). Young dreamers: An explorative study on how techno-starters look to the future. *Journal of Futures Studies*. 12(2): 23–36.

Fuller, T., Argyle, P. and Moran, T. P. (2004). 'Meta-rules for entrepreneurial foresight', in H. Tsoukas and J. Shepherd (eds), *Managing the Future: Foresight in the knowledge economy*. Oxford, UK: Blackwell Publishing, pp. 169–86.

Hamel, G. and Prahalad, C. K. (1994). Competing for the future. *Harvard Business Review*. July–Aug: 122–8.

Kauppila, O. (2010). Creating ambidexterity by integrating and balancing structurally separate interorganizational partnerships. *Strategic Organization*. 8(4): 283–312.

Kuosa, T. (2012). *The Evolution of Strategic Foresight: Navigating public policy making*. Farnham, UK: Gower Publishing.

O'Reilly III, C. and Tushman, M. L. (2004). The ambidextrous organization. *Harvard Business Review*. April: 74–81.

Porter, M. E. (1980). *Competitive Strategy: Techniques for analyzing industries and competitors*. New York: Free Press.

Schoemaker, P. J. H. (2002). *Profiting from Uncertainty*. New York: Free Press.

Schwartz, P. (1991). *The Art of the Longview: Three global scenarios to 2005*. New York: Currency Doubleday.

Tetlock, P. E. (2005). *Expert Political Judgment: How good is it? How can we know?* Princeton, NJ: Princeton University Press.

Thomas, W. I. (1903). *The Relation of the Medicine Man to the Origin of the Professional Occupations*. Chicago, IL: University of Chicago Press.

Tushman, M. L., Smith, W. K. and Bins, A. (2011). The ambidextrous CEO. *Harvard Business Review*. June: 74–80.

Van der Heijden, K. (1996). *Scenarios: The art of strategic conversation*. Chichester, UK: Wiley.

Further reading

Barker, J. (1996). *Paradigms: The business of discovering the future*. New York: HarperBusiness.

Duin, P. A. van der (ed.) (2007). *Knowing Tomorrow? How science deals with the future*. Delft, Netherlands: Eburon Academic Publishers.

Duin, P. A. van der (ed.) (forthcoming). *Foresight in Organizations*. Routledge.

Millett, S. M. (2011). *Managing the Future: A guide to forecasting and strategic planning in the 21st century*. Axminster, UK: Triarchy Press.

Rescher, N. (1998). *Predicting the Future: An introduction to the theory of forecasting*. New York: State University of New York Press.

Schnaars, S. P. (1989). *Megamistakes: Forecasting and the myth of rapid technological change*. London: Free Press.

Sherden, W. A. (1998). *The Fortune Sellers: The big business of buying and selling predictions*. New York: John Wiley.

Twiss, B. (1992). *Forecasting for Technologists and Engineers: A practical guide for better decisions*. London: Peter Peregrinus.

3 Inventive problem-solving and brainstorming

Rope problem

Imagine that you are locked in a room that is completely empty. From the ceiling hang two thin ropes. Your task is to tie the two ropes together. Only when you succeed in doing that will you be released from the room. Easy enough, it seems, but there are several problems. If you grab one rope and walk towards the other rope, you cannot reach it. The ropes are too lightweight to make them swing like a pendulum, and they are too thin for you to climb. The ropes must remain attached to the ceiling, and so you are not allowed to pull one off the ceiling. How can you connect the two ropes? Remember, the room is completely empty. Take a moment to think about it and try to solve this problem before reading on.

Have you solved the puzzle? If so, take another moment to reflect on how you accomplished that. How *did* you solve the problem? Was it a lucky guess? Probably not. Did you address the problem in a structured way? Did you relate the elements of the problem to another situation for which you already knew the solution? If you have not yet solved the puzzle, here are a few more hints. There are two different solutions to the problem, each of which can be discovered by focusing your attention on what actually prevents you from tying the two ropes together. What are the specific reasons that impede the task at hand, and how can you remove these obstacles? Maybe you want to give it another try before continuing to the answers?

Here is an example of how you could use logical reasoning to solve the problem:

> If only I could set the ropes in motion by swinging them, then I could stand in the middle and wait for them to swing towards me, grab them and tie them together. But I cannot swing the ropes because they are too lightweight. If only they were heavier, then I could swing them like a pendulum. If only they were heavier . . . if only I could make them heavier . . . by tying something to them . . . like my shoes!

Maybe you feel this is cheating, because the setting was a room that was completely empty. However, it was never implied that you were naked. Maybe you did not realize that you are wearing clothes that you can use to help you solve the problem. Maybe your mind interpreted the phrase 'completely empty' as 'there are no objects available, whatsoever'. Now that you have seen this solution, the other solution is much easier to find. The other obstacle that prevents you from tying the two ropes together is that the ropes are not long enough for you to hold one and reach the other one. If only the ropes were longer . . . if only you could make one of the ropes longer . . . by tying something to it that would increase its length . . . like your shirt or your trousers! Again, you find a solution by removing one of the reasons why the ropes could not be connected initially. The structured way of solving a problem like this one is to identify the obstacles that impede the straightforward solution and then focus on how to overcome these obstacles.

Problem-solving

Problem-solving is highly relevant to entrepreneurship, especially technology-based entrepreneurship. No matter how good the solution is that you think you have already developed, there will always be unexpected problems. Some may be minor problems that are easily fixed, but occasionally the problems can be so big that the continuity of the company is at stake. When a problem is purely technical, it seems unlikely that it could jeopardize the entire enterprise, because technical problems are meant to be solved, and experience shows that most technical problems can be solved. Peter Rem, a respected physicist and professor of recycling technology at TU Delft, once phrased it like this: 'If it is not in conflict with the laws of physics, it can be done in theory. And it can probably do it in practice as well, provided the motivation for doing so is big enough'. He proved his point by inventing a waste-separation technology only after an in-depth market analysis indicated that a viable business case could be made, once that technology existed. Box 3.1 presents this case in more detail.

Another example of the need for inventive problem-solving is Holland Container Innovations (www.hcinnovations.nl). This young company was founded by students who analysed the commercial potential of a new technology during the course Turning Technology into Business (see also Box 1.4). In this case, the technology already existed in the form of a Dutch patent describing a method to fold a cargo container (NL1017159: *Inklapbare container voor stukgoed*). This technology was developed (invented) by Ton Klein Breteler, at the Department of Marine and Transport Technology at TU Delft, and patented by the university and the Port of Rotterdam Authority. The container is folded to one-third of its original height by first pushing the long sidewalls inwards towards the bottom of the container, then raising the roof, which remains attached by cables to the sidewalls, and finally collapsing the roof with the sidewalls on to the bottom of the container. At the time, only a small wooden scale model existed that demonstrated the principle. Would it also work on a full-sized, 40-ft (12-m) steel cargo container? Before actually building a full-scale prototype, it is highly recommended to first analyse the potential market for the new product. What are the key advantages of a foldable container over a regular one? Can this competitive advantage be quantitatively expressed in terms of money? In other words, try to put a real price tag on advantages such as the need for less storage space, the use of fewer trucks, etc. How does that measure up to the (inevitable) higher cost of the foldable container over a standard container? How big is the potential market for foldable containers, and what are the specific requirements in terms of legislation and customer satisfaction? All these issues need to be

Box 3.1 Resteel

Ferrous scrap (iron and steel) is an important commodity in the manufacturing of steel. Contrary to what the word 'scrap' suggests, steel scrap is actually regarded as an important raw material and has become a globally traded commodity with an increasing demand. Shredded end-of-life cars are an important primary source of steel scrap. However, because of the increased use of electric motors in passenger cars, the amount of copper in car scrap has steadily increased over the years. Currently, an average passenger car contains about thirty electric motors, used for windshield wipers, electric windows, adjustable seats, etc. At the same time, the amount of steel used in the manufacturing of new cars is steadily decreasing, as steel is gradually being replaced by aluminium or a variety of plastics and composites. These two trends (more electric motors and less steel) have caused a sharp increase in the concentration of copper in steel car scrap. When this steel scrap is smelted, it produces a lower-grade steel. If the concentration of copper exceeds 0.2 per cent (Leroy *et al.*, 1995), the newly smelted steel is too brittle for any serious applications such as new cars. Even below this threshold there are serious problems, not least because this new steel now contains copper that cannot be separated in a cheap and easy way. So, when that steel reaches its end-of-life stage, it aggravates the problem in each next smelting cycle. If only the technology existed that could separate steel scrap that contains copper (the electric motors) from pure steel scrap. A search through the patent literature revealed that large companies such as British Steel had been trying to accomplish this for over a decade, as evidenced by their patents that claim to do just this. However, patents may claim whatever the inventor wants to claim, as long as they describe how it works. It is not required to prove that it actually works, as in this case, where none of the patents on technologies that claim to separate copper scrap from steel scrap actually do a good job.

What would be the market value of a technology that could separate copper and steel scrap? Students of the course Turning Technology into Business addressed this question and worked out a detailed market analysis for a technology that did not yet exist at that time. The results were very encouraging, and Peter Rem became sufficiently motivated to subsequently invent this technology. Although that sounds too good to be true, it was not the first time that Rem proved his ability to 'invent on demand'. An interesting aspect of this 'prospective entrepreneurship' was that the market analysis provided useful guidelines on the boundary conditions for the yet-to-be-invented technology, such as: What are the potential revenues as a function of the copper contamination (e.g. the added value of steel with only 0.05 per cent copper contamination over steel that contains 0.1 per cent copper)? What operational costs (euros per ton processed scrap) are acceptable to make this process economically viable? Also, the students explored various business models for the new enterprise. Should the new business become a processing plant where 'dirty' steel scrap is turned into 'clean' steel scrap, or should the company build and sell scrap separation machines? Maybe the best business opportunity is selling a licence to all existing scrap companies so they can build their own machines. An attractive licence strategy would be to relate the royalties to the amount of material processed. (Chapter 5 discusses licensing strategies in more detail.) The technology was developed by Peter Rem and patented by TU Delft (WO2010117273: Method and apparatus for separating a non-ferrous metal-comprising fraction from ferrous scrap). A new company, called ReSteel, was founded to exploit the commercial potential of this patent. In Febuary 2014, ReSteel was acquired by IFE Aufbereitungstechnik GmbH in Austria, one of the worldwide leading suppliers of machine components for the bulk materials industry.

Image 3.1 Scrap metal
© Mark Ahsmann

addressed and explored thoroughly before good money is spent on building even a full-scale prototype. The golden rule is to find a customer before you build the product. Once you have found a customer, you will be highly motivated to create the product in close collaboration with the customer. Nothing is more frustrating than searching for customers who might want to buy a product that you have already created. Chances are that your product is not exactly what the customers (if you find them) want. For a more detailed discussion on identifying customers and collaborative product development, see 'The lead user concept' in Chapter 8.

Because their market analysis indicated a great potential need for foldable cargo containers, the students, after they had graduated, founded the company Holland Container Innovations (HCI). A lead user was identified, and they worked collaboratively on reaching their first milestone: a full-sized foldable cargo container prototype. Immediately, two problems arose. First, legislation demands that all cargo sea containers are certified to remain afloat for at least one hour in the event that they fall overboard. Their current design for the foldable container would sink immediately. Second, and even more importantly, the current design was not robust enough, and the time it would take to fold and unfold the container was prohibitively long. These were two fatal blows to this promising business idea. Certainly, this was curtains for the enterprise. Unless . . . Unless the problems were solved, of course, which is precisely what HCI did. In collaboration with the faculty of mechanical engineering, a more robust concept was developed to fold a cargo container faster, so that it performed in the way that the market demanded. As an added bonus, the new design required less effort to fold, and, in the folded state, it measured only one-quarter of the original height. Now, four folded containers could be stacked and locked together to occupy the exact same volume as one unfolded container – a space saving of 75 per cent. The new design was patented (WO2010151116: Foldable container), and a first prototype was built. HCI acquired a full-sized (40-ft) cargo container, took it apart and implemented the folding mechanism. Quite a daunting task, as the inside dimensions of the container had to remain exactly the same, otherwise it would not blend in seamlessly in the world of cargo transport. Along the way, another problem was solved. Each of the container sidewalls weighs about 600 kg. How could these heavy sidewalls be lowered and lifted with the least amount of effort? A mechanism was invented to store the potential (gravitational) energy from the sidewalls during the folding process using a torsion spring mechanism. That energy is recovered when the sidewall is erected again. This technology enables a nearly effortless folding and unfolding process, and was patented (WO2009034142: Foldable container).

The example of HCI illustrates that new technological problems will arise no matter how well the original concept appears to solve the original problem. That means that you always have to be prepared to deal with unexpected problems, both emotionally (do not throw in the towel too soon when you encounter a setback) and technically (try and solve the problems by inventing solutions). The former requires a highly motivated team and a stimulating and proactive board of advisors; the latter needs an inventive problem-solving approach, which is what we will discuss next.

Inventive problem–solving

It is one thing to come up with a great innovative product for which you have established that a sizeable market exists. In other words, if you can deliver the product, there will be customers. But it is quite another thing to actually make this happen, to develop the new product that fulfils all of its promises and is readily accepted in the market. Take, for example, the invention of the incandescent light bulb. A great idea, but it proved quite a rocky road to make it happen. When asked who invented the light bulb, most people will probably answer that it was Thomas Edison. However, the invention of generating light by passing a current through a metal filament must be attributed to the British chemist and inventor Sir Humphry Davy, whose greatest claim to fame is the Davy lamp, an oil lamp that could safely be used in mines, where flammable gases (mine damp) frequently caused explosions. It also served as a detection device for the presence of these flammable gases (which caused the lamp to burn brighter and bluer) and for the presence of asphyxiating carbon dioxide (which would dim or extinguish the lamp). In 1802, almost 80 years before Edison invented and patented his light bulb, which contained a long-lasting filament, Davy was the first person to generate electric light by sending a current through a thin strip of platinum. Despite the high melting temperature of platinum, the strip did not last very long, nor did it generate a particularly bright light. It is unknown whether Davy foresaw a market opportunity for electric light, but it is very likely, because, in 1809, he also invented the first arc lamp. Even though there was a huge potential market for incandescent light bulbs, it took several inventors a very long time to overcome the problem of finding a durable filament, including John W. Star's patented charcoal filament (1845) and Alexander Lodygin's filaments made of chromium, iridium, rhodium, ruthenium, osmium, molybdenum and tungsten (all of which he patented – see Box 3.2). Finally, in 1878, the British physicist and chemist Joseph Wilson Swan demonstrated a prototype of an incandescent light bulb containing a carbon-fibre filament. The light bulb contained a vacuum and, therefore, no oxygen to ignite the filament. Swan had started working on the development of the light bulb in 1850 and, after 28 years of experimenting, he had finally succeeded.

On the other side of the Atlantic, Thomas Alva Edison (1847–1931) was also searching for the right material to make durable filaments for use in his light bulbs. Edison is regarded by many people as the prototypical inventor, although he frequently comes up second behind Gyro Gearloose (the fictional inventor from the Donald Duck comics) in a poll that I take among the students in my class Turning Technology into Business every year. Indeed, with more than 1,000 patents to his name, Edison is undoubtedly one of the most prolific inventors in history. Among the inventions ascribed to him are the telephone, phonograph, light bulb, electrical distribution system, electric vote recorder, stock ticker, quadruplex telegraph, motion-picture camera, fluoroscope and the dictating machine. Even though, as in the case of the light bulb, he was not always the original inventor of the technological principles underlying these inventions, he did improve and modify many of them for commercial use. In 1890, Edison founded Edison General Electric, which, after a merger with Thomson–Houston Electric Company 2 years later, became General Electric. According to *Forbes* (2014), GE was, in 2014, the eighth largest company (in market value) in the US and the seventh most valuable brand worldwide. One of Edison's most famous quotes is, 'Genius is one percent inspiration and ninety-nine percent perspiration'. Edison was certainly the prime example of this statistic. While searching for the right filament for incandescent light bulbs, he carried out more than 6,000 experiments, and, in the development of a nickel–iron battery, the number of experiments exceeded 10,000. Is that genius at work, or merely brute-force trial and error? One of Edison's big rivals and adversaries at the time was the Serbia-born physicist Nikola Tesla (1856–1943). Among his 'mere' 300 patents are inventions such as the alternating current (AC) motor, the AC polyphase power distribution system, radio frequency oscillators, an ozone generation apparatus, charged particle beam devices, high-voltage discharge devices, lightning protection devices, a bladeless turbine and a vertical takeoff and landing aircraft. And there is still an ongoing debate on who invented the radio – was it Guglielmo Marconi (1874–1937) or Nikola Tesla?

In 1884, Tesla moved to the United States and became an assistant to Edison, who had just perfected the light bulb and was now working on the electricity grid that was needed to bring electricity to consumers. Obviously, light bulbs by themselves were useless without a network to carry the electricity needed to light the bulbs. That is why the light bulb is really a 'system innovation', because, for it to be useful, the existing infrastructure of gas lighting needed to be replaced by an electricity network. Edison had designed a direct current (DC) generator that did not work very well. He asked Tesla to improve it and promised him a big reward if he succeeded. After Tesla had fixed the DC generator, he and Edison had an argument over the reward promised by Edison. Edison refused to pay, and Tesla quit. By 1888, Tesla had developed a much better electricity generator that produced alternating current (AC). This AC system had big advantages over Edison's DC system. It is more efficient (lower losses) to transport the electricity, and it is much easier to transform electricity to a higher or lower voltage. A long and bitter battle that became known as the 'War of the Currents' ensued over the establishment of the standard for electrical power distribution. Edison did everything in his power to discredit Tesla and George Westinghouse (1846–1914), an engineer and entrepreneur who had founded Westinghouse Electric Company in 1886

Box 3.2 Alexander Lodygin's patent

On 14 September 1888, Alexander Lodygin (who at the time resided in Paris and had changed his name to Alexandre de Lodyguine) applied for a US patent that was eventually granted as US 494,151 on 23 March 1893 and was titled 'Filament for incandescent lamps'. Old patents are far easier to read and comprehend than modern patents, in which the language has become highly specialized. Nineteenth-century patents read like a short narrative in which the inventor explains his invention. The full patent is only a page and a half (Lodygin, 1893). This is how it starts:

To all whom it may concern:

Be it known that I, Alexandre de Lodyguine, a citizen of Russia, residing at Paris, France, have invented a certain new and useful improvement in Incandescents for Electric Lamps, (Case No.223) of which the following is a specification.

The invention relates particularly to the manufacture of incandescents or filaments of incandescent electric lamps. I make use of any suitable organic substance such as silk, bamboo, thread, piassava, or other organic material capable of receiving the treatment hereinafter mentioned. In practice I have obtained especially good results from the use of silk. The material selected is reduced to the required shape and size in any of the usual ways employed in making the blanks from which such incandescents are generally formed. These blanks, having the required dimensions, are treated in the following manner. The material is first carbonized in any usual, well-known way, and it is then placed in a chamber from which the air is afterward exhausted. A current of electricity is then sent through the filament while *in vacuo*, and this is of such strength as to drive off the occluded gases contained therein. The vacuum pump employed for exhausting the air from the chamber may be kept in operation during this step of the process, if desired. After the filament has been thoroughly freed from the occluded gases, a current is passed through it of sufficient strength to change its character from the original carbonized filament, into the form of coke. This step is carried on *in vacuo*, and in practice it is found that it may be conveniently accomplished in about eight seconds. The strength of current used is as great as the filament will practically bear without breaking. In some instances the two steps may be combined. It is found that by thus coking the filament, its permanent or cold resistance is caused to change, being gradually reduced until it has become approximately the same as the hot resistance of the filament before it was coked. The coking may be stopped at this point, or before it has been reached, if desired, and for certain purposes it is found advantageous to arrest the operation at an intermediate point. When the resistance has reached its lowest point, it is found that it tends to again rise, if this step of the treatment is continued. The filament, after it has been thus electrically coked, may be placed in the bulb and the lamp finished and made ready for use in the usual way; or the coked filament may be further treated by the deposition of carbon upon its surface. This may be accomplished by placing it in a closed vessel charged with a hydrocarbon or other carbonaceous gas, and passing a current of electricity through it sufficient to heat it to such a temperature that the gas will be decomposed and carbon deposited on the coked core.

On account of the great uniformity of its texture or fiber, silk is found to be especially suited to the purposes of this invention and to the treatment described.

and had patented the AC system (US Patent 373,035: System of electrical distribution). To demonstrate how dangerous AC was, Edison staged public executions of cats, dogs, cattle and horses. Certainly, no one would want to have that happen in their home. On 4 January 1903, he even electrocuted an elephant in Luna Park Zoo on Coney Island (see Box 3.3). All to no avail, because the advantages of AC over DC were evident, and AC became the standard. AC is what households all over the world are still using today.

Tesla did not think highly of Edison the inventor:

> If Edison had the task of finding a needle in a haystack, he would not lose time determining the most probable location of it. He would immediately, with the diligence of a bee, begin picking up straw after straw until he found the object of his search.

Methodical, yes; smart, no. Tesla accused Edison of merely applying brute-force trial and error, instead of a more structured approach to problem-solving and inventing. Edison was

---

Box 3.3 The electrocution of Topsy the elephant

On 4 January 1903, Thomas Edison staged a highly publicized electrocution of an elephant to demonstrate the dangers of AC. Edison had established DC as the standard for electricity distribution and was living large off the patent royalties, royalties he was in no mood to lose when George Westinghouse and Nikola Tesla promoted AC. Edison's aggressive campaign to discredit the new current took the macabre form of a series of animal electrocutions using AC (a killing process that he referred to as getting 'Westinghoused'). Edison electrocuted squirrels, stray dogs and cats, but he also zapped a few cattle and horses. His 'biggest achievement' came when the Luna Park Zoo at Coney Island decided that Topsy, a cranky female elephant who had squashed three handlers in 3 years (including one idiot who tried feeding her a lighted cigarette), had to go. Park officials originally considered hanging Topsy, but the Society for the Prevention of Cruelty to Animals objected on humanitarian grounds, and so someone suggested having Topsy 'ride the lightning', a practice that had been used in the American penal system since 1890 to dispatch the condemned. Edison was happy to oblige. When the day came, Topsy was restrained using a ship's hawser fastened on one end to a donkey engine and on the other to a post. Wooden sandals with copper electrodes were attached to her feet, and a copper wire ran to Edison's electric light plant, where his technicians awaited the go-ahead. To make sure that Topsy emerged from this spectacle more than just singed and angry, she was fed cyanide-laced carrots moments before a 6,600-volt AC charge slammed through her body. Officials need not have worried. Topsy was killed instantly, and Edison, in his mind anyway, had proved his point. A crowd of 1,500 people witnessed Topsy's execution, which was filmed by Edison and released later that year as 'Electrocuting an elephant'. A short version of this video can be found on YouTube (2014). In the end, all Edison had to show for his efforts was a string of dead animals, including the unfortunate Topsy, and a current that quickly fell out of favour, as AC demonstrated its superiority in less lethal ways to become the standard.

Source: Text adapted from Wired.com (2008)

not impressed by this criticism and stated, 'I have not failed. I've just found 10,000 ways that won't work'. But Tesla was relentless:

> His methods were very inefficient. He would spend a lot of time and energy reaching nothing – unless luck was with him. In the beginning, it was sad watching him work, knowing that just a little theoretical knowledge and a few calculations could save him at least 30 per cent of his time. He despised education from books, and especially the knowledge of mathematics, trusting completely on his inventive intuition and American common sense.

The bottom line is that Tesla emphasized that a little elementary physics makes a big difference in solving technical problems. This is one of the key aspects of the Theory of Inventive Problem-solving, developed by Genrich Altshuller.

TRIZ

Genrich Saulovich Altshuller was born in Tashkent in the Uzbek Soviet Socialist Republic in 1926. While working as a patent inspector, he noticed that the inventive step in many patents involved the same basic physical principles. He studied some 200,000 patents, extracted what he called Principles of Inventing and argued that these methods could be applied in a systematic way to solve new technical problems. In 1948, he wrote a letter to Stalin in which he criticized the Soviet Union's ability to innovate and compete economically with the rest of the world. He offered to improve that situation by teaching the application of his Principles of Inventing. In those days, nobody openly criticized the Soviet Union, and Stalin was not a particularly forgiving man. Altshuller was arrested, interrogated, tortured and finally sentenced to 25 years' imprisonment in Siberia. After Stalin's death in 1954, Altshuller was released and rehabilitated. He continued to study more patents and refined his method, which he called *Teoriya Resheniya Izobreatatelskikh Zadach* (Theory of Inventive Problem-solving, or TRIZ). Two years later, he had developed the first algorithm for inventive problem-solving, which consisted of ten steps and five inventive principles. By 1968, TRIZ had expanded to twenty-five steps, thirty-five inventive principles and a 'Matrix for resolving technical contradictions', which consisted of 32×32 parameters.

In 1969, Altshuller founded the Azerbajdzhan Public Institute for Inventive Creativity, the first TRIZ training and research centre in the USSR. He also established the Public Laboratory of Invention Methodology, which was the first public open-source initiative aimed at unifying further TRIZ development nationwide. By 1971, TRIZ had expanded to include thirty-five steps, forty inventive principles (with eighty-eight sub-principles) and a matrix for resolving technical contradictions containing 39×39 parameters. This version of TRIZ formed the basis of a book that Altshuller published under his pen name H. Altov. After Perestroika, TRIZ came to the attention of the rest of the world, and, in 1993, Altshuller's book was translated into English and published as *And Suddenly the Inventor Appeared*. The book uses many examples to illustrate the various inventive principles. After working through a number of these problems, the reader develops a feeling for the TRIZ methodology and can try to apply these inventive principles to the other problems. It is a powerful, hands-on demonstration that problem-solving can be approached in a systematic way, by applying the generalized principles that Altshuller derived from studying a quarter of a million patents. In later years, Altshuller described TRIZ as follows: 'You can wait a hundred years for enlightenment, or you can solve the problem in 15 minutes with these principles'. It is reminiscent of how Tesla criticized Edison's approach to inventing and problem-solving.

One of the key elements in TRIZ is identifying 'technical contradictions' – reasons why a straightforward technical solution seems impossible – and attempting to remove these contradictions. Think back to the rope problem. The technical contradictions were that the ropes were too short (could not reach each other) and too light (could not swing like a pendulum). Once these contradictions were removed (increasing the length or increasing the weight of the rope), the problem was solved. The following example is taken from *And Suddenly the Inventor Appeared* (Altshuller, 1996). It does not deal with an unsolved problem, because, obviously, the problem is already solved. We are confronted with a product (chocolate candies) that was manufactured in some factory, and ask ourselves the question, 'How did they make these candies?':

> It was a young girl's birthday. One of the guests brought a big box of chocolate candies. The candies were shaped like small bottles, and filled with thick raspberry syrup. One of the guests said, 'I wonder how these candies are made?' 'First they make the bottles, and then they fill them with syrup', explained another guest.
>
> But the syrup is thick, and that makes it hard to pour it into the bottles. 'If you heat the syrup, it becomes more liquid', said a third guest. But then the syrup would melt the chocolate bottle.

So, the question remains: how do they make these chocolate candies? What are the technical contradictions that need to be removed? Which of the forty inventive principles (methods) can we apply to solve the mystery? The technical contradictions are that cold syrup is too thick to pour, and that hot syrup will melt the chocolate. Two methods that are appropriate for this problem are:

- Method 13: 'The other way around';
- Method 36: 'Phase transitions'.

Altshuller's book is full of such problems, which are presented as a challenge to the reader. A brief narrative describing a specific problem ends with the phrase from which the book derives its title: '*And Suddenly the Inventor Appeared*. "I have an idea!" he exclaimed. "I know how to make this type of candy quickly and without defects. The trick is to . . ."'. At that point, the reader is challenged to come up with the solution. Sometimes there are hints, but in most cases you are expected to try and apply the TRIZ methods to the problem. The two hints above (not given in the book) on which methods to apply make it relatively easy to solve this case. The solution is that you should freeze the syrup, in a mould that is shaped like a bottle, and then dip the bottle-shaped frozen syrup into molten chocolate. This is both doing it the other way around (cooling instead of heating) and changing the phase (state of matter) of the syrup (from liquid to solid). Applying the chocolate after shaping the syrup is also doing it the other way around.

It is useful to think about this process of inventive problem-solving. The more you think about it, the more you recognize that ingenious solutions to problems often can be categorized in this way. Thus, trying to apply the TRIZ principles (methods) to a new problem may indeed lead to a solution. In fact, these principles can also be found in the patents of TU Delft. For example, Geert Jan Witkamp of the Laboratory for Process Equipment has patented the process of eutectic freeze crystallization (EFC). When a salt (any salt – not just kitchen salt, NaCl) is dissolved in water, it is relatively expensive to recover it. The most common way to do this is to heat the solution to evaporate the water. The steam is condensed again, and the salt precipitates. The salt and the water are now separate again. Analysing this process, you may realize that it involves a phase transition for the water to free itself from the salt. Can Methods 13 and 36 also be applied here to find another way to recover the salt? What is the opposite of evaporating water? Freezing the water, obviously. That too is a phase transition. Can the water and the salt be separated through freezing? Indeed it can! Water is one of the very few substances for which the solid state has a lower density ('is lighter') than the liquid phase. Ice floats on water; almost every other solid sinks in its own liquid. Life on Earth would not be possible if ice did not float on water. Without this unique property, every pool, lake or sea would freeze solid. And without water, there cannot be life (as we know it).

EFC separates salts and water in the above-mentioned way. Witkamp patented the machine that makes this happen (WO2008113386: Crystallizer with internal scraped cooled wall and method of use thereof). It is interesting to observe that most people believe that cooling requires more energy than heating, and so EFC must be less efficient than evaporation. However, thermodynamically, the two processes require the same amount of energy. The only difference lies in the efficiency of the machinery. Energy is required to heat, and energy is required to cool. Theoretically, the amount of energy needed to raise the temperature of a salt solution by 1°C is the same as to decrease the temperature by 1°C. However, in most cases, a salt solution is initially at room temperature (20°C). That means that the temperature must be raised by 80°C to turn water into steam. However, the temperature needs only to be lowered by 20°C to freeze the water. So, in that case, theoretically, evaporation requires four times more energy than freezing. Even though the difference is a bit smaller in practice, it still makes EFC a commercially very interesting technology, especially because there are several other benefits, which we will not discuss here.

The forty principles of TRIZ are listed in Table 3.1. Except for a few obvious methods, such as Method 35, 'Parameter changes', or Method 18, 'Mechanical vibration', most of these methods require some explanation before a prospective inventor can try to apply them to the problem at hand. In his later book, *The Innovation Algorithm* (1999), Altshuller discusses each principle and supplies plenty of examples to illustrate them. For example, Method 7, 'Nested doll', got its name from the famous Russian Matryoshka dolls, which are cut from a single block of wood. This method includes (a) placing one object inside another object (for example, hiding a safe in a wall, or attaching a brush to the inside of the cap of a bottle of nail varnish); (b) placing one object inside a second object, which itself is placed inside a third object, and so on (for example, a folding telescope, or stackable chairs); and (c) one object passing through the cavity of another object (for example, the retractable power cord of a vacuum cleaner, or a tape measure).

One final example shows the great versatility of the TRIZ methodology. In *The Innovation Algorithm* (1999), Method 15, 'Dynamicity', is defined as follows:

> (a) Characteristics of an object, or outside environment, must be altered to provide optimal performance at each stage of an operation; (b) If an object is immobile, make it mobile. Make it interchangeable; (c) Divide an object into elements capable of changing their position relative to each other.

Figure 3.1 illustrates this powerful principle in an abstract way, transitioning in eight steps from a ridged, monolithic object to an intangible field. A practical application of the method

Table 3.1 The forty principles of TRIZ

1 Segmentation	2 Extraction
3 Local quality	4 Asymmetry
5 Consolidation	6 Universality
7 Nesting	8 Counterweight
9 Prior counteraction	10 Prior action
11 Cushion in advance	12 Equipotentiality
13 Do it in reverse	14 Spheroidality
15 Dynamicity	16 Partial or excessive action
17 Transition into a new dimension	18 Mechanical vibration
19 Periodic action	20 Continuity of useful action
21 Rushing through	22 Convert harm into blessing
23 Feedback	24 Mediator
25 Self-service	26 Copying
27 Dispose	28 Replacement of mechanical system
29 Pneumatics or hydraulic construction	30 Flexible films or thin membranes
31 Porous materials	32 Changing the colour
33 Homogeneity	34 Rejecting and regenerating parts
35 Transformation properties	36 Phase transition
37 Thermal expansion	38 Accelerated oxidation
39 Inert environment	40 Composite materials

is shown in Figure 3.2 as the increasing dynamicity of a measuring device. A ruler (monolith) is made more flexible by turning it into a foldable ruler (multi-joint). Even more flexible is a tape measure (which can also measure curved objects). The ultimate flexibility is achieved by a laser measure (field), which can operate from a distance. Although increasing the flexibility generally expands the useful applications of the device, it does not always include all prior possibilities. For example, the laser measure can measure distances more easily, quickly and accurately than a tape measure, but it cannot measure curved objects.

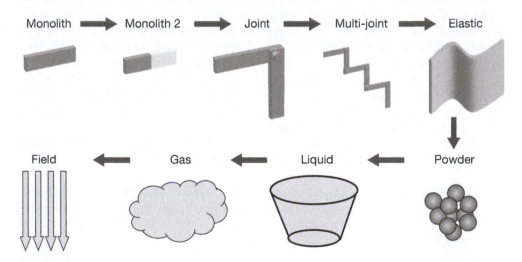

Figure 3.1 Method 15, 'Dynamicity', illustrated by the transitioning in eight steps from a ridged monolithic object to an intangible field

Monolith ruler   Multi-joint ruler   Tape ruler   Laser measure

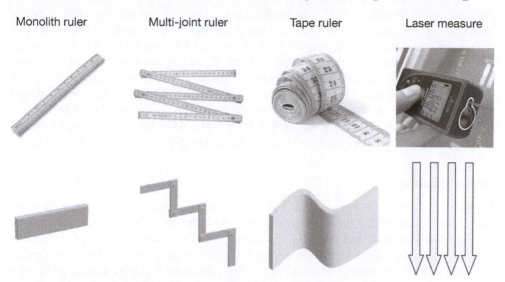

Figure 3.2 A practical example of Method 15, 'Dynamicity', increasing the dynamicity of a measuring device, starting from a ruler (monolith), via a foldable ruler (multi-joint) and a tape ruler (elastic) to a laser measure (field)

In addition to the forty methods, Altshuller identified thirty-nine parameters (factors) that are used to create a 39 × 39 matrix for resolving technical contradictions. The thirty-nine rows represent the parameters that need to be improved, and the thirty-nine columns are the features that are affected in a negative way. In this way, each element (cell) of the matrix constitutes a contradiction: if one parameter (row) is improved, another parameter (column) gets worse. Table 3.2 lists the thirty-nine parameters. Each cell in the matrix

Table 3.2 Altshuller's thirty-nine parameters

1 Weight of a mobile object	2 Weight of a stationary object
3 Length of mobile object	4 Length of a stationary object
5 Area of a mobile object	6 Area of a stationary object
7 Volume of a mobile object	8 Volume of a stationary object
9 Speed	10 Force
11 Tension/pressure	12 Shape
13 Stability of composition	14 Strength
15 Time of action of a mobile object	16 Time of action of a stationary object
17 Temperature	18 Brightness
19 Energy spent by a mobile object	20 Energy spent by a stationary object
21 Power	22 Loss of energy
23 Loss of a substance	24 Loss of information
25 Loss of time	26 Amount of substance
27 Reliability	28 Accuracy of measurement
29 Accuracy of manufacturing	30 Harmful factors acting on object from outside
31 Harmful factors developed by an object	32 Manufacturability
33 Convenience of use	34 Repairability
35 Adaptability	36 Complexity of a device
37 Complexity of control	38 Level of automation
39 Capacity/productivity	

indicates which of the forty TRIZ methods are most appropriate to eliminate that particular contradiction. For example, if an object is made stronger (improvement of Parameter 14), the weight might increase (diminution of Parameter 2). The best chance to eliminate this technical contradiction is to apply Methods 1, 26, 27 and 40 (in that order of decreasing priority/likelihood of success). Other examples of technical contradictions are as follows: A spy plane should fly high and fast to avoid detection and being shot down, and it should fly low and slowly to carry out detailed reconnaissance. A sports car should be light to improve acceleration, and it should be heavy for better road handling. A bigger battery increases the range of an electric car, but it takes up more space and adds more weight.

Brainstorming

A powerful tool to generate new ideas, especially solutions to specific problems, is a method called 'brainstorming' that was developed by Alex Osborne in the late 1930s. Osborne was an advertising executive and one of the founders of BBDO (Batten, Barton, Durstine and Osborne, Inc.), one of the largest advertising companies in the world (289 offices in eighty countries; 15,000 employees). He noticed that his employees had difficulties creating new ideas for advertising campaigns on their own. To overcome this problem, he organized group meetings in which the participants were asked to come up with as many ideas as they could. This approach increased both the quality and the quantity of new, creative ideas. In 1953, Osborne published his ideas in the book *Applied Imagination. Principles and procedures of creative problem solving*. Box 3.4 contains the origin and the key principles of the brainstorming process in Osborne's own words. In the same way that Altshuller believed that inventive problem-solving can be taught through TRIZ, Osborne was convinced that creativity could be taught. It is a matter of having a good set of tools and a lot of training in applying these tools in the real world. That is also how we teach children to play chess or to play the violin. That is how we teach people in art school how to paint a picture and people at a conservatory how to compose a piece of music. There is no guarantee that this will produce the next Kasparov, Menuhin, Van Gogh or Mozart, but, for those who possess the creative genius, a structured method, with an extensive set of tools and a lot of practice, will facilitate the rapid development of that talent.

The structured approach to brainstorming developed by Osborne consists of four steps. Following the description given by Altshuller in *The Innovation Algorithm*, these are as follows:

1 An idea-generating team should comprise people from different fields.
2 Ideas should be generated in such a way that anyone can express any idea – including errors, jokes and fantasies – within a 1-minute time limit. Ideas cannot be expressed without providing proof. All ideas are recorded.
3 No criticism is permitted during the generation of these ideas, either through words or through silence, or even in the form of sceptical smiles. Members should maintain a free and friendly relationship during the 'storm'. It is preferable that ideas proposed by one member should be picked up and developed by others.
4 During analysis, all ideas (even those that seem wrong or frivolous) should be attentively analysed.

The first requirement (a multidisciplinary team) is obvious, as people with different backgrounds have complementary knowledge and experiences. Often, the solution to a

Box 3.4 Alex Osborne on brainstorming

This is how Alex Osborne describes the origin of the brainstorming concept in Chapter XII of his book *Applied Imagination: Principles and procedures of creative problem solving* (1963): "It was in 1938 when I first employed organized ideation in the company I then headed. The early participants dubbed our efforts 'Brainstorm Sessions'; and quite aptly so because, in this case, 'brainstorm' means using the brain to storm a problem." Brainstorming has become so much a part of the American scene that the verb brainstorm, in the sense of creative effort, is now included in Webster's International Dictionary and defined as follows: 'To practice a conference technique by which a group attempts to find a solution for a specific problem by amassing all the ideas spontaneously contributed by its members.' This kind of conference is not entirely new. A similar procedure is known to have been used in India for more than 400 years as part of the technique of Hindu teachers while working with religious groups. The Indian name for this method is *Prai-Barshana*. *Prai* means 'outside yourself' and *Barshana* means 'question.' In such a session there is no discussion or criticism. Evaluation of ideas takes place at later meetings of the same group. The modern brainstorm session is nothing more than a creative conference for the sole purpose of producing a check-list of ideas – ideas which can serve as leads to problem solution – ideas which can *subsequently* be evaluated and further processed. No conference can be called a brainstorming session unless the deferment-of-judgement principle is strictly followed. In the early 50s brainstorming became too popular too fast, with the result that it was frequently misused. Too many people jumped at it as a panacea, then turned against it when no miracles resulted. Likewise, too many have erroneously regarded group brainstorming as a complete problem-solving process, whereas it is only one of several phases of idea-finding; and idea-finding is only one of the several phases of creative problem-solving. The principal value of group brainstorming is the fact that a brainstorming session, properly conducted, can produce far more good ideas than a conventional conference – and in less time.

specific problem in one field can be found in another field, as illustrated by the following example. InnoCentive (www.innocentive.com) is an open-innovation platform where problem owners (usually companies) post specific problems for which they offer cash rewards to whoever submits the best solution. An interesting sideline is that the idea for this concept came out of a brainstorm session in 1998 by Alpheus Bingham and Aaron Schacht, who both worked for Eli Lilly & Company. In 2005, InnoCentive was spun out of Eli Lilly and it is currently a privately held, venture-backed company. Since its foundation, more than 1,650 challenges in forty disciplines have been posted, which generated more than 40,000 solutions. More than 1,500 solutions were given cash awards ranging from US$5,000 to more than US$1,000,000. One of these challenges concerned the oil spill from the Exxon Valdez in 1989. In 2007, the Ocean Spill Recovery Institute in Alaska was looking for a method to separate oil and water from a frozen viscous mass, and this challenge was posted on the InnoCentive website. A few months later, a reward of US$20,000 was paid to a nanotechnology expert who suggested using a tool that is commonly applied in the concrete industry to keep cement in liquid form by means of vibration. It is a prime example of a problem in one domain for which a solution already exists in another domain. Recognizing the similarity between frozen oil plus water sludge and concrete, together with the knowledge of how to keep concrete a fluid, was the key to solving this problem.

The second requirement emphasizes that, in this phase of the brainstorm, basically anything goes. No idea is wild and crazy enough to be rejected up front, and all ideas must be recorded. Although the first two requirements are generally recognized as being important to the process of brainstorming, the third requirement is new to most people who are unfamiliar with Osborne's structured approach. Not immediately criticizing the ideas of the other participants takes quite a bit of self control, especially if those ideas appear to be crazy, far-fetched or simply wrong. Judgement should be postponed at all cost, because it will inhibit participants from speaking freely. Only in Step 4 will all the ideas be analysed and evaluated.

Box 3.5 contains an extract from an actual brainstorm session. Four people are brainstorming on the problem of how to separate ripe and unripe tomatoes. Their names have been omitted to show just the emergence of different ideas and how one idea leads to another. It also illustrates the concept of 'ideas cannot be expressed without providing proof', from the second of Osborne's four brainstorming requirements. It is not so much a rigorous proof, but is at least a useful method showing how to accomplish what is being proposed. For example, if you want to select on the basis of colour, you will need a colour sensor. Note also that, in this phase, the idea generation process is rather chaotic, with wild concepts

---

Box 3.5 Excerpt from an actual brainstorm session

This is an extract from an actual brainstorm session, taken from John Dickson's book *System Design: Inventing, analysis and decision making*, published in Moscow in 1969 and never (to our knowledge) translated into English. The names of the four participants have been omitted to enhance the stream of new ideas flying back and forth.

How to separate ripe and unripe tomatoes

'We can screen them by colour. Then we probably need a colour sensor.'
'Emitting or reflecting characteristics. Green tomatoes should have higher reflecting abilities.'
'Electric conductivity.'
'Magnetism.'
'Size. Are green tomatoes smaller in size?'
'Weight. Ripe tomatoes will be heavier.'
'Size and weight are codependent.'
'Size and weight give you density.'
'Specific gravity. Red tomatoes have a lot of water, therefore they have specific gravity closer to that of water.'
'Do they float or sink?'
'Maybe it's possible to screen by density if they float or not.'
'Not necessarily in water . . . Maybe other types of liquid.'

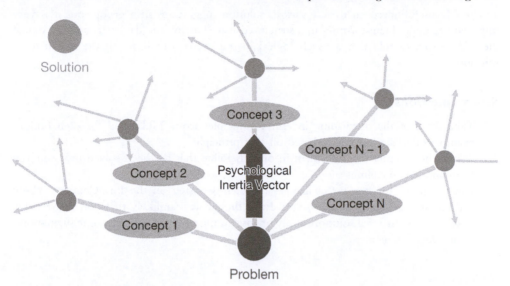

Figure 3.3 Solving problems by trial and error. Starting from the problem, various concepts in
subsequent iterations try to get closer to the solution. Beware of tunnel vision caused by
a psychological inertia vector

being forwarded without an apparent processing step. This may help to jog the creative
input from the other participants in the brainstorm.

The most promising results from a brainstorm session can be tested in practice to find
out whether a satisfactory solution can be obtained. Figure 3.3 illustrates the search for
a solution in a conceptual way. Starting from the problem, several concepts can be tried
in order to get closer to the solution. In most cases, additional efforts are required to get
closer to, and (hopefully) eventually arrive at, the solution. However, caution is advised
when, for some reason, the direction of the solution seems obvious. In that case, there is
a so-called psychological inertia vector, which pushes the creative process in a certain
direction (rightly or wrongly). Especially when dealing with technical contradictions,
one is tempted to ignore potential solutions that appear to be unlikely or simply impossible.
In the chocolate candy example, the psychological inertia vector is the preconception that
the thick syrup needs to get thinner to get into the chocolate bottle. The psychological
inertia vector prefers solutions that make the syrup thinner, for example by heating it. Only
after pursuing that solution further and discovering that this would melt the chocolate did
the prospective problem-solver revisit the problem. When suddenly the inventor appeared
. . .

Chapter summary

This chapter explained how innovative ideas can be turned into new products that solve
real customer problems. Identifying a customer problem is the easy part; the hard part is
actually solving that problem in an elegant way and for a price that the customer is willing
to pay. The Theory of Inventive Problem-solving (TRIZ) is presented as a powerful tool
to frame real-life problems as contradictions that can be resolved. Brainstorming is presented

as a highly useful approach to test various solution suggestions in a group, but it is very important to apply brainstorming in a structured way. Finally, the danger is pointed out of the stifling stranglehold that a psychological inertia vector can have on the search for a solution.

Study questions

1   Take three of the thirty-nine inventive principles from TRIZ and for each find an example of a solution that is based on that principle.
2   Search the Internet for a problem in one discipline that has been solved by a solution from another discipline.
3   Read some of the current challenges (problems) posted on the InnoCentive website and choose one that appeals to you. Even though it is unlikely that you will be able to come up with a real solution, apply brainstorming to come up with some suggestions. Write down your ideas.

References

Altshuller, G. (1996). *And Suddenly the Inventor Appeared: TRIZ, The theory of inventive problem solving* (2nd edn). Worcester, MA: Technical Innovation Center.

Altshuller, G. (1999). *The Innovation Algorithm: TRIZ, systematic innovation and technical creativity.* Worcester, MA: Technical Innovation Center.

Forbes. (2014). General Electric. Available at: www.forbes.com/companies/general-electric/ (accessed 31 December 2014).

Leroy, B., D'Haeyer, R., Defourny, J., Hoogendoorn, T., Birat, J. P., Grabke, H. J., Morrison, W. B., Henderson, N. G., Longbottom, R. D., Laux, T. and Les, I. (1995). *Effects of tramp elements in flat and long products.* Final Report, Directorate-General XII Science, Research and Development, ECSC-EC-EAEC, Brussels, Luxembourg. ISBN 92–827–5636–X.

Lodygin, A. (1893). *Filament for Incandescent Lamps.* US Patent 494,151. Available at: www.google.com/patents/US494151 (accessed 31 December 2014).

Osborne, A. (1963). *Applied Imagination: Principles and procedures of creative problem solving* (3rd rev. edn). New York: Charles Scribner.

Wired.com. (2008). Jan. 4, 1903: Edison fries an elephant to prove his point. Available at: www.wired.com/science/discoveries/news/2008/01/dayintech_0104 (accessed 31 December 2014).

YouTube. (2014). Electrocuting an elephant (1903). Available at: www.youtube.com/watch?v=NoKi4coyFw0 (accessed 31 December 2014).

Further reading

Hippel, E. von (1986). Lead users: An important source of novel product concepts. *Management Science.* 32(7): 791–805.

Hippel, E. von (1995). *The Sources of Innovation.* Oxford, UK: Oxford University Press.

Moore, G. A. (2014). *Crossing the Chasm: Marketing and selling disruptive products to mainstream customers* (3rd edn). New York: HarperBusiness.

Rogers, E. M. (2003). *Diffusion of Innovations* (5th edn). New York: Simon & Schuster.

4 The opportunity and the entrepreneur

When is an idea an opportunity?

Before we discuss what exactly an opportunity is, it is important to recognize the origin of entrepreneurship and how it can be defined. Many scholars have investigated the entrepreneur as a person having specific traits. These traits provide the person with the ability to bring value to society and, in doing so, they receive something in return. The essence here is that this person assumes that the returns for bringing value to society exceed the costs associated with producing that value. The word entrepreneur was derived from the old French verb *entreprendre*, which has a meaning related to an act such as 'to start with or to undertake'. The term was used for centuries to identify traders who connected two different worlds and brought goods from one world to the other. Marco Polo used the term *entreprendre* for those traders who brought spices, silk and other valuable goods from the Far East to Europe. Essentially, the word was used for people who bridged two worlds and took advantage of the opportunity where, in one world, few people knew exactly where and how the goods were collected or how much was paid for it. This gave the early entrepreneur the opportunity to ask higher prices for their goods, thereby creating an economic transaction. It was the French economist Richard Cantillon who coined the term entrepreneur in early 1700. Cantillon was among the first who studied entrepreneurship as an 'academic' area. He argued that the entrepreneur played a highly specialized role in society by bringing new, valuable goods, later referred to as innovations, into society. The entrepreneur did not earn fixed wages because of the speculative nature of the goods they brought into society.

The pioneering work of Cantillon was further discussed and refined by other economists such as Jean-Baptiste Say and, later in the twentieth century, Ludwig von Mises, who introduced the theory of uncertainty to the entrepreneur. While discussing the role of uncertainty, early entrepreneurship researchers began to discuss the variance of uncertainty that can be associated with the new goods that are brought to society. Whereas Cantillon argued that the entrepreneur brought equilibrium to a market by correctly predicting consumer preferences, others began to argue that the entrepreneur was someone who disturbed the economic equilibrium in the market by introducing new goods that replaced existing goods. Hence, a discussion emerged on the different types of opportunities and whether opportunities are created through technological discovery and development and social processes of evaluation, or whether opportunities exist objectively and wait to be discovered, depending on the alertness of an individual to spot an unanswered need.

Two Austrian economists, Schumpeter and Kirzner, further discussed the two views.

Schumpeter (1934) continued to elaborate on the uncertainty dimension. According to his view, not all entrepreneurs combine existing knowledge into new products or services, but the entrepreneur is someone who brings to society something that is completely new and, in doing so, reforms and revolutionizes a current situation and breaks with the past. His view is strongly based on the actions of an inventor – for instance, the invention of the steam engine by James Watt, which made tall ships redundant. The invention of the steam engine brought new applications into society. Schumpeter would argue that the innovation lies in something that is so radically new that it makes earlier applications useless. The steam engine was in itself a radical innovation, but the effect it had on industry was devastating as well. Figure 4.1 shows the transition from sail to steam, with the tonnage of goods transported by either sail or steam ships. Even knowing that companies might not immediately put their ships out of service, it still only needed some 20 years before steam ships took over the market. The shipbuilders who relied on sails and wind soon found out that their knowledge was pretty useless, because ship-owners replaced their sailing boats with steamships, for which the planning was more reliable and travelling time was shorter.

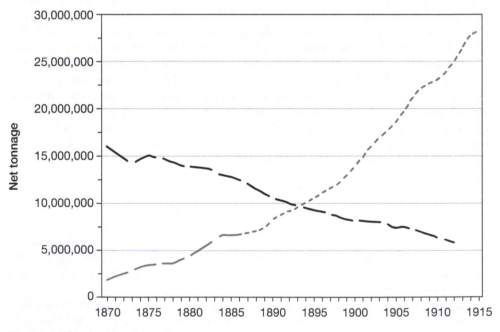

Figure 4.1 The transition from sail to steam

Source: http://homepages.ihug.co.nz/~j_lowe/C17Transition.htm

The whole industry, from shipbuilding to maintenance, as well as the training of crew and port services, changed and simultaneously destroyed the old way of doing things.

The term creative destruction emerged and was used to indicate that a new invention was replacing old products and services, and even people's habits and mindsets. This creative destruction could also affect the innovator, as can be seen in the case of the German motorcycle company NSU: although very successful just after the Second World War, this company fell on hard times owing to its innovative character and was bought by Volkswagen in 1969; see Box 4.1.

In contrast, Kirzner (1973) argued that the discovery of opportunities is the core issue of entrepreneurship. According to his view, entrepreneurs find and exploit opportunities by combining known products and services into new ones. Kirzner followed the argument of Herbert Simon. Herbert Simon is a sociologist who argued that people cannot possess all knowledge that is surrounding them, and, as a result, knowledge about products and services and how they can be combined is not equally distributed among people. Like the traders mentioned by Marco Polo, this asymmetry in information provided an opportunity to exploit for those who could bridge the knowledge asymmetry. In essence, the Kirzner opportunity is a combination of existing knowledge, and entrepreneurs who exploit Kirzner opportunities are alert to certain situations that may provide an opportunity. They have a superior perception of markets and customers and recognize that the needs of specific customer groups are not fully served, but can be by the transferral of ideas, knowledge, products or services from one market to another and their adaptation to the unmet needs. Economists argue that Kirzner entrepreneurs bring balance to markets by closing the information asymmetry that exists between the information levels available in various markets. They take advantage of economic disequilibria by knowing or recognizing things that others do not and by adjusting parts of information to the needs of certain customer groups. These Kirzner entrepreneurs are also called the 'agents of adjustment': they recognize new developments and customer needs and bring these together.

In the eyes of Joseph Schumpeter, the entrepreneur is someone who makes things work in the economy by reorganizing an industry based on innovations that lead to a disequilibrium in the economy. The disequilibrium is the gap that emerges as a result of the new innovation, e.g. a new product or a new development process in the market, between the entrepreneur and those who relied on the earlier products or services, also referred to as the followers. As such, the entrepreneur invents something truly novel, based on different combinations of resources. The result is that industries are revolutionized, reformed, or at least competition is redefined, and the dependencies between the organizations involved are reorganized. According to Schumpeter, this not only applies to products and services such as the tall ships and the NSU motorcycles but also to how businesses are organized, the business model or the business operation. For example, Southwest Airlines and, later, EasyJet and Ryanair did not alter the principal product/service they provide their customers, but the way they organized their business resulted in significantly lower prices on certain flight routes, which did put established airlines in difficulty. Also, companies such as Amazon, the Book Depository and Bol.com in the Netherlands introduced new business models for new and secondhand books that, in part, did push offline bookstores such as Borders in the US and Selexsyz in the Netherlands into bankruptcy.

Many have argued that the two views are the opposite of each other and are incommensurable. Cheah (1990), however, discussed the two views as complementary, arguing that economy follows a cyclic pattern in which Schumpeter and Kirzner opportunities and their entrepreneurs take turns. In essence, the Schumpeter entrepreneur often creates temporary

Box 4.1 Case description of innovation at NSU

Neckarsulm Strickmaschinen Union (NSU) was established in 1873 and specialized in maintaining knitting machines in the textile industry. Before the turn of the century, the company was completely focused on manufacturing motorcycles and also, later, building automobiles. Its motorcycles were most successful, and, after the Second World War, when its factory was completely destroyed, it restarted with some pre-war motorcycles. Its focus on innovation led to various innovations such as the monocoque frame of pressed steel, a central rear suspension unit and an overhead camshaft driven by eccentric connecting rods, instead of the commonly used bevel gears or chain belts. These innovations helped NSU to quickly become the biggest motorcycle producer in the world by 1955, and the company held a number of world records for speed in 1951, 1953, 1954 and 1955, and, in 1956, its motorcycle was the first to exceed the 200 mph (322 km/h) speed limit. Its car production also included some significant innovations, both in technology and design, of which the Wankel engine in the NSU Ro80 was the most remarkable. However, the innovations of the overhead camshaft

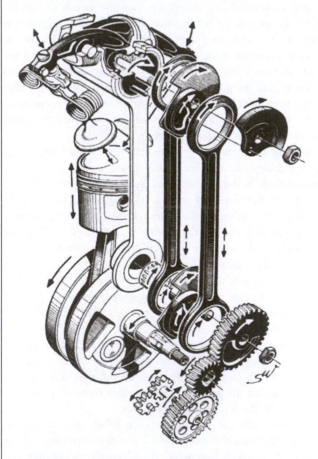

Figure 4.2 Complex system of connecting rods

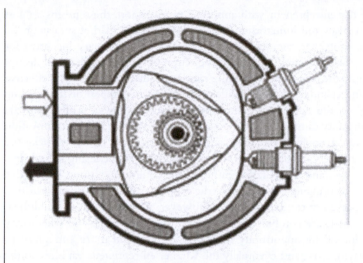

Figure 4.3 Wankel engine

using connecting rods and the Wankel engine brought about large concerns for NSU. First, after the Second World War, most motorcycles were sold by bicycle shops, which also carried out maintenance and repairs. However, with the introduction of the complex system of connecting rods (Figure 4.2), NSU could no longer fully rely on these shops to keep the engines in good shape. The company needed to invest in dealerships and training to teach mechanics about its system. Second, the many technical problems that came with the rotary engine (Figure 4.3), even with only low mileage, did not do the brand any good, and soon the company declined, owing to its honouring warranty claims while its financial position was already weakened by the formidable development and tooling expenses. Thus, the radical innovations that NSU implemented had an effect on how the car and motorcycle dealership and maintenance industry operated, which eventually affected not only other companies in these industries but the company itself as well.

Table 4.1 Kirzner and Schumpeter entrepreneurship and their characteristics

	Kirzner opportunities	*Schumpeter opportunities*
Description	Very nearly imitations of existing offerings, reproduced with minor variations	Truly novel, representing new and different combinations of resources
Characteristics	Alertness and ability to perceive opportunities before others	Reform and revolutionize
	Establish equilibrium	Creative destruction
	Opportunities as combinations of existing knowledge	Reorganizing industry
	Incrementalism	Disturb existing economic equilibrium

monopolies that provide the entrepreneur with abnormal profits; soon, these profits are lost to the competition when rivals and imitators are able to bring to the market similar or the same type of innovation. However, the temporary monopoly is the primary incentive for entrepreneurs to take the risk associated with the introduction of something that will disrupt and bring disequilibrium into the economy, by making existing products and services ineffective and changing people's mindset and behaviour. While more and more competitors are copying the Schumpeter innovation, the Schumpeter entrepreneur receives fewer profits, and the attractiveness of the opportunity diminishes. At the same time, we notice that the innovation is becoming more accepted in society, and more and more people are trying to make use of the new innovation in a variety of applications and to combine it with existing knowledge. Kirzner opportunities emerge, and the Kirzner entrepreneur combines existing knowledge with new knowledge, thereby bringing equilibrium to the economy. As long as the information asymmetry exists, the opportunity can be exploited. However, if equilibrium is established, everyone knows how products are combined based on existing knowledge and where they can be obtained. The value of the opportunity decreases, as more and more entrepreneurs exploit the information asymmetry, and eventually the Kirzner entrepreneur vanishes, as the information on which the opportunity was built is available to everyone, and eventually the opportunity to exploit disequilibria has disappeared. Entrepreneurial opportunities may then emerge when new and more radical innovations are brought to the market by Schumpeter entrepreneurs. These two types of entrepreneurial opportunity take turn, as Schumpeter entrepreneurs widen the gap between themselves and followers by bringing disequilibrium to society with their disruptive innovations. Subsequently, they are followed by Kirzner entrepreneurs who exploit the disequilibrium and make combinations of knowledge that are not equally spread among people and thereby restore equilibrium.

Differences in type of opportunity

The inclusion of the uncertainty dimension in entrepreneurial opportunities brought about different views on what opportunities actually are. Following the discussion of Schumpeter and Kirzner, we can distinguish between more incremental opportunities and more radical opportunities. Besides these two opportunity types, we can also identify opportunities that are not really innovation-based.

Incremental improvements as a source of opportunity

Kirzner opportunities reflect combinations of existing knowledge. In essence, they are the result of the entrepreneur's ability to evaluate customer behaviour, products and markets and identify the so-called white spots of underserviced customers. These white spots are then addressed by making combinations of existing products, technologies and service. The ability to identify valuable white spots is associated with the alertness of the entrepreneur. Many of the innovations are small improvements of existing products/processes.

Radical and disruptive innovations as a source of opportunity

The radical and disruptive innovations are related to the Schumpeter entrepreneur and represent a radical change to, and improvement of, existing knowledge about how to produce, organize or provide a service to clients. These innovations break with past experience and knowledge and require a new set of skills and knowledge and a different mindset.

Traditional, cognition-based thinking may lead to a dominant logic that is difficult for companies to abandon, thus making it difficult for them to take up more radical and disruptive innovations.

Imitation as a source of opportunity

Imitation often has this negative connotation that the entrepreneur takes advantage of a situation and misuses information to his own benefit. However, here we refer to the entrepreneurs who replicate proven business by exploiting the same products and services for another target group. These are often lifestyle businesses such as independent shops, but can also involve franchise businesses. Franchising involves entrepreneurs who take the opportunity to start a business using an already proven business concept. The entrepreneur buys a franchise opportunity that includes an existing business, with a solid business plan and process already in place. Many of the entrepreneurs operate their business under the umbrella of a recognized business name and receive support from the franchise headquarters, such as marketing and promotional materials, new business products or services, etc. Some examples are grocers and supermarkets such as Tesco, Albert Heijn and many others, but also many petrol stations are franchised to entrepreneurs but carry the name brand and sell the products of large oil companies such as BP, Shell, etc. Other types of imitation-based opportunity involve distributors and dealerships. These entrepreneurs have an agreement to sell products or services produced by another company. These distributors and dealers can be innovative when they provide specific features for the product, additional services or maintenance. In that respect, they can be like Kirzner entrepreneurs when they increase the service level and thereby meet customers' needs that have been thus far unmet. Similarly, with maintenance, the dealers and distributors often innovate in operations and work processes in order to provide more value to their customers. The last category of imitation-based opportunity is where the entrepreneur has a licence to produce and sell products or services that have been developed by another organization. Having a licence agreement gives the entrepreneur the opportunity to be creative and invent products or services, but retains the name brand, icon or trademark of the widely recognized business.

Rent-seeking as a source of opportunity

The last category of opportunities we discuss here are the rent-seeking opportunities. Essentially, these opportunities add little or no value, and often productivity increase is very low, but the entrepreneurs receive income based on the exploitation of goods. With rent-seeking opportunities, entrepreneurs deploy their resources to obtain an economic gain from others without reciprocating with any benefits to society through wealth creation. Examples here are the renting of land or accommodation to be used by others.

The cyclic nature of opportunities and the importance of platform ideas

Besides the fact that Kirzner and Schumpeter opportunities take turns and build upon each other, we can also recognize that Schumpeter opportunities can act as a platform idea. The introduction of the radical Schumpeter innovation may not only break with the past but also open up possibilities for many more Kirzner opportunities or incremental innovations in products and services. Clear examples in the past are the introductions of the personal computer (PC) and the mobile telephone. The introduction of the first semiconductors that were smaller and less expensive allowed the development of the PC, which can be considered a radical innovation. Hewlett Packard and WANG, in the early 1970s, introduced a relatively small programmable computer with devices such as a keyboard, display and printer. In the course of the early development, we saw a variety of hardware makers tapping into the opportunity to develop better and more diverse additional devices, such as hard disks, floppy disk drives, the mouse, expansion cards, etc. Similarly, a number of software developers saw the opportunity to develop programs that could run on the PC, but are actually digital programs based on physical applications that had been used for many years. Examples are text-writing programs based on the typewriter, spreadsheet programs based on the paper-based spreadsheets auditors had already been using, graphics-editing programs such as Adobe Photoshop, etc. These digital replacements of earlier physical applications gave rise to a large number of companies such as Novell Incorporation, Adobe Systems Incorporated, Lotus Software (today IBM), Oracle Corporation and Microsoft.

In the case of the mobile telephone, we see a similar interaction between Schumpeter and Kirzner opportunities and the role of the mobile telephone as a platform opportunity. Compared with the earliest mobile telephone, which could establish a phone connection between two people if they could afford the expensive and heavy devices. Today's smartphones allow for a wide range of tasks comparable to what computers can do and, in addition, they can run applications such as Global Positioning System (GPS), payment options, etc. A whole new industry has emerged in the telephone applications market, and, from the start of the App Store in 2008, close to 1.5 million apps were available by the end of 2014 for Apple's iPhone (http://www.statista.com/statistics/276623/).

Hence, we can see that radical, Schumpeter-type innovations initiated a large number of more incremental Kirzner-type innovations and provided a platform based on which many other entrepreneurs found opportunities to start their company. Similarly, the introduction of the microprocessor, which can be considered a Schumpeter-type innovation as well, led the way for entrepreneurs to use the microprocessor in applications that replaced a number of existing products, such as the typewriter, the spreadsheet book, the drawing table and many others. The Schumpeter-type innovations paved the way for a whole new industry to emerge that not only changed the products and services but also the business models these firms adopt to earn money.

Opportunity discovery and recognition

How opportunities come about is often discussed in research on entrepreneurship. Some authors focus on the sources of opportunities and argue that changes in technology, society or regulation provide openings for entrepreneurs to adapt to the new conditions. One straightforward example is the increase in a population due to urbanization. This triggers entrepreneurs to open a shop and provide services to local residents. This is a clear example of the Kirzner type of entrepreneur, who copies products, services and business models that already exist and transposes them to a new area. The other examples we have given, about NSU and the smartphone, are based on technological improvements that provided entrepreneurs with an opportunity to exploit. Developments in society such as ageing populations and the effect they have on the health-care system can stimulate entrepreneurs to find solutions to lower those costs or increase well-being. Also, governments can intervene with new regulations that sometimes restrict or stimulate certain technologies. One clear example is Germany's nuclear energy phase-out. Following Fukushima's nuclear

Image 4.1 iPhone

Box 4.2 Case study of the Post-it®

The Post-it case is illustrative of the differences between ideas and opportunities, as well as showing the process of opportunity recognition and an example of a platform opportunity.

Everyone knows the Post-it note as the small, yellow, paper strip that is re-adherable, with its adhesive on the back, and specially made for notes that can be temporarily attached to documents and other surfaces. The product is so common and so straightforward that one might forget how odd the process of discovery actually was.

In 1964, 3M aimed to develop stronger adhesive that would sustain larger stress. A project 'Polymers for Adhesives' was started. Dr Spence Silver was one of the engineers and, besides the regular experiments with mixing polymers, he tried, as a side project, several mixes of what he called 'wrong proportions of monomers just to see what the outcome could be'. Although the main project did not result in promising adhesives, the trial-and-error experiments were more fruitful in 1968, when Dr Silver discovered a 'low-tack', reusable, pressure-sensitive adhesive. The project 'Polymers for Adhesives' was, however, aimed at completely the opposite of what Dr Silver discovered in his side project, and the results of this project were considered unsatisfactory by 3M's managers, and they terminated the project in 1973. Meanwhile, Dr Silver promoted his low-tack glue within 3M at seminars and through informal talks, but he did not find any enthusiasm. 3M's managers did not think a low-tack glue would be of any use,

Image 4.2 Post-it notes
Source: © Ramesh NG

and even Dr Silver himself had little idea what the benefits of such a glue would be. In 1974, Art Fry, a colleague of Dr Silver, attended one of Silver's seminar presentations, and he had this idea to use the glue on small pieces of paper to be used in his hymnbooks. Art Fry sang in the local church choir and, every time he opened his hymnal to sing, his bookmarks would fall out on the floor. The glue discovered by Dr Silver could help to attach the small bookmarks temporarily, in places in his hymnal, any time he liked. Therefore, Fry improved the product slightly by covering only a small part of the paper with glue and not, as Silver proposed initially, covering the whole surface with the adhesive.

Fry developed this idea further at 3M; however, management did not see any business opportunity in the invention. How large could this market be, and, more importantly, how much could you ask for an adhesive paper, when a regular, non-adhesive piece of paper could do almost the same job and literally costs nothing? The managers, who normally decide on issues involving multiple millions, were concerned about the market potential; nevertheless, Art Fry could take advantage of the 'permitted bootlegging policy' at 3M that allowed employees to work on projects for a certain amount of time that may in future bring value to the firm. Being covered by 3M's permitted bootlegging policy, Fry introduced his product as 'Press 'n' Peel' in stores in four cities. To keep the costs low, he used scrap yellow paper, which is still the main colour today. The results were disappointing, because, as expected by upper management, people didn't want to pay for the adhesive paper strip. In order to get feedback on the product, Art Fry was giving away free samples among the residents in his hometown of Boise in Idaho. Also within 3M, Fry gave the staff the papers to use, and soon they found out how useful the invention was. The experience people had with the adhesive paper was astonishing, and almost 95 per cent of the people who tried the product indicated that they would buy it. The product was repositioned as Post-it®, and today, although the patent expired many years ago, 3M still leads the market. At the same time, 3M managed to develop a broad range of products based on the low-tack glue.

---

disaster in Japan in 2011, the German government decided to phase out its nuclear power plants by the end of 2022. Although some argue that coal plants will be used more intensively to generate energy, the decision also makes alternative energy sources more attractive and stimulates entrepreneurs to come up with new ideas for alternative energy production techniques and different business models, not only at firm level but also at the level of communities, as seen with the concept of the bioenergy village in Germany. A bioenergy village uses local biomass energy sources from agriculture and forestry for its energy and heat supply. Often, there is a local public–private partnership in which the local community invests in a biogas power plant to meet the complete energy requirements of a village and tries to operate independently from the national grid.

Idea or opportunity?

The Post-it case study provides us with insight into the processes of idea identification and opportunity recognition. However, questions may arise about when the idea turned into an opportunity, or, more generally, when do we actually speak of an opportunity, or is it

Table 4.2 An idea is not (yet) an opportunity

Ideas	Opportunities
Remain forever	Are temporal
Are free and unrestricted	Are subject to reality
Everyone can have them	Only a few can have them
Do not need clients to exist	Need clients to exist

still an idea, and how do opportunities differ from ideas? Can we consider every good idea an opportunity? And, if not all ideas are opportunities, when does an idea become an opportunity, or, maybe better, what are the conditions needed before an idea can be considered an opportunity? When we try to differentiate between ideas and opportunities, then at least four main characteristics can be considered where ideas and opportunities differ, and these are presented in Table 4.2.

Ideas generally remain over a longer period – in principle, forever – whereas a business opportunity is more temporal and fades away over time. That is, the activity underlying an opportunity may remain as a possibility for anyone to do, and yet its attraction diminishes when more people try to exploit and take advantage of the opportunity. For example, if someone discovered an ancient shipwreck in shallow water near one of Greece's islands, there would be an attractive opportunity to open a hotel with accommodation for scuba diving, and yet, as more people open hotels with comparable services, then competition increases, profits diminish, and, as a result, the opportunity gets smaller. Hence, opportunities are more temporal and, at the same time, need work before they can be exploited. Someone could have the idea to open a hotel on this Greek island, and yet, if no action is taken, the hotel will not be founded, and the opportunity cannot be exploited and thus only exists theoretically. Hence, work is needed before an idea becomes an opportunity, which is the second characteristic. One must open a hotel on the Greek island in order to be able to exploit the opportunity.

The third requirement is that an idea needs clients who appreciate the value they gain from an idea and are willing to buy it. For instance, someone could have the idea to build a hotel on Mars, and yet technologically it might not be feasible. Even if it were possible, then it would be very expensive and very uncomfortable to travel for at least 7 months to get there with conventional chemical rocket propulsion, and that's only when Mars is at its closest to Earth in its orbit. Hence, the idea to build a hotel on Mars remains an idea and is not considered an attractive opportunity, because it lacks clients who would be willing to buy this service.

However, coming back to the scuba-diving hotel on the Greek island, this opportunity may not be suitable for all of us to exploit. To open a hotel, one probably needs some experience of running and managing a hotel efficiently, and, to accommodate scuba-diving activities, one would also need a licence and years of experience of training people to dive and escorting them into the deeper water. This indicates the fourth characteristic an idea needs to become an opportunity, which is a fit between what is required to exploit the opportunity and the skills and experiences one has.

Opportunity identification

The above discussion shows that not every idea is an opportunity, and that the opportunity needs work before it can be exploited. Two streams of thought have emerged about the manner in which opportunities come about. Many argue that an opportunity is a favourable juncture of circumstances with a good chance for success or progress; others (Ardichvili, Cardozo and Ray, 2003) perceive an opportunity as an imprecisely defined market need or un- or under-employed resources or capabilities.

If an opportunity is a favourable juncture of circumstances, then this suggests that the opportunity already exists, and it is only a matter of recognition. Kirzner (1973) supports this view and poses the idea that an entrepreneur recognizes an opportunity as a result of his or her 'entrepreneurial alertness'. In his view, opportunities exist objectively and wait to be discovered. The prevailing theme in the literature is that ideas are plentiful and regularly encountered by the observant entrepreneur (Vesper, 1996; Timmons, 1999). This view is also posited by Kaish and Gilad (1991), but they argue that not everyone holding the same information is able to recognize the opportunity. They argue that entrepreneurs differ in the way they process information such that they are better able to recognize the opportunity. In their view, entrepreneurs (1) expose themselves in a different manner to the same information, (2) use specific parts or value specific parts of the same information differently, and (3) use different evaluation cues.

The other view, that an opportunity is an imprecisely defined market need, suggests that work is needed to find the opportunity, and this can be approached best through systematic searching. A systematic approach to opportunity recognition can be fuelled by two reasons. First, it is aimed at discovering where opportunities actually are, and, second, the aim is to fine-tune the opportunity in order to reduce the risks associated with the opportunity. Carl Vesper (1996) was among the first to discuss this process. In one of the earliest relevant writings on the subject, Vesper (1996) cited several ways that new venture ideas may be identified and suggested the possibility of a systematic search effort. However, systematically searching for ideas may not always be the best method of identifying entrepreneurial opportunities. Teach *et al.* (1989), for example, used field-survey data to examine how software firms identified their first market opportunity. They found that firms founded on 'accidentally' discovered venture ideas that had not been subjected to formal screening achieved break-even sales faster than those firms that had used more formal search and planning techniques. Teach *et al.* (1989) also found different styles of opportunity recognition among the software-firm presidents studied. Only about half favoured systematic approaches to searching for opportunities.

Timing of an opportunity

The temporal aspect of an opportunity implies that an opportunity does not last forever. The so-called window of opportunity is the time that it is indeed worthwhile pursuing an opportunity. When the window is closing, the opportunity no longer exists. Various factors influence this opening and closing of the window of opportunity, and it mainly has to do with the extent the problem exists and the extent that alternative solutions can address the problem.

The window of opportunity may not always be open immediately. Sometimes, the problem may be clear, and yet the solution to it is still not well developed. The difficulty may be that the technology is underdeveloped, or efficient distribution is not possible, or the solution is badly thought out. It may be also that customers are not aware they have a problem, and, although a solution is available, the need and urgency among customers have to be further articulated and understood. In the latter case, it will be difficult to set accurate price levels corresponding to the value that customers place on the solution for solving a latent problem. In these situations, the entrepreneur tries to enter the market too early, which we refer to as 'sinking the boat'. On the other hand, the entrepreneur might be too late entering the market and misses the boat. In these cases, the entrepreneur has often waited too long, and others have already exploited the opportunity. This often happens if the entrepreneur tries to reduce uncertainty by collecting more information about market size, customer preferences, etc. It may result from a tendency to look for resources before taking action. This is also an expression of uncertainty: to have control over resources makes it easier to make decisions and calculate costs. Stevenson and Gumpert (1985) argue that the heart of entrepreneurship is the pursuit of opportunity, regardless of the resources controlled.

However, if the entrepreneur has recognized an opportunity and tries exploiting it, it will be in their interest to make the window of opportunity longer – in other words, make sure that the opportunity is lasting. If the problem continues, then the opportunity can last for a long time, if only one solution best solves the problem. However, when competitors provide alternative solutions that solve the problem either at lower cost, more efficiently, more accurately or more quickly, then customers have alternatives to choose between. In these cases, the price of the solution decreases, or the costs of marketing or developing new features negatively affect the margin. Hence, the opportunity becomes less attractive to exploit.

Entrepreneurs can extend the window of opportunity by using or developing resources that are difficult to acquire or difficult for competitors to substitute. Barney (1991) argues that, if entrepreneurs can develop resources that meet the VRIN conditions, these resources will provide lasting benefits, which he claims will bring a sustainable competitive advantage. The VRIN conditions refer to the four criteria: valuable, rare, inimitable and non-substitutable:

- *Value* indicates that the resource should solve a significant problem that customers have.
- *Rare* indicates that the resources are not always or easily available. This could be a location that provides a unique selling point, e.g. an exclusive shop location, or, for example, a mining corporation that has access to rare materials.
- *Inimitable* refers to the difficulty of copying the same resource, e.g. a patent that prevents others from exploiting the technology.
- *Non-substitutable* refers to the absence of a similar resource that provides the same value to customers. Common ways for entrepreneurs to extend the opportunity window is by making the key resources difficult to copy. This can be done through legal mechanisms such as intellectual property rights (IPR), which include patents, trademarks, copyrights, industrial design rights and trade secrets.

IPRs have the disadvantage that they are accessible by others, who can acquire the same knowledge and know-how, although they are by law not allowed to exploit it. IPRs are applicable when the product can be reverse-engineered, and the entrepreneur needs to prevent that happening. Reverse engineering or back engineering is simply taking a device apart and seeing how it works. It would be more interesting if you could protect your product and thus your key resources from reverse engineering. Causal ambiguity is the key term here and occurs if the source that provides a firm with its competitive advantage is unknown. This could be the creativity of a team of designers that is the result of complex social interaction. Copying such a team or the conditions in which they work is hardly impossible. Causal ambiguity can also result from secrecy in the production process. For instance, an asphalt production company has found a new additive allowing it to work with rolled asphalt at a lower temperature. This can save the company a lot of money and gives more time and flexibility, or the distance between the production site and construction site can be greater. The working additive can be hidden by the asphalt being mixed with various other additives that have no function, but it would be impossible to reverse-engineer and find out which additive was added during production that gives asphalt the specific characteristic of working at a lower temperature.

Antecedents of idea identification (idea creation or opportunity identification)

Why do certain people have more ideas than others? Researchers have tried to answer this question, and various streams of research have emerged. In entrepreneurship research, the start-up firm is assumed to be an extension of the founder(s). Several studies have observed that team starters perform better than individuals, and, when they are more committed to the founding of the firm and expose a strong entrepreneurial orientation, they tend to start firms that grow faster than founders with lower commitment and less orientation. Regarding the experience of the founder(s), some studies have indicated that teams with experience in the technology are in a better position to exploit the discovery (Franklin *et al.*, 2001). Other studies continue that, besides experience in relevant knowledge fields, the complementarity among the team members' experience is important for successful early growth (Roberts, 1991; Shane, 2004). Other researchers refer to the importance of the start-up's network, the connections that provide novel information about opportunities or useful contacts to collaborate with or outsource activities to. The main theories here are the personal-traits view, the resource-based view and the social-network view (see Figure 4.4).

Personal-traits view

The personal-traits view focuses on the disposition of an individual to identify opportunities and act accordingly that distinguishes them from others. Studies at the individual level have mainly emphasized the behavioural factors and attributes of the entrepreneur (Bandura, 1997) and the decisions in the entrepreneurial process (Venkataraman, 1997) to explain the early

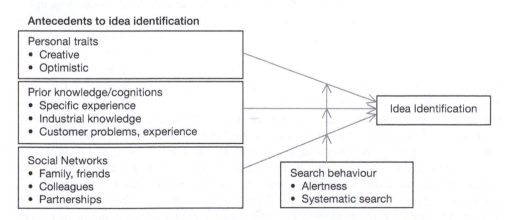

Figure 4.4 Simplified model for opportunity identification: Antecedents to idea identification

growth of the new firm. The behaviour theory focuses on psychological factors to explain who starts a new firm and why someone does and differentiates between successful and less successful entrepreneurs. The psychological factors address several human traits. Over the years, a large variety of factors have been investigated, such as the need for achievement, desire for independence (Cromie, 1987), internal locus of control (Cromie and Johns, 1983; Cromie, 1987), tolerance of ambiguity, (un)willingness to act in the face of uncertainty, even when risks are low, self-confidence that they can create their own luck, and self-efficacy (Bandura, 1997). This research approach is characterized by the collection of data among entrepreneurs and thus focuses on *ex post* situations. Gartner (1990) criticizes these studies for assuming that the entrepreneur's traits, attitudes and beliefs do not change because of the entrepreneurial experience itself. Individuals seldom behave consistently in different times and situations, and it is likely that the experience from the entrepreneurial event may affect the individual's behaviour. As a result, the behavioural theory is replaced by cognitive and attribution approaches. The cognitive approach suggests that the cognitive orientation (i.e. the way of thinking) of potential entrepreneurs influences their intention and persistence to act entrepreneurially (Gatewood *et al.*, 1995). The attribution approach refers to certain endowments that entrepreneurs possess and that put them into a position that makes them more suited to identifying certain opportunities and capitalizing on these opportunities (Shane, 2000; Shane and Stuart, 2002). The cognition and attributes of the potential entrepreneur may influence the entrepreneurial outcome, but their willingness and endowments cannot suffice 'if persistence merely results in potential entrepreneurs engaging in the wrong activities' (Gatewood *et al.*, 1995, p. 375). If the nascent entrepreneur allocates substantial time to a single activity and neglects other activities, a new business may not be created. The cognitive orientation and attributes of the entrepreneur are therefore believed to be mediating variables (Gatewood *et al.*, 1995). The extent that the entrepreneur is able successfully to exploit the opportunity is based on the organization of the entrepreneurial process (Venkataraman, 1997; Shane and Venkataraman, 2000). Organizing the entrepreneurial process involves evaluating the opportunity and engaging in activities such as gathering and acquiring resources to exploit the opportunity (Shane and Venkataraman, 2000).

Prior knowledge and cognitions

The prior knowledge and cognitions reflect the internal resources individuals can draw upon. This is often discussed in terms of the resources that can explain why a firm can be successful and exist (Wernerfelt, 1984; Barney, 1991). This so-called resource-based view is a reaction to the 'positioning' view that was dominant in the late 1970s (Mintzberg, 1990). The position view stresses that firms should identify attractive market opportunities with potential customers whose needs could be satisfied better than is currently being done by other firms. The firm's strategy should then be aimed at this market. This view was criticized because, if all firms identify the 'most attractive' niche, who will get it, and why would competition not destroy its attraction? The resource-based view emerged and builds on two assumptions. First, firms within an industry may be heterogeneous with respect to the resources they control, and, second, these resources may not be perfectly mobile across firms, and thus heterogeneity can be long-lasting. Based on these two assumptions, the resource-based view stresses that, rather than the external opportunities, a firm's own strengths should be the point of departure. The strengths of the firm are in its difficult-to-imitate competencies and unique resources. Firms can achieve an advantage by implementing value-creating strategies that cannot be duplicated by others. Thus, the resource-based view focuses on the rents flowing to the owners of scarce, firm-specific resources, rather than the economic profits from product-market positioning (Teece *et al.*, 1997). For start-ups, we focus on the resources, i.e. knowledge and capabilities, that the entrepreneur(s) possess themselves, as the start-up is considered to be an extension of its founders. Various scholars use the term prior experience to address this knowledge and ability of entrepreneurs. This leads to four types of experience that contribute to the resources that are considered important for technology-based start-ups, e.g. entrepreneurial, industry, research and management experience.

Start-up experience

Start-up experience is often mentioned as important for people starting a company. Start-ups need to overcome specific obstacles before they become a fledgling firm (Vohora *et al.*, 2004). Most important is the need to convince financiers, suppliers and customers of their abilities, even though they lack a track record. Having experience in start-ups and growing firms will help them to recognize that creating and building a new venture is a dynamic process, and they will understand the context in which their emerging firm will operate (Cooper *et al.*, 1994). Duchesneau and Gartner (1990) found that successful start-ups were able to plan the growth of their start-up better if they had considerable start-up experience. Chandler (1996) found evidence that prior ownership was positively related to venture performance, if the new business was connected to the experience gained in the entrepreneur's previous firm. Goslin (1987) found previous start-up experience to be the main characteristic of successful high-tech start-up firms. Thus, teams that include individuals with start-up experience are better suited to the changes and difficulties that have to be overcome during the start-up process.

Industry experience

Another type of experience that is often mentioned as facilitating start-ups is prior industry experience. Having industry experience makes it easier to adapt to the habits of that industry (Chandler, 1996). Founders who have experience in the same industry as that in which the start-up will operate have the benefit of knowing the competitive conditions and specific technologies in the industry. Industry experience allows entrepreneurs to identify emerging opportunities and position new products and services accordingly. In a study of seventy-eight MBA students, Shepherd and DeTienne (2005) observed that prior knowledge of the market was positively associated with the number of opportunities identified. And, in a large survey of 1,600 small firms and 105 large firms, Siegel *et al.* (1993) found that substantial industry experience was important for both high- and low-growth ventures to be profitable. Industry experience also helps firms to find ways to export their products (Westhead *et al.*, 2001) and facilitates start-ups' going public (Shane and Stuart, 2002).

Research experience

In technology-based start-ups, the prior research experience of the founders is viewed as beneficial to the early start (Shane, 2000). Start-ups that are based on technological findings need further research and development before the findings can be exploited commercially. Teams with members who have worked in technology before have the experience and skills to better translate the findings into various applications. Especially when it concerns complex knowledge with tacit components, the translation requires a specific research experience. Recent studies have found evidence that successful start-ups are founded by star scientists. The benefits result from the fact that star scientists operate at the forefront of their research field and they are more embedded in scientific networks that provide better access to expertise and more efficient collaboration (Murray, 2004). Vohora *et al.* (2004) observed among successful UK start-ups that they were founded by academic inventors who had a strong position in their research field and had created valuable know-how. More experienced scientists are in the best position to conduct radical innovations, which are more risky but also highly valuable (Corolleur *et al.*, 2004).

Management experience

Previous studies on entrepreneurial firms have shown that management experience is an important factor in explaining a new firm's performance. Firms that are founded by individuals with management experience are better suited to converting the firm's resources into value-generating activities. Also, management experience is important to the development and management of the start-up. Westhead *et al.* (2001) indicate that management experience is important for firms to develop export channels. Their management experience helps them to set up contracts and undertake negotiations. Furthermore, entrepreneurs with management experience have the know-how to introduce human-resource practices, carry out more effective administrative procedures, better control and monitor the work process and undertake more promising competitive-strategy tasks (Romanelli, 1989). However, one must be careful, as many of the management skills are important during later stages of the start-up. Managers have a tendency to control activities and feel more comfortable when they possess resources and organize procedures that can make the start-up less flexible, which is especially needed in the early stage of start-up growth, when the opportunity and its business model need to be developed. Several authors (e.g. Steen *et al.*, 2010) have found that management experience can be constraining for early start-up growth. Stevenson and Gumpert (1985) have discussed this view already in their article on the heart of entrepreneurship, where they argue that entrepreneurship is the pursuit of opportunity regardless of the resources controlled. They differentiate between the promotor and administrator types of manager. The promotor type is open to chance and tries to pursue the opportunity before collecting the required resources, whereas the administrator tries to mitigate risk and starts with the resources he controls before he exploits an opportunity.

Role of team diversity and cohesion

When discussing the prior experience of entrepreneurs, one can argue that, in teams of entrepreneurs, certain mixtures of prior experience are more suitable for carrying out the start-up of a new firm. This view is discussed in research on team diversity and cohesion. Diverse team members tap into the knowledge and experience they have obtained from a variety of information domains. The perceptions of work-related tasks are then differently assessed and evaluated. Priorities and assumptions about the future and actions to be taken can diverge and necessitate constructive debate before a common understanding is reached (Simons *et al.*, 1999). The diversity may then represent potential for more thoughtful decision-making. However, this may only be the case when diversity leads to what is called cognitive diversity. Cognitive diversity leads to diversity and maybe even cognitive conflicts in perceptions and understandings, but diversity may also manifest in affective conflict, which is personal dislike and is often not considered to contribute to constructive debate. However, if we focus on the diversity leading to cognitive conflict, then we can distinguish three types of diversity: tenure, function and industry. Tenure diversity expresses the difference in lengths of time that each member of the team has been associated with the team; functional diversity expresses the difference in the previous functions or positions of the team members; and industry diversity expresses the difference in experience in various sectors of industry.

Tenure diversity, the diversity of the moments when team members entered the spin-off, is important for strategic decision-making. Not constrained by previous thoughts or experiences, new members bring new views and perspectives to the discussion on strategic actions. They are more likely to question the strategic plan and to deviate from initial schedules or business plans. Ancona and Caldwell (1992, p. 325) found that, 'members who have entered the organisation at different times know a different set of people and often have different technical skills and different perspectives on the organisation's history'. Research on the role of tenure diversity shows that the more diverse teams are with respect to tenure, the more questions they ask about the intended strategy. In particular, when firms face environmental complexity or are active in R&D-intense industries, the diversity in tenure is positively associated with productive and innovative teams (Ancona and Caldwell, 1992; Reagans and Zuckerman, 2001), which has a positive effect on firm growth.

Functional diversity reflects the extent to which members span more and different functions, for example finance, marketing and technical experience. Diversity of function can be complementary and makes the execution of the various tasks more efficient. Especially in R&D-intense firms (Ancona and Caldwell, 1992) and in entrepreneurial teams (Ucbasaran *et al.*, 2003), functional diversity is associated with higher team productivity and larger sales growth.

Differences in industry experience result in different opinions and beliefs as to how to act, compete and approach business partners. In addition, diversity of industrial experience can be beneficial in identifying alternative opportunities in different industries (Shepherd and DeTienne, 2005), which in turn allows the team to choose the most attractive ones.

Team cohesion

The negative side of diversity, in general, is that the efficiency of communication and coordination of activities within a team are constrained by diversity among team members. If team members lack a common mindset or linguistic commonality, communication will be less efficient and more costly in terms of time. For teams that deal with complex knowledge and knowledge with a low level of codification, communication is hampered by difficult articulation. Team cohesiveness describes the close links between like-minded persons in an entrepreneurial team. Cohesive teams are closer to each other and share common beliefs and understandings that make the sharing of information smoother. The cohesion–performance effect has proven positive for entrepreneurial teams (Ensley *et al.*, 2002). Team cohesion was found to be related to venture performance and new venture growth (Ensley *et al.*, 2002).

Social networks

The entrepreneur's ability to build and maintain a network of relationships is increasingly viewed as key to identifying opportunities and exploiting them. The source of innovation does not exclusively reside in the firm, but instead it is commonly found at the intersection with actors such as competing firms, universities and business partners. Moreover, for entrepreneurial firms, relationships with external actors are important to gain access to resources such as finance, expertise and opportunities and to gain advice, guidance and endorsement (Aldrich and Zimmer, 1986). Entrepreneurs can draw upon their network contacts for emotional, material, social and creative support. Social networks play a significant role in the early growth of new firms, to overcome the liabilities of newness and smallness, and networks can help small and new firms to probe opportunities.

Compared with resources that are owned, such as capabilities and knowledge, network contacts are freer and are not possessed by the entrepreneur. As a result, the underlying principle of network contacts is social capital as goodwill – a valuable resource that others have towards each other (Adler and Kwon, 2002). Adler and Kwon argue that goodwill is the sympathy, trust and forgiveness offered us by friends and acquaintances. The effect of the goodwill is information, influence and solidarity. A large number of ways to measure a network of contacts have emerged, of which two approaches are mostly relevant for entrepreneurs: relational embeddedness and structural embeddedness. Relational embeddedness refers to the dyadic relationship between the actor, in our case the entrepreneur, and the network contacts, and structural embeddedness refers to the relationships among all the contacts of the actor in the network.

Relational embeddedness

The relational dimension refers to dyadic characteristics of the relationship, which are often expressed as the strength of the relationship (commonly referred to as the strength of tie) or content of the discussion with the relationship. Strong ties require fairly frequent contact, are usually of long duration and reciprocal and involve a strong degree of trust and emotional closeness. People rely on strong ties for (personal) advice and support and are less reserved about making heavy investments in this type of relationship. The strong-tie argument stresses that this type of relationship benefits the transfer of complex information (Hansen, 1999). Because people know each other quite well, they are more familiar with each other's interests, understand each other well, have shared beliefs and speak the same language, which makes the transfer of the information less puzzling. Strong ties are more reliable contacts, which yields three benefits: trust, predictability and voice. An exchange with a strong tie entails less potential for opportunism and uncertainty compared with market-mediated transactions. The trust in the relationship tells the entrepreneur on whom to count in difficult situations and, moreover, enhances predictability about how the contact will behave when the situation changes. Furthermore, using voice in a relationship means that the persons involved will make their complaints known and negotiate over them, rather than suddenly leave the arena.

Table 4.3 Advantages of strong and weak ties for identifying opportunities

Strong ties	*Weak ties*
More reliable and trustworthy information	New and novel information
Shared belief, same language makes communication easier	More information to choose from
More predictable	Information asymmetry
Easier to act upon	Time benefit

On the other hand, weak ties are more temporal and transient and normally involve little emotional investment. Communicating and exchanging ideas with people you don't meet that often and about whom you know little can provide you with novel information and new perspectives that support new arguments and debate. Granovetter (1973) coined the term 'strength of weak ties', in 1973, which he explains as a source of opportunities and unique resources. For entrepreneurs who have access to weak ties, their strength lies in the novel information that can lead to valuable information asymmetries to be exploited. Having more weak ties gives the advantage of more novel information that can reflect more opportunities, hence more to choose from to pursue, whereas start-ups without weak ties do not have access to these opportunities and consequently do not have that choice. Summing up, strong ties provide benefits in terms of trust and efficient collaboration, whereas weak ties give access to novel information, and, similarly, strong ties may constrain the search for novel information, whereas a weak tie will hamper the transfer of complex knowledge and reliable resources.

Besides the strength of the relationship, the content that is discussed within the relationship also matters. Adler and Kwon (2002, p. 23) refer to the abilities but also the norms and beliefs that are shared in the relationship. These may influence the value of the information or goods that are transferred. According to Podolny and Baron, 'the network structure most conducive to organizational advancement depends significantly on the content of the social tie involved' (1997, p. 674). In a study among Russian entrepreneurs, Batjargal (2003) stresses that the content of the tie is important for understanding the role of the relationship, for both strong and weak ties. Also, Hansen (1999) addresses benefits of both strong and weak ties for different types of business action. To find new information, weak ties are important, but strong ties are crucial for transferring that information. Gulati and Higgins (2003) analyse the role of endorsement that stems from relationships with venture capitalists and strategic alliance partnerships and found that the content of the tie can act as a contingent. In their study, Lechner *et al.* (2006) introduce the importance of the relational mix and discuss how, for different entrepreneurial activities, various compositions of network contacts, i.e. technology, marketing, finance contacts, are needed.

Structural embeddedness

The structural dimension refers to the amount of redundancy among network contacts. Contacts are redundant when they interact with each other, or at least are aware of each other. In an absolute redundant network, everyone is connected to each other, such that no one can escape the notice of others. This redundancy provides some benefits for entrepreneurs but also limitations, which are expressed by the closure argument and the structural-hole argument.

According to the closure argument, in a redundant network, the information known to one person is rapidly diffused to others and interpreted in similar ways (Granovetter, 1973). Network closure provides benefits in at least three ways. First, redundancy may facilitate trust among the people in the network (Coleman, 1988) and improve communication (Hansen, 1999). When firms interact with other firms in a group in which everyone knows what the others know, the fine tuning of activities is easier, more efficient and, thus, less costly. Second, in close networks, reputational effects can flow easily from one contact to another. The norms and behaviour of the participants in the network are clearly visible, and the mutual communication can facilitate effective sanctioning of opportunistic behaviour, but also rewards for high achievement. In redundant networks, it is less risky for people to

Table 4.4 Closure and brokerage argument for identifying opportunities

Closure argument	Brokerage argument
Rapid diffusion of knowledge	Diverse information
Facilitates trust	Control benefit and bargaining power
Prevents opportunistic behaviour	Time advantages
Redundancy if one contact is lost	Larger scope for referrals

trust one another (Coleman, 1988). Third, the redundancy in the network provides the firms with continuity (Steier and Greenwood, 2000). In redundant networks, contacts are redundant with respect to the sharing of information. When a partner withdraws from a relationship, the connection dissolves, but the redundancy allows the actor to switch easily to another contact and to maintain access to the resource, expertise or whatever.

The disadvantage of redundancy is that, with each tie that connects to the same kinds of people, the marginal value of each succeeding tie drops. Non-redundancy in the network increases the range of the network: a wider circle of information on opportunities such as potential markets, investors and business ideas is available to the entrepreneur. In non-redundant networks, people are not necessarily unaware of one another, but they are focused on their own activities and have no interest in the others' activities (Burt, 1992). The structural-hole argument claims that benefits result from the diversity of information and the brokerage opportunities created by the lack of connection between separate ties or clusters of ties in a social network. When firms exploit non-redundant networks through bridging structural holes (see Figure 4.5), they can have three benefits (Burt, 1992). First, the firm can profit from access to information and resources that are not available to other firms. The firm has a control benefit when two individuals (e.g. suppliers or buyers) have an interest in the same resource: a third individual can exploit the competitive relation between the two to play them off against one another. By exploiting the lack of connection between the two individuals, the third has bargaining power and can yield profit. Second, the firm can benefit from time advantages (Burt, 1992). The firm can use the separate contacts to scan for opportunities before others do. Third, the contacts in a non-redundant network reach out to a larger, more diverse network of contacts. Contacts in non-

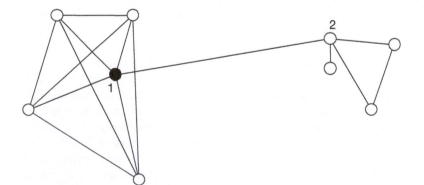

Figure 4.5 Bridging a structural hole

redundant networks can be used as referrals that provide the entrepreneur with more diverse opportunities and potential business partners that are beyond the network of the entrepreneur.

Thus, the structural dimension reflects the redundant–non-redundant continuum and consists of two diverging arguments at each end of the continuum. The closure argument, in sum, stresses that redundant network contacts can provide smooth communication, reputational effects and continuity in access to external resources. On the other hand, the structural-hole argument claims that a network rich in non-redundant contacts provides access to a wider circle of information about unique resources and opportunities, and the referrals provide a wider range of potential business partners. The social structure can be both a source of opportunities and a source of constraint.

Chapter summary

The question 'How can I find real problems to solve?' keeps many would-be entrepreneurs awake. An incredible number of exceptionally talented individuals try to find an 'opportunity' niche. The problem is that most don't know how to look. The source of entrepreneurial opportunities depends, in part, on the distribution of information in society. When people interact, they are exposed to new information. The combination of new information with existing knowledge can facilitate the emergence of new opportunities, but also the combination of existing parts of knowledge that are recombined into a new opportunity. Technology-based start-ups have the advantage of potentially valuable prior information and prior experience, which is important to the discovery of opportunities. However, many businesses, if not all business, start with a customer, not with know-how, not with the 'bright' idea. For inventor–entrepreneurs, the best approach to business is to find someone who will pay and help to develop something they need – and let you keep the rights to sell to others. In this chapter we have investigated when an idea becomes an opportunity, how to structure the search process, and how business planning, improvisation and the characteristics of the entrepreneur affect the outcome and framing of the opportunity.

Study questions

1   How do the Kirzner and Schumpeter types of entrepreneurship differ and interact with each other?
2   How can entrepreneurs extend the period where they can exploit opportunities?
3   Explain the role of network redundancy in view of entrepreneurial opportunity identification.
4   Explain the difficulty of timing an opportunity for an entrepreneur.

References

Adler, P. S. and Kwon, S. W. (2002). Social capital: Prospects for a new concept. *Academy of Management Review.* 27(1): 17–40.

Aldrich, H. E. and Zimmer, C. (1986). 'Entrepreneurship through social networks', in D. L. Sexton and R. W. Smilor (eds), *The Art and Science of Entrepreneurship.* Cambridge, MA: Ballinger, pp. 3–23.

Ancona, D. G. and Caldwell, D. F. (1992). Demography and design: Predictors of new product team performance. *Organization Science.* 3: 321–41.

Ardichvili, A., Cardozo, R. and Ray, S. (2003). A theory of entrepreneurial opportunity identification and development. *Journal of Business Venturing.* 18: 105–23.

Bandura, A. (1997). *Self-efficacy: The exercise of self-control.* New York: W. H. Freedman.

Barney, J. B. (1991). Firm resources and competitive advantage. *Journal of Management.* 171: 99–120.

Batjargal, B. (2003). Social capital and entrepreneurial performance in Russia: A longitudinal study. *Organization Studies.* 24(4): 535–56.

Burt, R. S. (1992). *Structural Holes.* Cambridge, MA: Harvard University Press.

Chandler, G. N. (1996). Business similarity as a moderator of the relationship between pre-ownership experience and venture performance. *Entrepreneurship Theory and Practice.* 20: 51–65.

Cheah, H-B. (1990). Schumpeterian and Austrian entrepreneurship: Unity within duality. *Journal of Business Venturing.* 5: 341–7.

Coleman, J. S. (1988). Social capital in the creation of human capital. *American Journal of Sociology.* 94(Supplement): S95–S120.

Cooper, A. C., Gimeno-Gascon, F. J. and Woo, C. Y. (1994). Initial human and financial capital as predictors of new venture performance. *Journal of Business Venturing.* 9: 371–95.

Corolleur, C. C. F., Carrere, M. and Mangematin, V. (2004). Turning scientific and technological capital into economic capital: The experience of biotech start-ups in France. *Research Policy.* 33: 631–42.

Cromie, S. (1987). Motivations of aspiring male and female entrepreneurs. *Journal of Organisational Behaviour.* 8: 251–61.

Cromie, S. and Johns, S. (1983). Irish entrepreneurs: Some personal characteristics. *Journal of Organisational Behaviour.* 4: 317–24.

Duchesneau, D. and Gartner, W. (1990). A profile of new venture success and failure in an emerging industry. *Journal of Business Venturing.* 5: 297–312.

Ensley, M. D., Pearson, A. W., and Amason, A. C. (2002). Understanding the dynamics of new venture top management teams: Cohesion, conflict, and new venture performance. *Journal of Business Venturing.* 17(4): 365–86.

Franklin, S., Lockett, A. and Wright, M. (2001). Academic and surrogate entrepreneurs in university spin-out companies. *Journal of Technology Transfer.* 26(1/2): 127–41.

Gartner, W. B. (1990). What are we talking about when we talk about entrepreneurship? *Journal of Business Venturing.* 5: 15–29.

Gatewood, E. J., Shaver, K. G. and Gartner, W. B. (1995). A longitudinal study of cognitive factors influencing start-up behaviours and success at venture creation. *Journal of Business Venturing,* 19: 371–91.

Goslin, L. N. (1987). 'Characteristics of successful high-tech start-up firms', in N. Churchill, B. Kirchhoff, W. Krasner and K. Vesper (eds), *Frontiers of Entrepreneurship Research.* Wellesley, MA: Babson College, pp. 452–63.

Granovetter, M. (1973). The strength of weak ties. *American Journal of Sociology.* 78: 1360–80.

Gulati, R. and Higgins, M. C. (2003). Which ties matter when? The contingent effects of interorganizational partnerships on IPO success. *Strategic Management Journal.* 24(2): 127–44.

Hansen, M. (1999). The search transfer problem: The role of weak ties in sharing knowledge across organization subunits. *Administrative Science Quarterly.* 44: 82–111.

Kaish, S. and Gilad, B. (1991). Characteristics of opportunity searches of entrepreneurs versus executives: Sources, interests, and general alertness. *Journal of Business Venturing.* 6: 45–61.

Kirzner, I. M. (1973). *Competition and Entrepreneurship.* Chicago, IL: University of Chicago Press.

Lechner, C., Dowling, M. and Welpe, I. (2006). Firm networks and firm development: The role of the relational mix. *Journal of Business Venturing.* 21(4): 514–40.

Mintzberg, H. (1990). The design school: Reconsidering the basic premises of strategic management. *Strategic Management Journal.* 11: 171–95.

Murray, F. (2004). The role of academic inventors in entrepreneurial firms: Sharing the laboratory life. *Research Policy.* 33(4): 643–59.

Podolny, J. M. and Baron, J. N. (1997). Resources and relationships: Social networks and the mobility in the workplace. *American Sociological Review.* 62: 673–93.

Reagans, R. and Zuckerman, E. W. (2001). Networks, diversity, and productivity: The social capital of corporate R&D teams. *Organization Science*. 12(4): 502–17.

Roberts, E. B. (1991). *Entrepreneurs in High-technology – Lessons from MIT and beyond*. New York: Oxford University Press.

Romanelli, E. (1989). Environments and strategies of organization start-up: Effects on early survival. *Administrative Science Quarterly*. 34: 369–87.

Schumpeter, J. A. (1934). *The Theory of Economic Development*. Cambridge, MA: Harvard University Press.

Shane, S. A. (2000). Prior knowledge and the discovery of entrepreneurial opportunities. *Organization Science*. 11: 448–69.

Shane, S. A. (2004). *Academic Entrepreneurship: University spin-offs and wealth creation*. Northampton, MA: Edward Elgar.

Shane, S. A. and Stuart, T. (2002). Organizational endowments and the performance of university startups. *Management Science*. 48(1): 154–70.

Shane, S. and Venkataraman, S. (2000). The promise of entrepreneurship as a field of research. *Academy of Management Review*. 25: 217–26.

Shepherd, D. A. and DeTienne, D. R. (2005). Prior knowledge, potential financial reward and opportunity identification. *Entrepreneurship Theory & Practice*. January: 91–112.

Siegel, R., Siegel, E. and MacMillan, I. C. (1993). Characteristics distinguishing high-growth ventures. *Journal of Business Venturing*. 8: 169–80.

Simons, T., Pelled, L. and Smith, K. (1999). Making use of difference: Diversity, debate, and decision comprehensiveness in top management teams. *Academy of Management Journal*. 42(6): 662–73.

Steen, M. van der, Ortt, R. and Scholten, V. (2010). Exploring determinants of life sciences spin-off creation: Empirical evidence from the Netherlands. *International Journal of Entrepreneurship & Small Business*. 10(1): 30–48.

Steier, L. and Greenwood, R. (2000). Entrepreneurship and the evolution of angel financial networks. *Organization Studies*. 21(1): 163–92.

Stevenson, H. H. and Gumpert, D. (1985). The heart of entrepreneurship. *Harvard Business Review*. 63(2): 85–94.

Teach, R. D., Schwartz, R. G. and Tarpley, F. A. (1989). 'The recognition and exploitation of opportunity in the software industry: A study of surviving firms', in R. H. Brockhaus, N. C. Churchill, J. A. Katz, B. A. Kirchhoff, K. H. Vesper and W. E. Wetzel (eds), *Frontiers of Entrepreneurship Research*. Wellesley, MA: Babson College, pp. 109–23.

Teece, D. J., Pisano, G. and Shuen, A. (1997). Dynamic capabilities and strategic management. *Strategic Management Journal*. 18(7): 509–33.

Timmons, J. A. (1999). *New Venture Creation* (5th edn). Boston, MA: Irwin McGraw Hill.

Ucbasaran, D., Lockett, A., Wright, M. and Westhead, P. (2003). Entrepreneurial founder teams: Factors associated with member entry and exit. *Entrepreneurship Theory & Practice*. Winter: 107–27.

Venkataraman, S. (1997). 'The instinctive domain of entrepreneurship research', in J. A. Katz (ed.), *Advances in Entrepreneurship, Firm Emergence and Growth*, Vol. 3. London: JAI Press, pp. 119–38.

Vesper, K. H. (1996). *New Venture Experience* (rev. edn). Seattle, WA: Vector Books.

Vohora, A., Wright, M. and Lockett, A. (2004). Critical junctures in the development of university high-tech spin-out companies. *Research Policy*. 33: 147–75.

Wernerfelt, B. (1984). A resource-based view of the firm. *Strategic Management Journal*. 5: 171–80.

Westhead, P., Wright, M. and Ucbasaran, D. (2001). The internationalization of new and small firms: A resource-based view. *Journal of Business Venturing*. 16: 333–58.

Further reading

Burt, R. S. (2004). Structural holes and good ideas. *American Journal of Sociology*. 110(2): 349–99.

Kirzner, I. M. (1997). Entrepreneurial discovery and the competitive market process: An Austrian approach. *Journal of Economic Literature*, 35: 60–85.

Knight, F. H. (1921). *Risk, Uncertainty and Profit*. Washington, DC: Beard Books.

Lumpkin, G. T. and Dess, G. G. (1996). Clarifying the entrepreneurial orientation construct and linking it to performance. *Academy of Management Review*. 21: 135–72.

McMullen, J. and Shepherd, D. A. (2006). Entrepreneurial action and the role of uncertainty in the theory of the entrepreneur. *Academy of Management Review*. 31(1): 132–52.

Mises, L. V. (1949). *Human Action: A treatise on economics* (4th rev. edn). San Francisco, CA: Fox & Wilkes.

Part II

Developing the venture

The opening chapter of Part II builds on Part I by examining business models and, in particular, addressing the question of how this business will make money. Once you have a clear idea about what problem is being addressed and how the new venture plans to make money, the next stage is to generate customers who will pay for your products and services. Chapter 6 looks at the wider innovation system into which the venture will be launched. Entrepreneurs must have the ability to explore and use the knowledge, expertise and capital of others. This requires not only technological expertise but also managerial and social skills to connect with other entrepreneurs and other organizations and build relationships.

Chapter 7 explores academic spin-outs, how they contribute to society and the main difficulties that they face in their early development. Chapter 8 explores how some users are inclined to modify an existing product so that it better suits their needs. Unmet customer needs are an important target for aspiring entrepreneurs and may be indicative of a much larger customer base of people who are also not satisfied with the current product but do not modify it themselves.

Part II

Developing the venture

5   Developing a business model

This chapter helps entrepreneurs consider how their new venture will make money. This may seem like an obvious question with an equally obvious answer, but it should not be overlooked, for there is much room for creativity on the entrepreneur's part. For example, it may be that the techno-starter believes it has developed a better product than the existing products on the market. It will, therefore, simply offer its product at a competitive price relative to the competition. However, this would overlook other possibilities for the business. Are there opportunities for leasing rather than simply selling? Can the business adopt a landlord business model? Famous examples abound where start-ups have developed new business models that challenge existing, dominant business models in an industry. Table 5.1 shows a wide range of new services that have been created that also led to the creation of new business models. These range from eBay to Facebook. Figure 5.1 shows the eBay business model. Clearly, this model is dependent on a stable technology platform, but at its heart is a simple transaction fee revenue model.

Business models are fundamentally linked to technological innovation, and yet the business model construct is essentially separable from technology. According to Baden-Fuller and Haefliger (2013), business models mediate the link between technology and firm performance. Second, developing the right technology is a matter of a business model decision regarding openness and user engagement.

Table 5.1 A range of new services that also created new business models

Company	Industry sector	New service/new business model
eBay	Online auction	A new way of buying and selling through a community of individual users
Ryanair	Airline	A new way of offering air travel with no-frills service and emphasis on economy
netflix	Online movie and TV series rental	A monthly subscription service providing members with fast and easy access to movies and television programmes
Amazon	Retailer	New way to buy goods – online retailer
Napster, iTunes	Music retailer	New way to buy and download music
Google/ Bing	Internet search engine	A fast way to search for information on the Internet
PartyGaming	Online gambling, e.g. poker	Gambling and gaming from the comfort of your own home
Twitter/ Facebook	Social networking	A community of online users who can chat and share music, images, news from their own home
YouTube	Online video and film archive	A community of users sharing home-made video clips plus recorded favourite clips from movies

Figure 5.1 An overview of the eBay business model

What is a business model?

A *business model* describes the value an organization offers to its customers. It illustrates the capabilities and resources required to create, market and deliver this value, and to generate profitable, sustainable revenue streams. It is the revenue stream that is key here. Where is the money going to come from, and how much of it will the business be able to retain? It includes considering issues such as margins and allocation of profits to those in the supply chain. For example, Apple is extremely profitable partly because its margins on its products are so much higher than its competitors'. So, there is a key question that needs to be addressed: How will this business make money?

To answer this question, it is necessary to address a series of additional questions, such as:

- Who is the target customer?
- What customer problem or challenge does the business solve?
- What value does it deliver?
- How does it reach, acquire and keep customers?
- How does it define and differentiate its offering?
- How does it generate revenue?
- What is the cost structure?
- What is the profit margin?

In principle, a business model does not matter to customers; it is important to the company and the organization of its business. The business model determines the external relationships with suppliers, customers and partners. However, it is primarily focused on the company's business processes. Box 5.1 explains the different component parts of a business model.

Box 5.1 Parts of the business model

1   *Value proposition*: a description of the customer problem, the product that addresses the problem and the value of the product from the customer's perspective.
2   *Market segment*: the group of customers to target; sometimes the potential of an innovation is unlocked only when a different market segment is targeted.
3   *Value chain structure*: the firm's position and activities in the value chain and how the firm will capture part of the value that it creates in the chain.
4   *Revenue generation and margins*: how revenue is generated (sales, leasing, subscription, support, etc.), the cost structure and target profit margins.
5   *Position in value network*: identification of competitors, partners and any network effects that can be utilized to deliver more value to the customer.
6   *Competitive strategy*: how the company will attempt to develop a sustainable competitive advantage, for example, by means of a cost, differentiation or niche strategy.

Source: Chesbrough and Rosenbloom, 2002;
Shafer *et al*., 2005; Watson, 2005

In a seminal article in *Long Range Planning*, Professor David Teece argued that, whatever the business enterprise, it either explicitly or implicitly employs a particular business model that describes the design or architecture of the value-creation, delivery and capture mechanisms it employs. This provides a useful definition of a business model (see Teece, 2010).

The business model is the key factor that leads to success in start-ups. It provides the starting point that allows a company to maximize its profits – the sooner the business model is in place, the easier it will be for the start-up to obtain support and funding. Investors will be seeking to ensure that the model is scalable. This will help reassure them that the business can grow exponentially. Investors must be able to envisage a start-up's business model (from an organizational and process perspective) as the company grows.

Many of the business models that we see today are influenced by Michael Porter's value chain (primary and support activities; Porter, 1980). To these key activities are added additional operational flows such as: plan, create demand, produce, sell/fulfil order (satisfy demand), charge, bill and accrue revenue, and provide after-sales service (and reverse supply chain). There are many other key activities and factors that are not mentioned, even though they may be more important than items identified. For example, the enterprise interacts with many stakeholders in such fields as technology, labour and capital markets. It is also affected by such external factors as regulation, competitors and new entrants. In the brewing industry, for example, a change in the excise applied to beer can dramatically alter revenues and profits. Indeed, some UK brewers are now producing low-alcohol beers of less than 3 per cent alcohol by volume because the excise is half that for higher-strength beer (*The Economist*, 2012).

There are many different styles of business model. There are also a wide variety of frameworks available to help firms develop their own business model. All business models are representations of an architecture, because they consist of both *functions* and *flows* in interconnection. Business models typically exhibit a rather abstract process taxonomy that may not align well to the enterprise structure, end flows and existing systems. As such, these models have limited practical value for the business owner or manager. For further explanation on this, see Shafer *et al.* (2005), Zott and Amit (2007), Mason and Leek (2008), Patzelt *et al.* (2008) and Richardson (2008).

The business model and the business plan

The terms business model and business plan are similar, but they are different. A business plan is a detailed document, typically 50–100 pages, with a lot of financial projections. If someone sets up a new business and applies for a loan, the lending institution will demand a business plan. The lender wants to assess whether its customers will be able to repay the loan. A business model is much less detailed. A business model describes the specific way the business expects to make money. It should be on one page, and it would be more clearly shown as a diagram. The business model itself is a single concept.

The concept of a business model is most useful for a new business (which explains the predominance of ecommerce-related references in recent years), and it is essential for a new business to establish a positive feedback loop. For example, word of mouth has to be effective, and customers have to recommend other customers. Without that kind of acceleration, a business will never get off the ground. As many owners of websites found in the early years of the World Wide Web (mid-1990s), their original business model didn't work, and the business soon failed: a classic example of that was boo.com. Other businesses found their customers adapted the products for a use that the business had not expected. This suggests that, when a business model is developed, it should be flexible, so that it can be modified easily should financial growth not meet expectations. It is, therefore, useful for the business model to include methods for its own evaluation. If a model is displayed as a series of 'boxes and arrows', the boxes represent activities, the arrows represent causal links between the boxes, and the strength of each link can be measured – or at least estimated. To help firms develop a business model, the following guidelines may help. The business model should contain:

1   a graphical representation (usually in the form of a flow chart);
2   a list of activities, on the part of both the business owner and potential customers;
3   a likely sequence for those activities (which may later be altered in the light of customer behaviour);
4   a set of indicators or metrics for measuring the linkage between the activities.

Figure 5.2 is a simple flow diagram that captures a series of activities showing how a technology-based start-up uses its technical expertise and entrepreneurial skills to develop a product or service that is made available to the market. Revenues are then used to reinvest into the company and to further reinforce the firm's advantage.

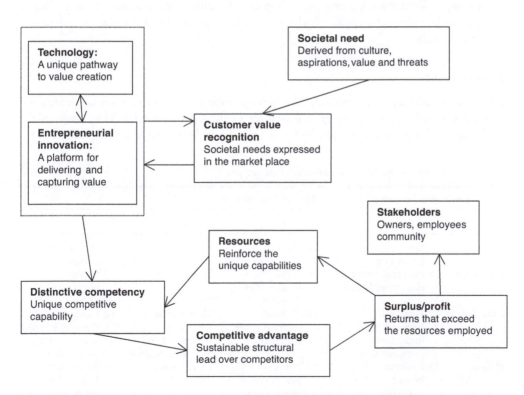

Figure 5.2 A business process showing how a firm uses its resources to create value

The range of business models

Clearly, there is a wide range of different business models applicable across all industries. A useful classification is provided by Weill and Vitale (2001; see Table 5.2). This shows sixteen different business models, including models such as human trafficking, which is clearly illegal. It is worthy of note that those firms that innovate on a business-model level are able to experience greater growth rates than companies that focus on innovation in products and operations. For example, the list of firms in Table 5.1 shows a range of different industry sectors in which these firms were able to develop new business models. Johnson *et al.* (2008) illustrate how firms can reinvent business models. There are several methods that start-ups can use to create an innovative business model:

- *Revenue/pricing model*: change how revenue is generated through new value propositions and new pricing models (to take advantage of economies of scale). This was the Ryanair approach to developing no-frills air travel.
- *Enterprise model*: specialize and configure the business to deliver greater value by rethinking what is done in-house and through collaboration. For example, Innocent Drinks, maker of fruit smoothies, was able to compete with industry giants such as Coca-Cola and others by outsourcing production and distribution, and also through building effective relationships with retailers.
- *Industry model*: redefine an existing industry, move into a new industry or create a new industry. Better Place is doing this with its electric vehicle infrastructure. It has developed a complete national electric vehicle infrastructure for Israel and has plans for Denmark and Australia.

Revenue models

Revenue models are often mistaken for business models. However, revenue models are concerned specifically with the pricing element of the business model. They concern the establishing of a price for the product and will clearly be dependent on reliable market

Table 5.2 The sixteen detailed business model archetypes

Basic business model archetype	Type of asset involved			
	Financial	*Physical*	*Intangible*	*Human*
Creator	1 Entrepreneur (serial entrepreneurs)	2 Manufacturer (VW automobiles)	3 Inventor (Trevor Bayliss)	4 Human creator (illegal)
Distributor	5 Financial trader (investment banks)	6 Wholesaler/ retailer (Tesco, Amazon)	7 IP trader (Logicalis)	8 Human distributor (illegal)
Landlord	9 Financial landlord (banks, insurance companies)	10 Physical landlord (hotel, car rental)	11 Intellectual landlord (publisher, brand manager)	12 Contractor (Federal Express, management consultancy)
Broker	13 Financial broker (insurance brokers)	14 Physical broker (eBay, estate agents)	15 IP broker (3i)	16 HR broker (employment agent)

Source: Weill and Vitale, 2001; Trott, 2011

Box 5.2 The bait and hook revenue model

The *bait and hook* business model is also referred to as the 'tied products business model'. It involves offering a basic product at a very low cost, sometimes at a loss (the 'bait'), and then charging compensatory recurring amounts for refills or associated products or services (the 'hook'). Examples include: razor (bait) and blades (hook); mobile phones (bait) and airtime (hook); computer printers (bait) and ink-cartridge refills (hook); and cameras (bait) and film (hook). An interesting variant of this model is Adobe, a software developer that gives away its document reader free of charge, but charges several hundred euros for its document writer.

Image 5.1 Hook
Source: © Emmanuel Ramos

intelligence. The 'bait and hook' revenue model is a good example of how firms can set a low price for part of their product to ensure that future substantial revenues are established (see Box 5.2). This model was clearly extremely successful for Gillette and Kodak. A wide range of revenue models are evident within online businesses. Table 5.3 illustrates five different such revenue models.

For a useful overview of developing business models, see Johnson *et al.* (2008).

The parts of the business model

A company's strategy defines its target market segment and customers and determines the value proposition for the customer's business. The business model focuses on how a

Table 5.3 Online revenue models

Type of revenue model	Approach	Examples
Advertising	Customers pay to be visible on your site/web pages	Google and Yahoo
Subscription	Customers pay a regular fee for access to information, content	*The Economist*, adult porn sites
Transaction fee	Customers pay a commission fee for using your services	eBay, lastminute.com
Retail	Customers pay for goods, similar to high-street retailer	Amazon
Affiliate	Customers pay if you send traffic to their sites	Google

start-up captures some of the value for itself (i.e. how the company makes money) and determines the viability of the company. The business model also focuses on coordinating internal and external processes to determine how the start-up interacts with partners, distribution channels and customers (Dubosson-Torbay *et al.*, 2002).

According to Alex Osterwalder (2004), there are four key aspects to any business model:

1   offer;
2   customer;
3   infrastructure;
4   finance.

Start-up ventures need to consider each of these in turn and build their business model accordingly. Figure 5.3 illustrates the business model framework and shows how each part interrelates. The business model describes, as a system, how the components of the business (i.e. organizational strategy, business processes) fit together to produce a profit. It answers the key question for investors: 'How does this business work?' The answer to the question consists of two parts:

1   It includes a description of the efforts that generate sales, which produce revenue. The value proposition is delivered to the target customer through a distribution channel. The flow and update of the value proposition are influenced by the relationship capital created through the company's marketing activities. Clearly, Mozilla has developed a unique value proposition through its development of open-source software. It receives donations from satisfied users, as well as income from other sites to which it sends traffic from its Firefox Internet browser.
2   It includes a description of the value-generating parts that make up the cost structure. A company's value proposition is created by the application of its key functions and abilities, through a configuration of operational activities that includes inputs and interaction with partners. A simple example is Toyota and its web of suppliers, with whom Toyota works closely to ensure incredible quality and reliability within its vehicles.

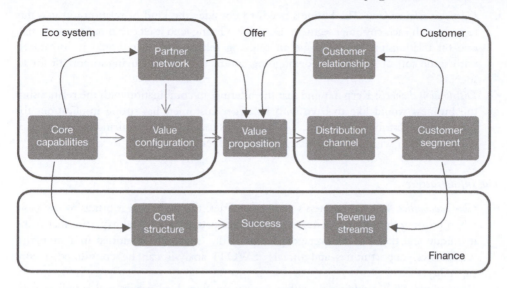

Figure 5.3 Business model framework
Source: Adapted from Osterwalder and Pigneur, 2013

The offering

The value proposition is the central piece that illustrates how the business plans to bind the supply side to the demand side. Value must always be considered from the buyer's perspective. Any functional, emotional or self-expressive value will vary depending on the customer's specific situation. Understanding the customer's role (e.g. economic buyer, technical buyer, end-user), as well as where the customer belongs on the technology adoption life cycle, is critical when developing a value proposition. For the customer to consider buying a product, its value proposition must be superior to: (1) the competition, and (2) doing nothing. It must set it apart from the competition and focus on its product's unique benefits. The value proposition also requires an understanding of what your customers are trying to achieve through their strategy and actions (see Shafer *et al.*, 2005; Mason and Leek, 2008; Richardson, 2008).

The value proposition statement consists of several key components:

- what is on offer, and how it is offered to customers;
- what type of value or benefit is associated with the offering, and how much (e.g. cost savings, time savings, revenue increase, customer/employee satisfaction);
- how the value is generated;
- why it is different from anything else on the market.

The customer side

- *Target market segment*: Defining the value proposition leads naturally to a discussion about who is the target market segment and what characterizes the ideal customer. Specifically, it should have a clear understanding of the target customer's motivation to buy.

- *Customer relationships*: The business needs to consider the kind of relationship it wants to have with each customer segment. Does the offering lend itself to a more transactional, one-off relationship, or will it be an ongoing relationship that should be organized with some sort of subscription or ongoing contract? Is repeat buying important for its success?
- *Distribution channels*: Keep in mind that the offering, in combination with the relationship the business would like to have with its target customer, has strong implications for the choice of distribution channel. The trade-off is usually about balancing the complexity of the solution with the complexity of the marketing.

The infrastructure

- *Core capabilities*: List the business's core capabilities: the assets that it brings to the table when creating the offering. These include skills, patents, assets and expertise that make it unique and that can be leveraged. Some of the 'strengths' identified in a strengths, weaknesses, opportunities and threats (SWOT) analysis can be considered a core capability.
- *Partners and allies*: Building the offering may involve third parties and suppliers who have key capabilities to complement it. Understand how to integrate these in the offering and the processes is critical.
- *Value configuration*: Describe how all the components together create the product and serve customers. Explain the most important activities and processes needed to implement the business model, including critical tasks and timelines, the people and skills required, and the organization's core processes.

The finances

- *Revenue streams*: Evaluate the streams through which the business will earn revenues from value-creating and customer-facing activities. Is it possible to price the product in such a way that optimizes the volume?
- *Cost structure*: Calculate the costs that will be incurred to run the business model as determined by its infrastructure (above). Does the cost structure offer a reasonable profit?

Examining the finances at the end of the process allows the business to ensure that it has a balanced business model that produces value for its customers and profits for its shareholders at the same time.

Considerations in designing a business model

Switching costs

The time, effort or money a customer has to spend to switch from one product or service provider to another is called 'switching costs'. The higher the switching costs, the likelier a customer is to stick to one provider, rather than leave for the products or services of a competitor. A great example of designing switching costs into a business model is Apple's introduction of the iPod in 2001. Steve Jobs heralded his new product with the catchphrase '1,000 songs in your pocket'. Well, that was more than a product innovation focusing on storage. It was a business model strategy to get customers to copy all their music on to iTunes and their iPod, which would make it more difficult for them to switch to competing digital music players. In a time when little more than brand preferences were preventing people from switching from one player to another, this was a smart move and laid the foundation for Apple's subsequent stronghold on music and later innovations.

Scalability

Scalability describes how easy it is to expand a business model without equally increasing its cost base. Consultancy is a well-understood business model and can be attractive and lucrative for techno start-ups, but it suffers from limits on scalability. Of course software- and web-based business models are naturally more scalable than those based on bricks and mortar, but, even among digital business models, there are large differences. An impressive example of scalability is Facebook. With only a few thousand engineers, it creates value for hundreds of millions of users. Only a few other companies in the world have such a ratio of users per employee. A company that has pushed the limits even further is the social-gaming company Zynga. By building games such as Farmville or Cityville on the back of Facebook, the world's largest social network, it could benefit from Facebook's reach (and scale), without having to build it itself.

A company that quickly learned its lessons regarding scalability was peer-to-peer communication company Skype. Its customer relationship collapsed under the weight of large numbers, when it was signing up tens of thousands of users per day. It quickly had to adapt its business model to become more scalable.

Recurring revenues

Recurring revenues are best explained through a simple example. When a newspaper earns revenues from sales at a news-stand, those revenues are transactional, whereas revenues from a subscription are recurring. Recurring revenues have two major advantages. First, the costs of sales incur only once for repetitive revenues. Second, with recurring revenues, the business will have a better idea of how much it will earn in the future.

A nice example of recurring revenues concerns Red Hat, which provides open-source software and support to enterprises based on a continuous subscription basis. In this model, clients don't pay for new software versions because software is continuously updated. In the world of software as a service, these types of subscription are now the norm. This contrasts with Microsoft, which sells most of its software in the form of licences for every major release.

However, another aspect of recurring revenues concerns additional revenues generated from initial sales. This is the 'bait and hook' revenue model. For example, when you buy a printer, you continue to spend on cartridges, or, when you buy a game console, you'll continue to spend on games. This revenue model has not gone unnoticed by large corporations such as Apple: although Apple still earns most of its revenues from hardware sales, the recurring revenues from content and apps are steadily growing.

Cash flow

Specifically, the more the business can earn before spending, the better. Dell pioneered this model in the computer hardware manufacturing industry. By assembling on order after selling directly, it managed to escape the terrible inventory depreciation costs of the hardware industry. Its impressive results showed how powerful it is to earn before spending.

Getting others to do the work

This is probably one of the least-publicized weapons of mass destruction in business model design. What could be more powerful than getting others to do the work, while you earn the money? For example, IKEA gets us to assemble the furniture we buy from it. We do the work. It saves money in transportation and storage costs. Similarly, eBay get us to do the work of posting details of the items we want to sell, and then it gets paid for any sale. Another more obvious example is open-source software, where firms generate cash from a community of users developing the software.

Protecting the business from competitors

A great business model can provide a longer-term protection from competition than just a great product. An elaborate supply-chain network, such as those developed by Toyota, offers it additional protection from competitors. Furthermore, Apple's main competitive advantage arises more from its powerful business model than purely from its innovative products. It's easier for Samsung, for instance, to copy the iPhone than to build an ecosystem such as Apple's appstore, which caters to developers and users alike and hosts hundreds of thousands of applications.

Changing the cost structure

Cutting costs is a long-practised sport in business. Some business models, however, go beyond cost cutting by creating value based on a totally different cost structure. This is what Ryanair did with its no-frills airline. The newspaper industry has also changed the cost structure of its industry by making content available online and making people pay for access via a subscription charge. In addition, many daily newspapers are now given away free, with advertising paying for the production costs. Another example is Skype. It provides calls and communication almost like a conventional telecommunications company, but for free or for a very low cost. It can do this because its business model has a very different cost structure. In fact, Skype's model is based on the economics of a software company, whereas a telecommunications provider's model is based on the economics of a network company. The former's costs are mainly people, whereas the latter's costs include huge capital expenditures on infrastructure.

Intellectual property is an asset

IP is a company asset and should be treated and managed as such. Owning and acquiring IP will not overcome poor business strategy and make a company successful. There are many examples of firms with exciting technology that failed to profit from it. Classic cases such as the EMI scanner (MRI) are told to business students. This technology was developed by EMI, but it failed to develop a business model to exploit it. The licensing business model is well understood and well known, but the variety of ways the licensing arrangement is organized is almost limitless.

IP is a broad concept and includes many different intangibles, such as patents (inventions), copyright (works of authorship, software, drawings, etc.) know-how (e.g. expertise, skilled craftsmanship, training capability, understanding of how something works), trade secrets (a protected formula or method), trademarks (logos, distinctive names), industrial design (the unique external appearance) and semiconductor mask works (the physical design of semiconductor circuits).

The technology licence and business relationships

Although not immediately apparent when reading an impressive-looking licence agreement, it is quickly realized and understood by all businesses that, with a licence, must come other very practical agreements that will help both parties succeed. Let us take an example. The Red Software Company decides to collaborate with the Blue Software Company to develop a new computer game, provisionally labelled Galaxywars. This will involve collaborative R&D activities. So, they sign a technology licence that gives each company rights to use each other's technology (software). In addition, they need to negotiate an R&D agreement to specify the terms of the collaboration, that is, length of time, level of investment required, resources that each company will have to make available, etc. Furthermore, what will happen to all the outputs from the collaboration? Red Software Company may be able to utilize some of the outputs in its own range of computer games, whereas Blue Software Company may be unable to use any of the outputs. Also, who is going to manufacture, market and distribute Galaxywars? An IP licence is interrelated to many other agreements.

Continual adaptation of the business model

Developing a business model is all well and good, but sustained success comes from changing it and continually adaptating it. Companies that manage to create value over extended periods of time successfully shape, adapt and renew their business models to fuel such value creation. One only has to consider General Electric, IBM or Apple and one quickly realizes that the business model in place today for these firms is very different to the one in place 10 or 20 years ago. Achtenhagen *et al.* (2013) identify three capabilities critical to achieve this:

1   an orientation towards experimenting with and exploiting new business opportunities;
2   a balanced use of resources;
3   coherence between leadership, culture and employee commitment.

The licensing business model

A licence is a consent by the owner for the use of IP in exchange for money or something else of value (Boyle, 2004). The owner of a licence is known as the licenser, and the purchaser and user of the licence is known as the licensee.

Technology-based start-up ventures inevitably involve scientists and inventors who are interested in seeing their research or inventions commercialized for use; usually, however, they are also equally interested in the intellectual challenge of the research. In such cases, licensing a technology idea might make good sense. Licensing allows technology producers to generate cash from their innovations by licensing them to other companies so that they may be integrated into an end product.

Licensing is most commonly applied to innovations that involve sophisticated technology protected by IP agreements. The innovation itself may not be a complete product and may need to be integrated into a broader offering in order to create value for the end-user. For example, the case study at the end of Chapter 1 illustrates the challenge faced by the business of securing a licensing deal with shipping firms.

It is worthy of note and consideration by the start-up that technology-based licensing agreements rely on relatively intimate, long-term relationships with customers. This is because all parties must exchange certain (confidential) information, and because the fundamental economics of a licensing arrangement are long-term in nature. The idea that business negotiations over licensing deals are won and lost through good and bad negotiations is overstated. There is a mutual interest in both parties surviving and thriving, and, hence, most technology-based licensing deals are beneficial for both parties.

Bear in mind, however, that it is possible that a potentially attractive licensing agreement can result in very poor results for a start-up. Such a situation could occur, for example, if a start-up signs an exclusive licence with a partner in order to secure a royalty stream, but then actions do not live up to the promises, because, for example, the partner doesn't invest sufficiently in marketing or developing the technology. In these situations, sales and income levels will be low. This could, in turn, prevent the company from moving forward with other more productive partnerships. An alternative solution might be a licensing agreement that clearly accounts for the above situation. See the section on payments later in this chapter.

Income from licensing

Licensing income usually involves a fee paid upfront to the inventor through a signed licensing agreement between the parties. These agreements may also include milestone payments that become due as the technology or innovation is commercialized, and/or a royalty fee set at a percentage of the revenue or earnings from the eventual sale of products or services. The amount of the upfront fee, milestone payments and royalties are negotiated between the parties and generally reflect the effort and stage of commercialization. In other words, the more developed a product or service, the higher the proceeds tend to be.

There exist a number of organizations interested in licensing innovative technology and inventions that complement their existing products and services for a specific purpose or market. The organization that licenses the technology usually assumes all responsibility for subsequent costs of developing, marketing, selling and distributing the product or service.

Marketing issues related to the licensing model

The goal of marketing technology for licensing is to create a deep understanding of the potential applications of the innovation among key industry insiders. Successful marketing for technology licensing focuses on creating visibility for the technology through industry presentations, establishing a presence in academic and industry journals, authoring white papers and otherwise evangelizing the innovation. For example, the pharmaceutical industry uses academic conferences to promote awareness of new drugs. Frequently, news organizations will select articles from key academic journals that have newsworthy stories (see Box 5.3).

Box 5.3 *Los Angeles Times* **reports on research results**

'Huge' results raise hope for cancer breakthrough

In early results from a clinical trial, genetically engineered T cells eradicate leukemia cells and thrive. Two of three patients studied have been cancer-free for more than a year.

In a potential breakthrough in cancer research, scientists at the University of Pennsylvania have genetically engineered patients' T cells—a type of white blood cell— to attack cancer cells in advanced cases of a common type of leukemia. Two of the three patients who received doses of the designer T cells in a clinical trial have remained cancer-free for more than a year, the researchers said.

(Eryn Brown, *Los Angeles Times*, 11 August 2011)

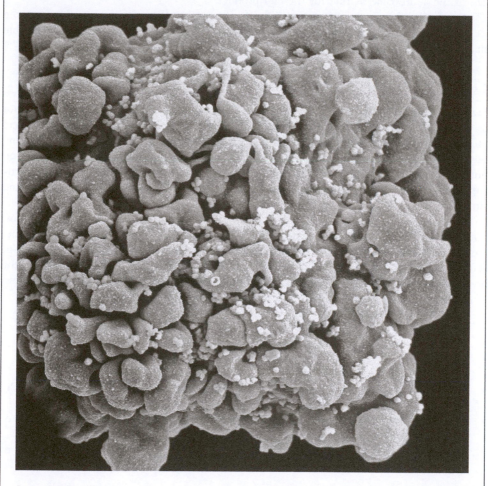

Image 5.2 T cells
Source: © NIAID

Financial and strategic implications

Licensing revenues can be structured in different ways, with upfront payments by the licensee or with payments that are revenue-dependent. In order to license successfully, a company will require the funding necessary to develop their technology to the point where it becomes a suitable add-on to the offering of its licensee partner. If the licensed product is a tangible item, costs are the most important metric to monitor. Royalty fees may accompany licensing revenue on a per-unit-sale basis, or the parties may use some other transparent means of measuring usage of the licensed technology. For example, the fabric manufacturer Gore-Tex may structure a licensing deal whereby it receives a percentage of the wholesale price of the item sold, or it may decide to agree a fixed price with, say, Nike for a wide range of products.

An important consideration in structuring licensing agreements is the portion of income derived from licensing revenue versus that deriving from royalties. Royalty revenue is dependent on the selling ability of the party integrating the licensed technology and the size of the addressable market for the end product.

Strategically, licensing may involve the risk of exposing IP to the party integrating the technology into their products. It is, therefore, important to ensure that patents are defensible and that other IP is protected.

Costs and benefits of the licensing model

Licensing works well in situations where developing an entire product independently is not feasible. The trade-off is that, as the offering comprises only one element of a complete product, it may hinder the development of a strong company profile, unless a co-branding option is available, like 'Intel inside'. It is not uncommon for very successful firms to go unrecognized by the public. ARM, a chip producer from the UK, is the world's second-largest developer of computer chips. Its microprocessors are found in all Apple iPhones and almost all smartphones, and yet few people have heard of the company.

Within a licence agreement, the royalty rate may be interlinked with other factors, most notably minimum royalty commitments and decreased royalty rates once certain volumes are reached. Minimum royalties are often a commitment to some form of exclusivity or access to the brand in a market. Decreasing royalty rates could be used to incentivize the licensee to achieve higher volumes, as the unit cost of branded products then becomes less.

Licence agreements usually include a number of other considerations, such as:

- definition of the brand being licensed;
- definition of the sales to which the royalty percentage is to be applied;
- A restriction of the use of the brand to specific products, channels and territories;
- a specific time period, say 3 years;
- brand use and authorization procedures to ensure that the use of the brand by the licensee is consistent with that of the brand owner;
- commitments by licensee to brand marketing; this can also be a percentage of sales or a fixed amount;
- other legal rights and obligations, such as necessary records and returns and access to audit each other's accounts.

These factors will also influence, to a greater or lesser extent, the royalty rate. If a licensee agrees, for example, to contribute to brand marketing, then the royalty rate might be reduced to compensate for this.

Table 5.4 Typical royalty rates in technology sectors

Industry	Royalty rate (%)					
	0–2%	2–5%	5–10%	10–15%	15–20%	20–25%
Aerospace	50.0	50.0				
Chemical	16.5	58.1	24.3	0.8	0.4	
Computer	62.5	31.3	6.3			
Electronics		50.0	25.0	25.0		
Healthcare	3.3	51.7	45.0			
Pharmaceuticals	23.6	32.1	29.3	12.5	1.1	0.7
Telecommunications	40.0	37.3	23.6			

Source: Parr, 2007

Table 5.4 illustrates the wide range of royalty rates that exist across a broad range of different industries. The rates differ for a variety of reasons, including historical working practices. Usually, however, there is a link to the typical length of time the licenser can earn income before the technology is superseded or becomes obsolete. Other influences can be the level of upfront R&D costs and volume of sales (few units of aircraft are sold compared with units of gaming software). In Table 5.4, we can see that the aerospace industry seems very conservative, paying royalty rates of up to 5 per cent. Electronics, on the other hand, looks more lucrative, with 25 per cent of royalties achieving a rate of between 10 and 15 per cent.

Other strategic uses of licensing

A start-up business may consider licensing a technology or the right to use a technology in a specific field or geographic area as a means to obtain funding for its core product.

Life-science companies, particularly those developing therapeutic products, generally use licensing as a sales and marketing strategy for their products owing to the very significant costs of development and clinical trials, as well as the eventual marketing, sale and distribution of the product.

Licensing a technology may also be used as a way to create an exit for a business, if it becomes clear that the business cannot fund the marketing, sales and distribution of the product from existing resources and additional financing is not available. Generally, in 'stalled or failed' technology businesses that have been backed with equity investment, the shareholders will request that management or a third party attempt to license or sell the technology in an effort to provide some return on investment to shareholders.

Negotiating a licensing deal

Licensing deals are just that – a deal struck between two parties. There is no correct deal, nor an incorrect one. It is simply an agreement where both parties agree to do business that will usually result in benefits for both. For example, the licensing deal struck between Bill Gates and his tiny Microsoft company and the mighty IBM in the 1980s is regarded by many as the one single act of genius on Gates's part that helped to launch Microsoft (see Box 5.4). Similarly, the licensing deal struck by J. K. Rowling's agent and the publisher, where the author held on to the film rights, was another decision of inspired brilliance.

Box 5.4 The infamous IBM–Microsoft MS-DOS licensing deal

Development of the Microsoft Disk Operating System (MS-DOS) began in October 1980, when IBM began searching the market for an operating system for the yet-to-be-introduced IBM Personal Computer. IBM had originally intended to use a simple system developed by the respected firm Digital Research. IBM then talked to a small company called Microsoft. Microsoft was a language vendor. Bill Gates and Paul Allen had written Microsoft BASIC and were selling it on punched tape or disk to early PC hobbyists. Prior to this, the company's original name was Traf-O-Data, and its goal was making car counters for highway departments.

Microsoft had no real operating system to sell, but quickly made a deal to license Seattle Computer Products' 86-DOS operating system (also called QDOS, for Quick and Dirty Operating System), which had been written by Tim Paterson earlier in 1980 for use on that company's line of 8086 computers. Fortunately for Microsoft, Digital Research was showing no hurry in introducing its operating system. Paterson's DOS 1.0 was approximately 4,000 lines of assembler source. This code was quickly polished up and presented to IBM for evaluation. IBM found itself left with Microsoft's offering of 'Microsoft Disk Operating System 1.0'. An agreement was reached between the two, and IBM agreed to accept 86-DOS as the main operating system for its new PC. Microsoft purchased all rights to 86-DOS from Seattle Computer Products in July 1981, and 'IBM Personal Computer DOS 1.0' was ready for the introduction of the IBM PC in October 1981. IBM subjected the operating system to an extensive quality-assurance program, reportedly found well over 300 bugs, and decided to rewrite the programs. This is why PC DOS is copyrighted by both IBM and Microsoft.

Image 5.3 IBM PC

Source: © Boffy b

As most people engaged in deal making are involved in multiple deals at the same time, important aspects can be forgotten or overlooked at any time and for any deal. The following is an inexhaustive list that provides an insight into the areas that need to be agreed upon. Most firms that are involved in licensing will ensure they have people in such positions that are well educated and experienced in dealing with the scientific, legal and business arenas, all at the same time. After all, as experienced negotiators will testify, there is only one thing more expensive than a patent agent and that is a bad patent agent. Simple mistakes can be costly, and what is crucial to one party may not be to the other.

Terms for the agreement

Each licence will have its own specific set of definitions. All other appropriate terms should be listed and defined. Clear definitions will add great clarity to a licence. For example, if dealing with a company, is it the company and all its affiliates? All of its subsidiaries? Or only the parent company? Products/processes licensed should be specifically defined as Licensed Products or Licensed Processes. If only certain types of invention are covered, these need to be referred to as Inventions, including the patent number and/or patent application number that is being licensed. The agreement must also specify whether know-how is included.

Licensee, sales, net sales, profit, territory, field, patents, patent rights, intellectual property and non-profit are examples of other relatively common terms, and there are many more. Once defined, these terms will usually appear throughout the rest of the contract.

Rights granted

The agreement should also include which IPR the licence is given under: patent right only, or know-how right, or both, and exclusive right, co-exclusive with the licenser, or non-exclusive. The licence agreement should also specify the term of the exclusivity and/or non-exclusivity, whether such right is irrevocable, and if there is a right to grant sublicences.

Scope of rights

A licence with broad scope gives flexibility; a licence with narrow scope will be less flexible but will be less expensive. An IP licence gives several different 'grants' of rights, such as:

- to reproduce the technology;
- to display it;
- to modify it;
- to make derivative works from it (new versions or entirely new products);
- to use it for research or product development;
- to make it or have it made by a contractor;
- to distribute or sell it;
- to import it; and
- to sublicense it to another who can do any or all of the above.

Licensee restrictions

Either of the parties may also wish to include licensee restrictions concerning the industry or market, territory, prior licensee's rights, and the commercial rights retained by the licenser.

Territory

IPR are often territorial. It is possible to negotiate a licence for the same IP to different firms in different regions of the world. Also, some firms will be given rights to manufacture, whereas others are given rights to distribute and sell. For example, Nike negotiates distribution and sales rights for its products with retailers all over the world.

Improvements

The agreement needs to address any improvements made and/or patented (by whom and paid for by whom) during the term of the licence, by either the licenser or licensee, and what obligations are present in the deal as to whether or not to include future technology under the present licence or to have future technology fall under the reservation of rights to the licenser.

Consideration (monetary value)

The consideration is relatively involved and can be cut back if equity is not part of the payment for the licence. Royalty, milestone payments, type of currency, determining rate of exchange, and equity-ownership issues all need to be considered, as they can result in substantial differences in payments. The issue of minimum annual payments is particularly important in the case of an exclusive licence, as it is effectively the only income stream.

The licenser has to ensure that the costs of developing the technology are covered and that the deal is worthwhile. The licensee, on the other hand, has to consider how much he/she can afford. How much will the licence add to the cost of the product? This is a better question than the abstract one of what the technology is worth. There are three main methods used to establish a value for a licence:

1   *The cost method*: This involves simply calculating how much the licenser has invested in developing the technology and the IP.
2   *The income method*: This involves calculating how much each party expects to earn from the licensed technology and then discounting this, based on time before income is received, level of further investment required, level of further R&D required, level of manufacturing required, etc.
3   *The comparables or market method*: This means establishing a value based on a similar example. The difficulty is finding a licence or transaction that is comparable in all respects.

Payments

The most common payments are royalties and lump sum.

Royalties may be based on a per unit royalty, where the licensee (purchaser and user) pays a set amount, usually a percentage figure; see Table 5.4. Alternatively, the royalty may be a percentage of revenues from sold or sublicensed products that incorporate the technology. It will usually be necessary to specify exactly how the royalty will be calculated: for example, whether royalty payments are based on retail or wholesale prices – there can be a 100 per cent difference!

There is often scope for capping the royalties paid, so that the licensee will pay up to an agreed level, say €1 million. This is usually beneficial to both parties, as it encourages the licensee to achieve sales beyond this cap so that thereafter the technology is effectively free. Equally the licenser (owner of the technology) is usually reassured that the licensee is maximizing effort to hit the cap and thus deliver income to the licenser. Conversely, there is the notion of a minimum fee that should be paid. This is beneficial to the licenser, as it guarantees an income, even if the licensee is unsuccessful or decides to direct effort and resources away from the project into other products. It is also possible to use an adjustable royalty scale, dependent on volume. So, for example, the royalty may begin at 5 per cent but decrease to 2 per cent once sales pass a set figure.

Lump-sum payments may also be used with royalties or instead of royalties. Such payments may be in instalments, linked to revenue or product development milestones. Sometimes, where there is a technology start-up that has technology but not money, the licenser may be willing to pay an advance to help the licensee continue to develop the technology. Usually, this advance will be offset against future royalties. For example, a technology start-up firm at the TU Delft incubator had developed an interesting new process for filtering air and dust particles. A Dutch industrial chicken farm was willing to pay an advance to the start-up to help it develop the air purifying system specifically for the farm's industrial farming needs.

Reports and auditing of accounts

The issue of establishing the level of royalties can be tricky. Firms rely on the licensee to inform them of the actual level of sales achieved. Hence, royalties based on any measure tied to a product's sales need to be paid to the licenser accompanied by a report stating how the royalty was calculated. The agreement should also specify how often and when these reports (and royalties) are due. Additionally, the right of the licenser to audit the books that generate these reports can be a part of the licence agreement.

Representations/warranties

Certain basic representations and warranties need to be given by each party to the other, such as the ability to enter into the agreement, the validity of the intellectual property, and a standard warranty disclaimer.

Infringement

The agreement needs to address issues associated with infringement, such as: if the IP is infringed by third parties, how such infringement will be handled, and, if there is a recovery cost for the infringement, how that will be divided between the licenser and licensee.

Confidentiality

A confidentiality, or nondisclosure, agreement will usually have been signed prior to the licensee agreement to enable exploration of terms of business, etc. This should remain effective during the term of the licence agreement.

Arbitration

In the case of a major disagreement about the terms of an agreement, parties may wish to take the issue to arbitration. Arbitration can be carried out in many different ways, and it is easier to specify the rules to be used for arbitration in the agreement, before there is an issue to arbitrate. A trade body or other independent organization could perform this role. This should help avoid expensive legal costs.

Termination

Areas to consider include the right of either party to end the agreement for no reason at all; the rights of the party that has performed when confronted with a party that refuses to perform; material breach issues; and length of notification of breaching activity and time given to the breaching party to cure the breach, before losing rights and/or being charged penalties. Issues dealing with the natural expiration of the licence should be considered, as well. What happens to the know-how (if any) upon the expiration of all patents? And what are the confidentiality provisions?

Chapter summary

This chapter has shown the importance of developing a clear business model for the enterprise. It is a simple, powerful tool to remind entrepreneurs how their ideas will make money. We showed that business models are fundamentally linked to technological innovation, and yet the business model construct is essentially separable from the technology. More importantly, developing the right technology is a matter of a business model decision regarding openness and user engagement. The licensing business model is common for technology-based ventures, and all aspects of licensing have been considered.

Study questions

1   For start-ups, the need to scale up can be costly; discuss how business model design can help overcome this.
2   Selling a product is great, but generating recurring revenues is better. Discuss the value of developing a 'mobile phone monthly subscription' business model.
3   Is it possible to receive payment before incurring expenditure?
4   Why are switching costs useful to consider in the design of a business model?
5   Is it possible to limit the threat of competition within your business model?

References

Achtenhagen, L., Melin, L. and Naldi, L. (2013). Dynamics of business models – Strategizing, critical capabilities and activities for sustained value creation. *Long Range Planning.* 46: 427–42.

Baden-Fuller, C. and Haefliger, S. (2013). Business models and technological innovation. *Long Range Planning.* 46: 419–26.

Boyle, J. (2004). A manifesto on WIPO and the future of intellectual property. *Duke Law & Technology Review.* 9: 1–13.

Chesbrough, H. and Rosenbloom, R. S. (2002). The role of the business model in capturing value from innovation: Evidence from Xerox Corporation's technology spin-off companies. *Industrial and Corporate Change.* 11(3): 529–55.

Dubosson-Torbay, M., Osterwalder, A. and Pigneur, Y. (2002). E-business model design, classification and measurements. *Thunderbird International Business Review.* 44(1): 5–23.

Economist, The (2012). Brewers droop. Britain section, 11 February.

Johnson, M. W., Christensen, C. M. and Kagermann, H. (2008). Reinventing your business model. *Harvard Business Review.* Dec: 51–9.

Mason, K. and Leek, S. (2008). Learning to build a supply network: An exploration of dynamic business models. *Journal of Management Studies*. 45(4): 774–99.

Osterwalder, A. (2004). The business model ontology. A proposition in a design science approach. Thesis presented to l'Ecole des Hautes Etudes Commerciales de l'Université de Lausanne.

Osterwalder, A. and Pigneur, Y. (2013). Designing business models and similar strategic objects: The contribution of IS. *Journal of the Association for Information Systems*. 14(5): 237–44.

Parr, R. L. (2007). *Royalty Rates for Licensing Intellectual Property*. Hoboken, NJ: John Wiley.

Patzelt, H., zu Knyphausen-Aufseß, D. and Nikol, P. (2008). Top management teams, business models, and performance of biotechnology ventures: An upper echelon perspective. *British Journal of Management*. 19: 205–21.

Porter, M. E. (1980). *Competitive Strategy: Techniques for analyzing industries and competitors*. New York: Free Press.

Richardson, J. (2008). The business model: An integrative framework for strategy execution. *Strategic Change*. 17(5–6): 133–44.

Shafer, S. M., Smith, H. J. and Linder, J. C. (2005). The power of business models. *Business Horizons*. 48(3): 199–207.

Teece, D. (2010). Business models, business strategy and innovation. *Long Range Planning*. 43(2–3): 172–94.

Trott, P. (2011). *Managing Innovation and New Product Development* (5th edn). London: Prentice Hall.

Watson, D. (2005). *Business Models*. Petersfield, UK: Harriman House.

Weill, P. and Vitale, M. R. (2001). *Place to Space: Migrating to ebusiness models*. Boston, MA: Harvard Business School Press.

Weill, P., Malone, T. W., D'Urso, V. T., Herman, G. and Woerner, S. (2005). Do some business models perform better than others? A study of the 1000 largest US firms. MIT Center for coordination science working paper, 226.

Zott, C. and Amit, R. (2007). Business model design and the performance of entrepreneurial firms. *Organization Science*. 18(2): 181–99.

Further reading

Achtenhagen, L., Melin, L., Naldi L. (2013) Dynamics of Business Models – Strategizing, Critical Capabilities and Activities for Sustained Value Creation, *Long Range Planning*, 46, 427–442.

Afuah, A. and Tucci, C. (2000). *Internet Business Models and Strategies*. New York: Irwin McGraw-Hill.

Amit, R. and Zott, C. (2001). Value creation in e-business. *Strategic Management Journal*. 22(6/7): 493–520.

Baden-Fuller, C. and Haefliger S. (2013) Business Models and Technological Innovation, *Long Range Planning*, 46, 419–426.

Betz, F. (2002). Strategic business model. *Engineering Management Journal*. 14(1): 21–7.

Chesbrough, H. (2003). *Open Innovation: The new imperative for creating and profiting from technology*. Boston, MA: Harvard Business School Press.

Chesbrough, H. W. (2006). *Open Business Models. How to thrive in the new innovation landscape*. Boston, MA: Harvard Business School Press.

Chesbrough, H. W. (2007). Why companies should have open business models. *MIT Sloan Management Review*. 48(2). Available at: http://sloanreview.mit.edu/article/why-companies-should-have-open-business-models/ (accessed 10 August 2015).

De, R., Mathew, B. and Abraham, D. M. (2001). Critical construct for analyzing e-business: Investment, user experience and revenue models. *Logistics Information Management*. 14(1/2): 137–48.

Gordijn, J., Akkermans, H. and van Vliet, H. (2000). 'Business modelling is not process modelling', in S. Liddle, H. Mayr and B. Thalheim (eds), *Conceptual Modeling for E-Business and the Web*. Berlin: Springer, pp. 40–51.

Hedman, J. and Kalling, T. (2003). The business model concept: Theoretical underpinnings and empirical illustrations. *European Journal of Information Systems*. 12: 49–59.

Jørgensen, F. and Ulhøi, J. (2009). Entrepreneurial emergence in the field of m-commerce: A generic business model reconceptualization. *Proceedings of The International Academy of E-Business 9th Annual Conference*, April 9–12.

Magretta, J. (2002). Why business models matter. *Harvard Business Review*. 80: 86–92.

Malackowski, J. E. (2009). 'IP asset sales, still a work in progress', in B. Berman (ed.), *From Assets to Profits: Competing for IP value & return*. Hoboken, NJ: John Wiley, pp. 193–214.

Mitchell, D. W. and Coles, C. B. (2004). Establishing a continuing business model innovation process. *Journal of Business Strategy*. 25(3): 39–49.

Morris, M., Schindehutte, M. and Allen, J. (2005). The entrepreneur's business model: Toward a unified perspective. *Journal of Business Research*. 58(6): 726–35.

Onetti, A., Talaia, M., Presutti, V., Odorici, M. and Verma, S. (2010). The role of serial entrepreneurs in the internationalization of global start-ups: A business case. *Journal of Strategic Management Education*. 6(1): 79–94.

Osterwalder, A. and Pigneur, Y. (2002). An e-business model ontology for modelling e-business. *15th Bled Electronic Commerce Conference, E-reality: Constructing the e-economy*. Slovenia: Bled, pp. 1–12.

Osterwalder, A., Pigneur, Y. and Tucci, C. L. (2005). Clarifying business models: Origins, present, and future of the concept. *Communications of AIS, the Association for Information Systems*. 15: 1–40.

Spieth, P., Schneckenberg, D. and Ricart, J. E. (2014). Business model innovation–state of the art and future challenges for the field. *R&D Management*, 44(3): 237–247.

Tongur, S. and Engwall, M. (2014). The business model dilemma of technology shifts. *Technovation*, 34(9): 525–535.

6 Innovation systems

Embedding the entrepreneur

Nowadays, entrepreneurship is no longer for those who like to operate alone and think they have all the knowledge they need to be successful. Entrepreneurs must have the ability to explore and to use the knowledge, expertise and capital of others. They need to position themselves as best they can in their surrounding *innovation system*. This not only requires technological expertise, but also managerial and social skills to connect with other entrepreneurs and organizations and build relationships. In this chapter, we dismiss the myth of the 'lone entrepreneur' and place the entrepreneur within the framework of an innovation system. We discuss the concept of the innovation system and look more extensively at the Cyclic Innovation Model, a framework that entrepreneurs can use to describe and manage 'their' innovation system.

Introduction

An important topic in the area of developing new products and services is the innovation system. Briefly put, it means that companies increasingly work together when they innovate. There are various kinds of innovation system. Some innovation systems focus on geographical aspects, such as national or regional, whereas others emphasize the content of the future innovation: for instance, the *food* innovation system. Innovation systems can also relate to a specific sector (such as the ICT sector) or be based on a certain technology (such as nano-technology).

With regard to a definition of an innovation system, we refer to Fischer and Fröhlich (2001, p. 1):

A *system of innovation* [italics in original] can be thought of as consisting of a set of actors or entities such as firms, organizations, and institutions that interact in the generation, use and diffusion of new – and economically – useful knowledge.

This definition has a strong focus on actors, which very much appeals to us. Innovation processes in general and innovation systems in particular do not fall from the sky, but are largely the outcome of human action. According to Fischer and Fröhlich, again: 'The concept of "innovation systems" carries the idea that innovations do not originate as isolated discrete phenomena, but are generated through the interaction of a number of actors or agents'. Zahra and Nambisan (2012) use a different, but very closely related, term, namely *business ecosystems*: 'A *business ecosystem* is a group of companies – and other entities including individuals, too, perhaps – that interacts and shares a set of dependencies as it produces the goods, technologies, and services customers need' (p. 220). They state that, 'Creating, shaping, navigating, and exploiting business ecosystems requires entrepreneurial insight, coupled with strategic thinking' (p. 219). Furthermore, they state that, in this business ecosystem, entrepreneurs cooperate, not only with other entrepreneurs, but also with existing businesses, and that entrepreneurs (new ventures) 'work on the fringes of their respective industries' (p. 221). Both the concepts of innovation system and business ecosystem are an alternative to categorizing companies in fixed industries and stress that innovation processes go beyond these industry borders and require intensive cooperation from organizations with different backgrounds (e.g. profit versus non-profit), knowledge bases, skills, etc. However, despite the necessity of cooperation between different organizations from different industries and sectors, it does not make innovation easier. For instance, in an application of the CIM to the development of a mobile data service (Berkhout and Duin, 2007), it appeared that the required cooperation between a telecommunications company and a software company could be very difficult. In its innovation processes, a telecommunications company is used to doing (and obliged to do) extensive testing, making sure that the service works in every part of the geographical region it services, whereas the software company wants to implement the service as soon as possible, enabling feedback from users as quickly as possible, so that it can improve the service and implement a new version of it.

Innovation systems are very much inspired by science and technology literature, which discusses the development of innovations and the relationship between technology and society. Management science has also looked at the increasing collaboration between companies in the area of innovation. The most popular current development from that perspective is 'open innovation', as described by Henry Chesbrough (2003). According to Chesbrough, it is no longer smart for companies to keep knowledge to themselves and not share it. In our society, where boundaries between countries and between companies are blurring more and more, a strategy based on secrecy has become pointless. The 'open innovation' concept is based on the following principles:

- The vast majority of the required knowledge and skills is located outside the organization.
- Share, license, sell and buy patents and other kinds of knowledge.
- An organization does not have to take part in the entire innovation process, but can get in or out along the way.
- The success of many innovations can be explained by the right business model (revenue model). The right business model has to be worked out at an early stage of the innovation process.

From a historical perspective, collaborations in innovation are nothing new. Jørn Bang Andersen places the start of thinking in innovation systems as early as around 1850, when the German economist George Friedrich List felt that Germany needed a 'national system' to compete with the British economically. Shortly after, Alfred Marshall spoke of 'agglomerations', by which he meant that companies tend to locate in proximity to each other to benefit from each other's presence. Although Western society is becoming more and more virtual, physical proximity is still important, as becomes clear in innovative areas such as Silicon Valley in the United States and Food Valley in Wageningen (the Netherlands). Then, in 1950, Eric Dahmén introduced the term 'development blocks', in which innovation and entrepreneurship were positioned mainly in certain industries that were supposed to contribute to national economic growth. After that came Michael Porter (1990), who again paid more attention to regions, which he views as areas that can become competing through specialization.

Almost at the same time as Porter, the term 'innovation system' was introduced through the work of Chris Freeman, John Clark and Luc Soete (1982). Up until that time, scientific research into innovation primarily adopted an economic perspective, which meant that innovation was seen as a 'black box' connecting input and output. In 1997, the OECD defined a (national) innovation system as follows: 'The study of *national innovation systems* [italics in original] directs attention to the linkages or web of interaction within the overall innovation systems' (OECD, 1997, p. 3). In addition, Andrew Van de Ven *et al.* (1999) subscribe to that definition and propose a process-oriented approach to innovation that involves mapping the various actors who together form a network and should be examined from a qualitative perspective.

Carlsson *et al.* (2002) argue that innovation systems contain three elements:

1 Components: these are the 'operating parts' of the system, such as actors or organizations (companies, financial institutions, universities, government organizations, non-profit organizations), but also technical artefacts (such as medical instruments, telecommunications platforms) and institutions (such as legislation and social values).

2 Relationships: these are the connections between the components. The feedback relationships between the components make the system dynamic. The relationships are also interactive in nature, which means they are cyclical. The relationships themselves are also subject to change and, as such, change the system: 'One result of the interaction (feedback) among actors is that capabilities shift and grow over time, and therefore, the system configuration also changes' (Carlsson *et al.*, 2002, p. 234).

3 Attributes: these are the qualities and features of the components and relationships, and of the system. They refer to the characteristics and dimensions of the system, its purpose and the extent to which it manages to develop and implement innovations.

The CIM, Level 1: Innovating for the future

Now we provide a framework with which entrepreneurs can set up and manage their own innovation system. Although various systems are available, we choose the CIM (Berkhout, 2000), because of its focus on actors, the room it provides for technology, as well as other sources of innovation (cf. Hippel, 1998), and the fact that it is very visual, which offers entrepreneurs a quick and accurate overview of the various parties that are (or ought to be) involved.

The main principles of the CIM are as follows:

* Innovation is predominantly a process between different actors exchanging knowledge and information.
* Innovation is not a linear but a cyclic process (with feedback and feed-forward).
* Every well-functioning innovation process should be based on a clear view of the future: innovation and looking to the future are two sides of the same coin.
* Every innovation system needs an *entrepreneur* to set it up and manage it.
* Every node of CIM (science, technology, product, market) can be a source of innovation (cf. Hippel, 1998).

The CIM can be described on two different levels:

* Level 1, which links 'the' future to innovation processes;
* Level 2, which structures the partners involved in the innovation network and links them in a cyclic way. This cyclic nature of the relationships between the different actors means that there is constant feedback and feed-forward between the actors.

Level 1 of the CIM is illustrated in Figure 6.1. This 'futures research' part of CIM is made up of four components:

1   *The image(s) of the future*, which function(s) as a kind of leitmotiv for all innovation-related activities, is fed both by the organization's *internal ambitions* for the future and by an awareness of *external developments* that may influence the organization's future goals and performance.
2   To carry out innovation processes, the organization needs an *innovation process model* to guide these processes.
3   The ongoing innovation processes together constitute a *transition path* that leads the organization from the present to the future.
4   The component of *leadership* is important, because it links the first three nodes, making sure they are consistent, interconnected and balanced. Leadership in this sense means setting out an inspiring *vision* of the future (see also the chapter on looking to the future), while making sure that the future vision is *strategically* aligned with the innovation processes, and that a sound process model is used to manage and *execute* these innovation processes.

The CIM emphasizes strong, balanced connections between the vision of the future of the innovation network, the innovation process model used to guide the execution of the innovation processes of the innovation network, and the transition path illustrating to what extent the visualized future is realized. Leadership, at the centre of the framework, is responsible for facilitating the connections between these three elements and providing connections to other innovation systems.

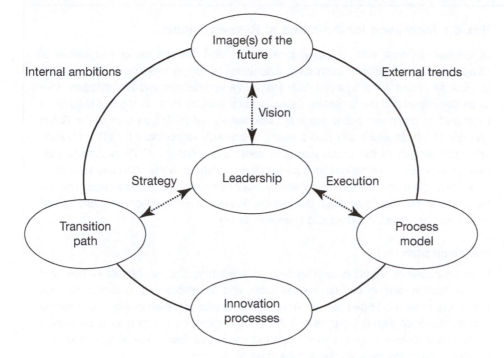

Figure 6.1 Level 1 of the Cyclic Innovation Model: The connection between innovation and the future

The CIM, Level 2: A network of actors

Next to connecting future developments with innovation (Level 1), CIM considers an innovation system as a set of actors who are structurally related to each other: Level 2. This Level 2 is the *process model* of Level 1 and is grounded in the empirical observation that involving more actors in the innovation process (system) means that innovation processes (systems) become more complex and, thereby, more difficult to set up and to manage. This increasing complexity is mainly caused by the fact that innovations contain more and more technological components. For example, the first generations of mobile telephony were based on dozens of patents, whereas the third generation (i.e. mobile broadband) contained hundreds of patents. From the visualization below of the innovation system of the Dutch energy industry, it can be concluded that clustering different actors in the innovation system and (thereby) simplifying it is no luxury.

At Level 2, CIM emphasizes that:

- innovation processes are inherently cyclic;
- the essence of every innovation process (system) is that different actors constantly develop and exchange information and knowledge;
- hard knowledge of emerging technologies is complemented by soft knowledge of emerging markets (combining technology push and market pull);
- every node (science, technology, product/service, market) is a potential 'source of innovation'.

Box 6.1 Innovation for the future at Rijkswaterstaat

Deltas have to cope with increasing pressure on land use and the consequences of rising sea levels. Traditional methods and solutions no longer meet the challenges and political ambitions. Consequently, truly innovative approaches and technologies have to be developed and implemented, especially in a country such as the Netherlands, a large part of which lies below sea level. Rijkswaterstaat (RWS), as part of the Dutch Ministry of Infrastructure and Environment, is primarily responsible for the realization and management of the Dutch road and water infrastructure. RWS is continuously looking for innovative solutions to cope with the challenges in the short and long term, to which end the organization has initiated various innovative programmes and projects, for example the Water Innovation programme (WINN). This innovation programme was evaluated using the CIM (Duin and Hermeler, 2014).

Transition path

Most interviewees regard innovation only as something that is completely new and believe that innovation can be both tangible and intangible (e.g. business models, concepts). From a CIM perspective, using such a broad definition of innovation means that the transition path is broad as well. Also, the emphasis on innovation as something really new implies a lengthy transition period and a possible vision of the future that is significantly different from the current state of affairs.

Process model

The interviewees stated that WINN did not have a formalized innovation process model, by which they meant that there was no single innovation process model, and that various implicit innovation process models were present. From a CIM perspective, this means that no innovation process model was actually used.

Leadership and vision of the future

The involvement of commercial organizations in the WINN programme was limited. As a consequence, the input into the vision of the future consisted mainly of internal ambitions rather than external trends. Also, leadership was focused internally and less 'open' than one might expect or perhaps desire. The innovation processes were not sufficiently populated with external parties. Although, for a government organization such as Rijkswaterstaat, sharing its innovation programme with an external organization might be an exciting first step, from an innovation network (and 'open innovation') perspective, it is still rather limited.

Vision of the future

From the interviews, a mixed picture emerged with regard to the presence and use of a vision of the future regarding the innovation processes of WINN. Our conclusion was that, if a vision of the future was indeed used for innovation, a consensus was required as to its mere existence. Because such a consensus was lacking, that vision, at least from a CIM perspective, did not explicitly exist.

Leadership

WINN did not function in a vacuum, but as part of a government organization. As a consequence, the innovation processes came under considerable political scrutiny.

With regard to the CIM, leadership has the task to 'manage' this political context and to explain what innovation actually is and which risks it entails. That is, the 'leader' or 'innovation network manager' has to act as a guard against bad, outside political influences, as well as making sure that the 'internal' components of the innovation systems are aligned.

Furthermore, WINN has had a lot of contact with different levels of management within RWS. The interviewees did not agree on which management level was the best level to approach. To implement the outcomes of innovation processes, lower levels of management might be best, whereas, when it came to securing support for the innovation programme in general, approaching higher management levels might be more productive.

Once again, from a CIM perspective, this means that the leadership has to 'sell' its innovation programme to various managers at different management levels within the client organization. In particular, in contacts with higher management levels, the vision and strategy of the innovation programme (system) will be important topics.

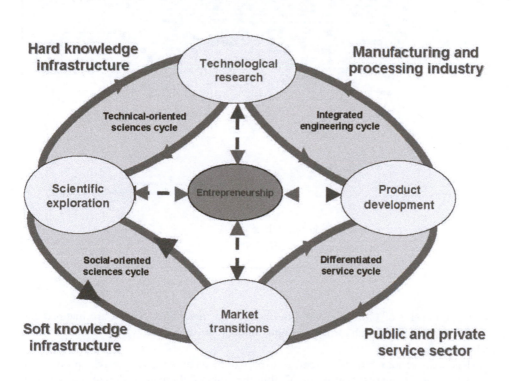

Figure 6.2 Visualization of Level 2 of CIM: The actors in the 'innovation arena'

In 2011, the Dutch government started to redefine its innovation policy. One of its elements was to define a limited amount of industries, so-called 'top industries', to focus the governmental 'policy on innovation'. Furthermore, to address the 'innovation paradox' (see below), the topics of the additional governmental spending on innovation were decided by consortia consisting of representatives of the chosen 'top industries' and academics. For one of the top industries, energy, the map of *scheidingstechnologie*, shown in Figure 6.3, was made, which looks rather complex, almost chaotic.

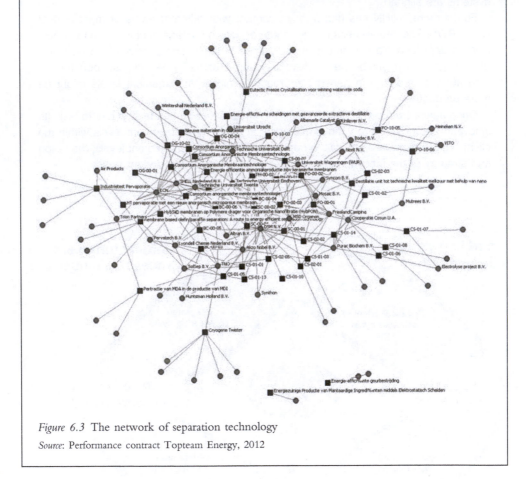

Figure 6.3 The network of separation technology

Source: Performance contract Topteam Energy, 2012

In short, at Level 2 of CIM, the various actors of an innovation system are mapped and cyclically connected to each other through different types of knowledge cycle. CIM is visualized in Figure 6.2.

CIM consists of four 'nodes': scientific exploration, technological research, product (or service) creation and market transitions. Within these nodes, there are different organizations that develop and have knowledge of these four nodes. In CIM, innovation can start anywhere, and so the first step for setting up an innovation system can be made in any node.

The more nodes involved, the more radical the innovation will be. For an incremental innovation, only changes in the market-transitions node and in the product-creation node are necessary. However, for a more profound innovation process, such as a system innovation or transition – for instance, a transition to fuel cell-driven cars – or the setting up of a completely new innovation system – for instance, the development of wind-turbine innovation systems after the oil crises in the 1970s – changes in every node of the CIM are required. For such a profound innovation process, scientific exploration, technological research, product development and market transitions have to go hand in hand in a process of co-evolution.

Detecting innovation system failures using CIM

A well-functioning innovation system is crucial to the successful development of innovations. When, for example, the right conditions have not been created, or the right actors have not been involved, or the communication between the actors involved does not run smoothly, the innovation system cannot develop properly. To determine whether or not an innovation system is of good quality, the potential system errors need to be mapped, allowing entrepreneurs to correct those errors. Below, we describe five innovation system failures that can occur and illustrate them using the CIM.

The 'innovation paradox'

One of the best-known system errors is the 'innovation paradox', which is based on the notion that some innovation systems may be successful from a scientific point of view, while performing poorly from a commercial perspective. This paradox appears to apply to the European economy, which is why some speak of the 'European innovation paradox'. We would like to remark that, strictly speaking, this is not a paradox, but at the most a contradiction. In addition, this system error is based on the erroneous thought that innovation systems always start with scientific discoveries, which ignores the fact that technological knowledge and social changes can also lead to innovation. Nevertheless, it is unfortunate when the scientific side and the business side are not connected, because it means that science is not inspired by developments and product development, and the business side does not use scientific solutions. CIM illustrates the innovation paradox as shown in Figure 6.5.

The next question is how the gap between science and business emerged. To a large extent, this can be explained by the fact that the motives and stimuli of the people on both sides are probably different. Scientists are assessed based on the quantity and quality of their scientific publications. Often, these publications are very specialized and will most likely be read by only a handful of fellow scientists. Those who are not a part of the scientific community will find it hard to see the practical use of these publications, which is not all that surprising, as the aim of these publications is not to develop innovations or give advice to companies, but to present and validate scientific knowledge. Scientists are often not encouraged to contact companies, because it would not directly benefit their publication record. Needless to say, more applied science narrows the gap, because this type of research requires input from companies, which makes it easier to make a practical translation.

We also believe that the gap between science and business is wider for beta sciences than it is for the other sciences, which often study society and social phenomena and as such are more closely connected. However, science and business remain two separate worlds.

A second important cause is the difference in speed and dynamics. Scientific research requires a lot of patience, in terms of the time it both takes to conduct the research and in getting the results published. In the business community, targets tend to be shorter term, often no longer than a year.

Box 6.2 Thixomolding and CIM

Magnesium is one of the commonest elements on Earth. It is the lightest construction material that retains its strength and rigidity. The relative mass of magnesium is about 30 per cent lighter than aluminium. A known disadvantage of magnesium is its sensitivity to oxidation, which is why magnesium is alloyed with aluminium and zinc. At certain temperatures, this alloy takes on a doughy quality, which makes it possible to inject the alloy. Thixomolding is a combination of different existing technologies, including injection, matrix building and finishing. The name Thixo is derived from the chemical term thixotrope, which refers to the change in viscosity of liquids owing to movement. A well-known example is ketchup. Thixomolding creates a unique, tough, molecular structure with a high density and without entrapped air. Owing to the limited shrinking when cooling, less finishing is required, and it offers greater moulding freedom.

A group of entrepreneurs in the province of Flevoland (in the Netherlands) decided to investigate how this technology could be converted into innovations in the area of lightweight constructions. Because they wanted to know how and what each company could contribute to the development of thixomolding, and because they wanted to know how they were related to each other, they decided to map their innovation system according to the CIM: see Figure 6.4.

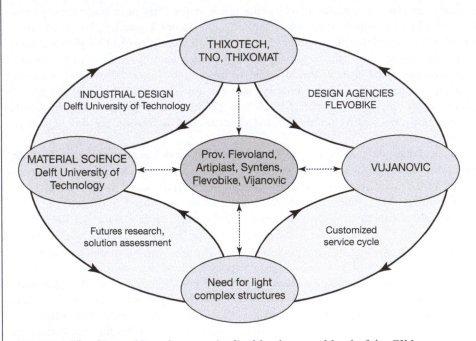

Figure 6.4 The thixomolding cluster as visualized by the second level of the CIM

Source: Duin *et al.*, 2007, p. 209

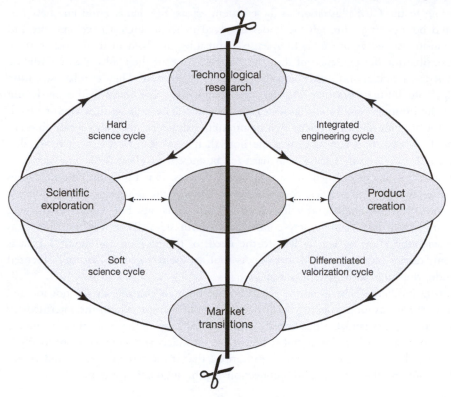

Figure 6.5 The 'innovation paradox' as illustrated by CIM

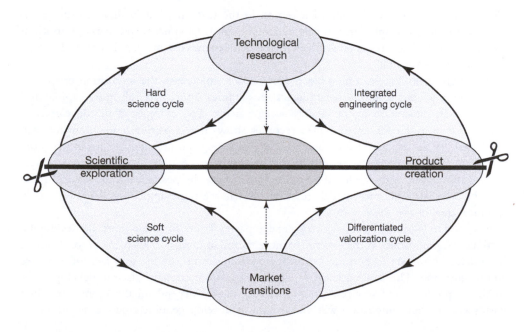

Figure 6.6 The gap between technology push and market pull as illustrated by CIM

According to the CIM illustration of these system errors, the demarcation line between science and business runs through the nodes involved in technological developments and market transitions (see Figure 6.6). In a sense, companies involved in these areas can be held responsible for the existence of the gap. After all, one of their jobs is to coordinate the knowledge activities and needs between science and business. They translate scientific knowledge into business practice. On the other hand, they also translate the needs and wishes of the business community into scientific practice. The translation is almost literal, because, not only are the aims of the two communities different, they also speak different languages. It is hard for scientists to imagine how their work can have commercial value for companies. On the other hand, it is hard for businesses to know what knowledge is available and how it can be used in an innovation process. It is up to the intermediaries between the scientific and business communities to connect the two sides. This requires a kind of Janus head: the ability and will to look in both directions. For employees of these intermediaries, it is important to stay connected to both sides. That way, everyone has access to scientific knowledge as well as to the needs of the business community. That is why intermediaries must never split in two. As soon as their employees are only focused on one side, the innovation system falls apart.

The intrinsic difference between the scientific and business communities is not in itself the cause of the innovation paradox, but it does cause the division within the intermediary companies. It is understandable that science and business keep doing what they do best – conducting (fundamental) research and selling (new) products and services, respectively – which is why there is a real need for organizations that, to a certain extent, understand both sides, allowing them to establish connections in the innovation system.

The gap between market and technology

The second system error is somewhat related to the first one, but in this case the gap is not vertical but horizontal. In this case, technological developments and market transitions are not connected, as a result of which an innovation depends too much either on technology push or on market pull.

Although technology can be a more than valuable input into the innovation process, it is not smart to start from the technological possibilities alone. After all, the technological quality of an innovation is not its only success factor. The example of the development and market introduction of the video recorder shows that a particular functionality (e.g. the length of the tape) and the content of the tape (e.g. pornography) were much more important than the technical performance of the recorder. A more contemporary example is the MP3 player, with Apple's iPod in the lead, where the possibility to download music and the associated business model (revenue model) are more important than the purely technical qualities of the device.

It is good to listen to customers, as long as companies do not focus too much on developing incremental innovations at the expense of more radical innovations. Such an approach makes it hard for customers to become aware of new innovations, owing to a lack of expertise and imagination. This is not a criticism, because it is not customers' place to develop (ideas for) new products and services. Companies that mostly depend on the opinion of their customers for their innovation will find it hard to develop genuinely new innovations.

Philips has taken an overly technical approach to the innovation process on several occasions. Fortunately, the company has learned to pay more attention to the non-technical aspects of innovation and to emphasize the design and marketing of its products. The most notorious example of a company that has overemphasized technology is Xerox. Although its Palo Alto Research Center is responsible for many innovations (such as the graphical user interface and the laser printer), the company never succeeded in making them commercially successful. For a long time, Xerox kept trying to sell its photocopiers to companies, when leasing them and making companies pay for each copy they made was the right business model. Putting too much emphasis on technical aspects in innovation can prevent a company from reaching its customers in the right way.

On the other hand, putting too much emphasis on marketing and customer needs can lead to a situation where technical possibilities are underestimated. The classic example is the Swiss watch industry, where watchmakers failed to take digital technology into account, because they assumed their customers were happy with the existing mechanical technology.[1]

No balance between the feedback loops

The third system error has to do with the feedback loops between the nodes of the innovation system. The essence of CIM is the existence of constant feedback of information and knowledge between the nodes, allowing people to learn from each other and knowledge to develop and grow. When that feedback is absent, the system practically comes to a halt. However, even when there is feedback, that is no guarantee that the innovation system is running smoothly. An important condition is that feedback loops between the nodes have to be balanced, which means that the exchange of information has to take place on an equal footing. If one of the loops becomes dominant, the innovation system becomes lopsided. An example is the loops between scientific exploration, technological development and product development. The emphasis on the commercial exploitation of scientific knowledge means that universities are bound too much by what the business community needs. As a result, scientific independence is compromised, and we can no longer trust the objectivity of scientists, and the scientists themselves are forced to conduct research the results of which are known in advance. This may be acceptable when it comes to developing incremental innovations, because they require little genuine scientific curiosity. However, when the aim is to develop more radical innovations, fundamental research is needed, which means research that does not necessarily focus on social requirements but that is about satisfying scientific curiosity; research that is purely theoretical in nature and that has no immediate practical use. Placing too much emphasis on the needs of product development (and technological development) curtails the independent scientific spirit.

On the other hand, obviously, focusing too much on fundamental research alone means losing touch with society and the business community altogether. We do want to point out, however, that, at this point, the influence of the business community on the scientific community is far greater than it is the other way around. This is caused by the above-mentioned need to commercialize technological developments, to the extent that scientists are often asked to indicate how they plan to exploit their discoveries commercially, which

Box 6.3 The innovators' dilemma of Clayton Christensen

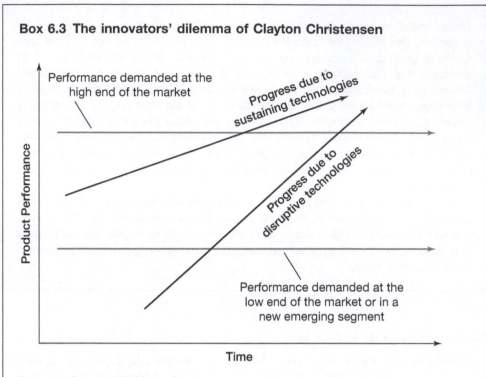

Figure 6.7 'Innovator's dilemma'

It is not always easy to distinguish technology push and market pull and their effect on innovation, as is illustrated by the concept of 'innovator's dilemma', which was developed by Clayton Christensen (1997), who argued that many companies simply follow the prevailing technological paradigm in their industry. As a result, they ignore new technologies that may perform less well initially but, in time, may replace the existing paradigm. The main explanation is that companies find it hard to imagine that their customers would want to use an inferior technology. However, the essence is that a certain portion of the market may actually be content with a (temporarily) lower quality and is unwilling to pay more for technological functionalities that offer no added value to them. A company that enters a sector (market) can tap into this target group by offering an inferior technology. As soon as the new technology improves and overtakes the existing paradigm, the new entrant can also target other groups that will benefit from an improved technology. Companies who stick to the existing technological paradigm will find it hard to switch to the new paradigm, because the new and improved technology also poses large-scale organizational and business demands, as well as requiring a different business model. Although it may not be hard to acquire the new technological expertise, it is more difficult to acquire other knowledge, which is often based on tacit knowledge. One option is to go for the financial solution and simply buy an existing competitor.

An example of the 'innovator's dilemma' is telephony using the Internet. Traditionally, telephony was based on analogue technologies. The initial experiments with (digital) telephony over the Internet were very disappointing. The quality of a call is largely determined by how much of what is being said is actually transmitted. In that regard, with digital telephony, which involves the transmission of packages of data, often not everything is transmitted. Initially, that meant that people only heard a portion of what was being said, often in the wrong order and with too many delays. This made it hard to have a normal conversation. However, subsequent improvements remedied these flaws and produced a technology that rivalled the existing technology, at a much lower price and with greater functionality. By that time, many telecommunications companies had decided not to invest in this technology, which meant they missed out on a technology that would end up defeating theirs.

Digital technology led to a large number of changes. Whereas telephony was the core product at first, with Internet access merely a side business, this was turned on its head as a result of the digitization process. These days, the Internet is the main product, with fixed telephony a virtually free addition. All this was made possible by a switch from analogue to digital.

---

is a lot to ask of people whose primary task it is to conduct research, rather than set up new businesses.

To a degree, this system error is the opposite of the innovation paradox. In this case, the link between the scientific and business communities, rather than being non-existent, tends to be too close, which is an argument against the notion that different parties in an innovation system should operate in close proximity. To allow each organization to flourish, it is important that there be a certain level of autonomy and independence. Organizations need to take part in innovation systems from a position of strength. Science can play a valuable role, owing to its independence and theoretical knowledge. If science only plays that role to provide other parties in the system with knowledge, the temptation exists to engage in (too many) other activities, for which it was not originally designed. Doing something other than what you are good at is never a smart strategy, and so its role as a partner in the innovation system will gradually be eroded. That does not mean that organizations should never switch roles, but doing something for which the organization is not optimally equipped will ultimately lead to the demise of the organization.

In shifting from fundamental research towards applied research, universities run the risk of being overtaken by non-profit research organizations, business laboratories and consultants, who have much more experience in developing applied knowledge. The strength of CIM is that it offers room to intermediaries, whose main task it is to translate between the various types of organization who need to work together to ensure a successful innovation process.

In short, organizations need to trust their own strengths to avoid creating an imbalance between the various feedback loops and to make sure the innovation does not become lopsided.

No innovation system manager or entrepreneur

One of the main advantages of the traditional 'closed' approach to innovation is that people mainly deal with the organization's own employees, who are easier to manage than those of other organizations, and internal processes are easier to manage than external processes.

In the case of 'open' innovation, innovation within systems or networks, an organization has to deal with several organizations that all have their own competences and agendas. This means that, in a well-functioning innovation network (and, in fact, in any kind of network), the parties involved have to trust one another. To promote trust, it is smart to appoint an impartial party to make sure organizations honour their agreements and give each party in the network its fair share. However, trust is not something that can only be given; it has to be earned as well, which means that the innovation network has to continue growing, which brings us to another role of the 'system entrepreneur', that of *manager* of the innovation system. Innovation systems can become highly complex, owing to the fact that many parties are involved. To guard the big picture, make sure all the required knowledge is available and carry out many other tasks, there has to be a party who is in charge. In a sense, this party has to make sure that no system errors occur or, when they do, that they are fixed in time.

In the thixomolding case (Box 6.2), for a brief while, there was no innovation manager. The initial innovation manager was forced to terminate his activities owing to institutional restrictions. Fortunately, the other organizations were able to secure the management with the financial support of the Dutch province of Flevoland, without which the innovation system surrounding thixomolding would not have got off the ground.

The lack of an innovation manager is a good opportunity for government to stimulate innovation without the need for large-scale investments. After all, the government can make a meaningful contribution by playing the role of innovation manager early on in the

---

When there is no innovation manager, there is a risk the innovation system will fall apart. However, especially during the start-up phase, it is important to have a party who is above the other parties, because, in that phase, the parties involved are likely to be sceptical about each other. They do not know each other well enough and will tend to be suspicious about the innovation process, because the outcomes at that stage are far from certain. In a sense, the organizations in the system network face a prisoner's dilemma. Although the organizations involved obviously want to innovate, they will try to avoid risks and prefer other organizations to assume any risks. As soon as more information becomes available about the potential success of the innovation, it is more interesting to be a part of the innovation system or to broaden one's activities within the system. However, until that time, any organization will tend to wait and see. It is up to the innovation manager to break this stalemate and bring the organizations together to try and create trust. Table 6.1 shows this stalemate with regard to collaborative innovation.

Table 6.1 The prisoner's dilemma applied to collaboration in innovation

	Party 1 wants change	*Party 1 does not want change*
Party 2 wants change	Uncertainty about outcome; risk-seeking	Advantage for 2; disadvantage for 1
Party 2 does not want change	Advantage for 1; disadvantage for 2	Status quo; risk-avoiding

innovation process. As soon as the innovation process is well and truly underway, another party, for instance a consultancy, can take over the role of innovation manager and consolidate the system.

Missing cycles

In recent years, innovation science has focused more and more on the subject of innovation systems. Although various definitions have been suggested, the essence is that there needs to be a certain coherence between specific parts. There may be few or many parts, their coherence may be simple or complex, but the main question is whether or not the innovation system is complete. From the perspective of CIM, the first counter-question is: how incremental or radical is the innovation? In the case of incremental innovations, (relatively) few actors are involved, and the coherence will be less complex. Incremental innovations require little in terms of new knowledge and often use existing collaborations that usually do not require the participation of new actors. In the case of more radical innovations, things are different. They require a great deal of new knowledge and collaboration with unknown entities that may behave in unpredictable ways in a risky relationship.

Whether or not a system is complete according to CIM depends on the ambition with regard to the future innovation. In the case of incremental innovations, CIM will not be filled in completely, whereas, in the case of radical innovations, every aspect will be addressed. Obviously, in the case of incremental innovations, it is important to make sure the proper elements of CIM are filled in. In most cases, the aspects in question will have to do with product development and market transitions. Radical innovations are often scientifically inspired and technological in nature and often play a decidedly less important role compared with incremental innovations, which are often market- and/or product-oriented. This means that market and product aspects are less important. In the thixomolding-case, failure to address the 'softer' aspects of CIM led to the failure of the innovation system. System innovations often start in science and technology, but, eventually, market and product aspects need to be addressed as well.

When a cycle is missing, CIM in a sense goes off course. Similar to what happens with the feedback loops, certain aspects of CIM are made too important compared with other aspects that may not be filled in completely. One might also argue that, even in the case of incremental innovations, it is important to take technology into account, perhaps not with the aim of improving the existing innovation (again), but to understand where new, competing innovations will originate. After all, those innovations will not be able to use existing technologies, but will instead have to look for new scientific and technological

---

Radical innovations are often called system innovations, which means that they are not just about renewing individual products or services, but about renewing the surrounding 'system'. Developing and implementing an electric car involves more than developing a new, different prototype of car. For instance, for electric cars to be able to run, recharging stations have to be designed and built (because the existing infrastructure is insufficient), and a solution has to be found for the fact that electric cars produce very little noise, which has serious road safety implications. In short, a system innovation requires an overhaul of pretty much all aspects of the innovation system.

insights. Above, we have described the theory suggested by Christensen, who argues that a new technological paradigm is needed to generate genuinely new innovations. To set up a CIM for an incremental innovation, it is still wise to look at science and technology to look for potential threats (and perhaps even opportunities).

Incidentally, experience teaches us that the bottom-left cycle is ignored most often (see Figure 6.2). Organizations, including those that operate in a technological environment, may feel that the market is quite important, but often they do not look for feedback from the social sciences. The lack of cycles is, therefore, closely connected to the absence of actors. Often, CIM is built by naming actors that are then positioned correctly in relation to each other, which of course means that the cycles do not emerge automatically, but instead need to be initiated by the actors themselves, coached and facilitated by the innovation system manager. To determine the 'completeness' of CIM, we first need to be clear whether enough and the right actors are present.

Innovation systems do not emerge from nowhere, but develop over time. This development can happen for a number of reasons:

*   A new scientific insight can lead to the creation of an innovation system because there is a desire to commercialize the knowledge.
*   A technical discovery can be applied in a product or service.
*   A new social problem can also lead to the setting up of all kinds of innovation activity to deal with the problem.

So, all CIM nodes can serve as a starting point for the development of an innovation system.

The development of innovation systems applied to CIM

We have seen that the development of innovations takes time, which means that innovations go through a certain development as well. There are various kinds of development, and, to map them, we use a categorization developed by Andrew Van de Ven and Marshall Scott Poole (1995). They distinguished four types of development:

1   life cycle;
2   teleological;
3   dialectical;
4   evolution.

These types of development are not autonomous but are the result of entrepreneurial actions. So, the type of development could be chosen by the entrepreneur, although every entrepreneur operates in a societal and business environment that has great influence on their degrees of freedom in the way they choose to develop the required innovation system for entrepreneurial activity.

Life-cycle development

A life-cycle development means that the change in the innovation system has a logic of its own that provides direction to the change from the outset. Although there are external influences, they will always be accommodated by the logic and rules of the change itself. To use the (somewhat abstract) words of Van de Ven and Poole (1995):

According to life-cycle theory, change is imminent: that is, the developing entity has within it an underlying form, logic, program, or code that regulates the process of change and moves the entity from a given point of departure towards a subsequent end that is prefigured in the present state. Thus, the form that lies latent, becomes progressively more realized, mature, and differentiated.

According to the authors, an example of such a development is the five layers of diffusion that Everett Rogers applies to innovation: need recognition, research on problem, development of idea into useful form, commercialization, and diffusion. According to the life-cycle theory, this order is necessary and, according to Van de Ven and Poole (1995), it is based on 'the natural order of Western business practices'.

Teleological development

A teleological development is based on the assumption that the development of an entity (such as an innovation system) is steered by a certain goal, which is formulated explicitly and informs the activities that should lead to its realization. This does not have to mean that the activities have to have a fixed order, but it does mean that they are designed to achieve the goal that has been formulated. This does not take place in a vacuum: the development is influenced by the environment in which it takes place, which can either have a hampering or encouraging effect. Either way, the entity or actor needs to make sure to use the given circumstances as well as possible. Examples of teleological developments are the formulation of certain policy objectives and the associated action plan – for instance, those of the Lisbon Agreement or the Kyoto Treaty.

Dialectical development

The dialectical approach is based on the assumption that a development is the result of opposing forces and mechanisms, either outside or within the entity. As a result, the development does not have to be gradual, but the speed and direction of the development are determined by the moment when the conflicting forces have reconciled and are taken to a higher level. In dialectical terms: the thesis has an antithesis, which eventually results in a synthesis. It is that synthesis that shapes the development and leads to the change. An example of a dialectical development is a political decision-making process involving opposing opinions and interests that eventually (must) result in a consensus that satisfies the representatives of the different opinions and interests and that can lead to other (legislative and executive) processes.

Evolutionary development

Evolutionary developments are (usually) characterized by gradual and cumulative processes, in which variation, selection and preservation play an important role, giving rise – spontaneously or accidentally – to forms and a subsequent competitive process in which the 'best' forms survive. These new forms coexist next to older, existing forms that have (also) managed to survive. In the case of an evolutionary process, it is important for the entity to adapt well and in time to changes in its environment. Biological processes are, of course, the best-known examples of evolutionary processes, but the emergence of new companies and sectors can also often be described adequately using evolution as a metaphor.

We now take a look at these four developments from the perspective of CIM.

CIM and life-cycle development

The life cycle can provide information about the speed of the development of the innovation system according to CIM. When we interpret the life cycle as an S-curve, this means that the start-up phase of CIM will take some time. During that time, the future vision has to be made concrete and attractive enough for potential participants. Not only will it take some time to persuade them to take part in the innovation system, it also takes time to assess their suitability as potential participants: Do they possess the right knowledge? Do they have enough quality? Are they reliable partners who will commit to the goal of the innovation system? After the assessment has taken place, it will take some time to get the innovation system underway. After that, with the contours of the innovation system in place, things can speed up, and the focus can shift towards the content of the innovation. In later phases of the process, delays that may be understandable in the initial phase are undesirable, because there may be competing innovation systems that will also want to benefit from first-mover advantage. Of course, the acceleration of the innovation system is not infinite, as the S-curve also shows. At the end of the development of the innovation system, the pace of the development will slacken, at which point development becomes diffusion, and it is up to more operational departments, such as marketing and sales, to sell the innovation successfully and make good on its promise.

CIM and teleological development

Teleological development assumes that a development has a goal. With regard to an innovation system according to CIM, that would mean that it is known in advance what the innovation is exactly and how it should be developed. Because, as we have indicated earlier, uncertainty and creativity are essential to innovation, this type of development is not entirely compatible with the principles of CIM. Innovation processes often turn out different from what was expected.

For instance, Viagra was meant for people with heart conditions, but, ultimately, men with erectile problems benefited the most. Text messaging, to name another example, was originally designed with business people in mind. In the end, youngsters turned out to be the heaviest users. And, in fact, with regard to the telephone, it was originally thought it could be used to tell people a telegram had arrived for them. Innovation processes, then, are inherently uncertain (as we keep repeating), and their outcome is unknown in advance. In some cases, they are downright chaotic.

However, that does not mean that the entire innovation process takes place without meaningful intervention by the parties involved. There is a reason that people often speak of innovation *management*. Although innovations cannot be controlled, innovation managers have the ability to steer them through informed decisions and actions. In the initial phases of the process, the so-called fuzzy front end, that is not easy, because there is little reliable information on which to base decisions. However, during the innovation process, when the innovation has a more solid foundation, there is more information available that innovation managers can use.

With CIM, the vision of the future plays a crucial role in the innovation system (see Level 1 of the CIM). It is used as a source of inspiration and as a leitmotiv throughout the innovation process. However, this vision of the future does not provide a blueprint, which means that there has to be enough room to adjust the vision, should the need arise. The point is that innovation managers need to find a workable compromise between a vision that inspires and binds them and the actors in the innovation system on the one hand, and a vision that is open enough to new social and technological developments that can be used to adjust the course of the innovation.

CIM and dialectical development

The dialectical development is heavily based on conflicts and opposing forces and on conquering them. At face value, one might conclude that such a development is not suitable for an innovation system according to CIM. After all, an innovation system is largely based on trust, and emphasizing differences is subjugated to that. However, a dialectical perspective can be helpful in describing and explaining the development of an innovation system according to CIM.

First of all, it would be naïve to assume that all the actors in an innovation system have the same ideas and objectives regarding the course of the innovation system. An innovation system by definition consists of various actors, and it will also benefit from this diversity. In that sense, it is important to have a clear vision for the future, because that will appeal to the various actors. This shared vision represents a 'common interest' that indicates which role an actor can play in the innovation system and on the basis of which it can be determined what the innovation system can mean for the actors themselves. Although dialectics are not aimed at balance (but rather at dynamics through 'conquering' differences), it is important to make sure that, for every actor, there is an acceptable balance between what they invest and what they get out of the innovation system. If the costs outweigh the benefits, there is a good chance the actor will leave the innovation system. In itself, that does not have to be a problem. In the general opinions about innovations and 'open innovation', it is argued that it is common for actors to take part in innovation systems temporarily. In the days of 'closed', linear innovation, it was more common to take part in the entire process. As far as the innovation manager is concerned, it is important to keep track of the considerations of the various actors. Actors for whom the costs outweigh the benefits are a potential risk, especially when they see others benefit more.

To handle dialectic tensions within an innovation well, feedback and feed-forward between the nodes are crucial. The cyclical connections between the nodes first of all make the differences between the nodes visible and knowable. Through the exchange of information (for instance, questions about each other's knowledge), it becomes clear what the mutual expectations are. Based on that, new knowledge can be developed to broaden one's own knowledge base. It is possible to interpret the various kinds of knowledge in the different nodes as opposing forces that are reconciled through the development and feedback of new knowledge. In other words, people learn from each other. Often, innovation processes are also seen as learning processes. So, although, in CIM, contradictions are acceptable, they need to be removed by setting in motion the (cyclical) learning process and bringing together different actors (in different nodes), who can then develop and exchange information.

CIM and evolutionary development

With regard to evolutionary developments, from the perspective of innovation systems, we can say that they can mainly be interpreted as gradual developments in which there are various competing ideas for innovations. An evolutionary development of an innovation system is certainly possible with CIM. Involving actors in the innovation process can be a gradual process that starts with looking for potential candidates. However, this selection process cannot take place entirely in advance. Only time will tell which actors actually bring added value to the innovation system. The fact that an actor leaves the innovation system in itself does not have to be a bad thing. Unlike in the past, when organizations needed to be involved from start to finish, nowadays it is not uncommon for organizations to enter and leave the innovation system along the way. Incidentally, this does not mean that every innovation system will develop gradually. It is quite possible for one organization to speed up the process considerably. The evolutionary process means that the selection process will continue throughout the life cycle of the innovation system.

Another aspect by which evolution can be linked to CIM is the influence the environment has on the development of an innovation system. Modern innovation systems, as described and analysed using CIM, are in essence 'open systems' (see also Chapter 10, 'Entrepreneurship in context'), in which the actors respond to both internal and external influences, be they social or technological changes or competing innovation systems. The innovation system therefore has to adapt to its environment and it has to do so in time. As far as CIM is concerned, the nodes must also be related to other innovation systems, to make sure that the actors in the nodes are aware of developments in other innovation systems (whether competing or not) and use the information from those other innovation systems in their own system.

Concluding remarks

We think it is important to make it clear that the nodes of the CIM do not automatically set an innovation system in motion. That is, a scientific insight in itself cannot start up an innovation system; that will always require people with the ideas and ambition to shape the scientific insight, technological discovery and/or social problem and to involve other parties. These people come from a certain node and assume the role of innovation manager to further build the innovation system. This means that this role can be temporary, because, owing to the specific background and function of these people, building an innovation system is not part of their expertise. After a while, these people return to 'their' nodes, and their role has to be taken over by others who are specialized in that area. Of course, the role of innovation manager can also be taken on immediately by someone 'outside' the system, meaning a person or organization who did not directly acquire the scientific insight, think of the technical application or notice the social problem, but who sees the potential for innovation. Important characteristics of 'real' entrepreneurs are their powers of observation and their ability to connect what they see to a possible innovation, their ability to – as it were – build a bridge from an idea to the ultimate innovation. This not only requires vision for the future, but creativity and imagination as well.

The development of an innovation system according to CIM can start in two ways: top–down and bottom–up:

1   Top–down means that an entrepreneur with a vision for the future goes looking for possible scientific insights, technological applications and/or social problems that can lead to the creation of an innovation system. This person's first task is to involve actors in the innovation system who can be expected to offer a useful contribution. The innovation system manager functions as a spider in a web, weaving the threads of the innovation system, to complete the metaphor.

2   The bottom–up approach, on the other hand, starts from one of the 'nodes' itself.

With both types of approach, it has to be decided in which order to involve the actors:

- With regard to the *bottom–up approach*, based on our experience with applying CIM, the first actor who needs to be approached should be located in the node that is nearest to the 'starting node'. In the case of the scientific node, for example, that would either be the technology development node or the market transitions node. In the first phases of the development of an innovation system according to CIM, it can be too early to connect to the product development node, because the nodes are too different in nature (academic versus business) and with regard to their role in the innovation system. In addition, when the innovation system starts in 'hard' science, there will have to be contact with the technology node first and later, via the social sciences, with the market transitions node.
- With regard to the *top–down approach*, it is harder to determine what the correct order is, as it is unclear in which node the innovation system originates. It is possible to determine, however, that an entrepreneur with a technologically inspired vision of the future is very likely to go looking for actors who are located in the technology development node. From that point onwards, the development will be similar to that of a bottom–up approach: start with the nearest node and try to involve the other nodes from there, thus creating a larger system that includes all the necessary disciplines and knowledge.

Chapter summary

Entrepreneurship is not a solitary activity. Input from various sources and partners are required to develop innovative ideas into profitable ventures. The ability to set up, coordinate and manage an innovation network or system, therefore, has become a vital process skill for every entrepreneur.

Study questions

1   Why should an entrepreneur consider him/herself as part of a system?
2   Describe in your own words the characteristics of the Cyclic Innovation Model.
3   Design an innovation of your own business (idea) using CIM.
4   What are the most relevant failures of your innovation system? How do you address these?

Note

1   We need to add, of course, that the Swiss watchmakers made an excellent comeback with the design of beautiful watches – a classic example of high-quality market research and marketing.

References

Berkhout, A. J. (2000). *The Dynamic Role of Knowledge in Innovation: An integrated framework of cyclic networks for the assessment of technological change and sustainable growth*. Delft, Netherlands: Delft University Press.

Berkhout, A. J. and Duin, P. A. van der (2007). New ways of innovation: An application of the cyclic innovation model to the mobile telecom industry. *International Journal of Technology Management*. 40(4): 294–309.

Carlsson, B., Jacobson, S., Holmén, M. and Rickne, A. (2002). Innovation systems: Analytical and methodological issues. *Research Policy*. 31: 233–45.

Chesbrough, H. (2003). *Open Innovation*. Boston, MA: Harvard Business School Press.

Christensen, C. (1997). *The Innovator's Dilemma: When new technologies cause great firms to fail*. Boston, MA: Harvard Business School Press.

Dahmén, E. (1950). *Svensk industriell företagarverksamhet: kausalanalys av den industriella utvecklingen 1919-1939* (Entrepreneurial activity in Swedish industry in the period 1919-1939; with an English summary; Vol. 3). Industriens utrednings-institut.

Duin, P. A. van der and Hermeler, H. (2014). Innovating in a government context: An evaluation of a Dutch water program using the Cyclic Innovation Model. *International Journal of Innovation and Technology Management*. 11(3): 1–22.

Duin, P. A. van der, Heger, T. and Schlesinger, M. D. (2014). Toward networked foresight? Exploring the use of futures research in innovation networks. *Futures*. 59: 62–78.

Duin, P. A. van der, Ortt, J. R. and Kok, M. (2007). The Cyclic Innovation Model: A new challenge for a regional approach to innovation systems? *European Planning Studies*. 15(2): 195–215.

Fischer, M. M. and Fröhlich, J. (eds) (2001). *Knowledge, Complexity and Innovation Systems*. Berlin: Springer.

Freeman, C., Clark, J. and Soete, L. (1982). *Unemployment and Technical Innovation: A study of long waves and economic development*. London: Burns & Oates.

Hippel, E. von (1998). Economics of product development by users: The impact of 'sticky' local information. *Management Science*. 44(5): 629–44.

OECD. (1997). *National Innovation Systems*. Paris: OECD.

Porter, M. E. (1990). The competitive advantage of nations. *Harvard Business Review*. 68(2): 73–93.

Van de Ven, A. H. and Poole, M. S. (1995). Explaining development and change in organizations. *Academy of Management Review*. 20(3): 510–40.

Van de Ven, A. H., Polley, D. E., Garud, R. and Venkataraman, S. (1999). *The Innovation Journey*. Oxford, UK: Oxford University Press.

Zahra, S. A. and Nambisan, S. (2012). Entrepreneurship and strategic thinking in business ecosystems. *Business Horizons*. 55: 219–29.

Further reading

Berkhout, A. J., Duin, P. van der, Hartmann, D. and Ortt, J. R. (2007). *The Cyclic Nature of Innovation*. Amsterdam: Elsevier Science.

Duin, P. A. van der (2010). 'The Dutch innovation system: Raising the lowland?' in V. K. Narayanan and G. O'Connor (eds), *Encyclopedia of Technology and Innovation Management*. Chichester, UK: Wiley, pp. 403–418.

Duin, P. A. van der, Sule, M. and Bruggeman, W. (2011). Deltas for the future: Lessons learned in a water innovation programme. *Irrigation & Drainage*. 60(Suppl.1): 122–8.

Kamp, L. and Duin, P. A. van der (2010). Analyzing the innovation system of wind turbine development 1973–2000 using the Cyclic Innovation Model. IAMOT Conference, Cairo, Egypt, March.

7 Academic spin-outs

What is an academic spin-out?

Academic spin-outs are new firms that are typically founded by one or more scientists who have participated in academic research programmes. Their research has resulted in a specific scientific finding that can be exploited commercially and has led to the founding of the new firm. To successfully exploit the scientific finding, it is important for scientists to understand the opportunities in the market. Scientists bring to the spin-off their scientific experience and expert skills, which might be different from the skills and expertise that are required to run a commercial, new venture successfully. Despite their strong reputation in academe, it does not guarantee success in the business environment.

Academic spin-out is a term for new ventures that have originated in academic research. In general, we speak of academic spin-outs when three conditions are met (Pirnay *et al.*, 2003):

1   the new venture is based on a scientific finding;
2   the new venture is an autonomous entity; and

3   the new venture is founded by one or more scientists who have participated in academic research programmes that resulted in the scientific finding that shaped the basis for the spin-off.

The *scientific finding* can be the result of a deliberate research investigation or a finding that emerges in the course of a research project. In the case of the deliberate research project, it is often driven by contract research or consultancy work. This research has the intention to bring about clear scientific findings that have commercial applications and are brought to the market by profit-driven companies. This *deliberate creation* of knowledge in academic environments and its exploitation in industry are often referred to as *knowledge and technology transfer*.

> Example: A research group identifies new materials for photovoltaic cells, which can be transferred to a company that commercially exploits the technology. In such a case, the research group or department often agrees to an arrangement such as a licence in order to capture some of the value that is generated with the new material for photovoltaic cells.

It may also happen that, in the process of conducting the research, new insights or new test procedures are developed that can be articulated into commercial applications. Although it was not intended, and the findings have emerged in the process of conducting the research, they can still be transferred to a commercial company. These cases are referred to as knowledge spillovers, with technology spinning off from a research programme.

> Example: The same research department likes to know exactly the efficiency of the photovoltaic cells and develops a model to simulate and test the cells. These additional research activities may not be the core of the research project but bring about new insights or test procedures for measuring the efficiency of photovoltaic cells under different circumstances and over longer periods.

It might happen that basic research has led to a scientific finding that existing companies are not willing to exploit. This could be for a variety of reasons: for instance, the early stage of the technology and absence of operational proof. In such a case, the research group might decide to start a new company based on the spin-off technology. This new venture is often known as a *spin-out* company. The new company is based on the scientific finding that has been developed by a research group and is spun out into a new entity. Now, depending on the person who initiates the founding of the new company, further specification can be made. If the scientific finding is transferred to individuals within the research group, and they start a new firm, this firm is often referred to as a *faculty-based spin-out* company, whereas, if someone outside the research department starts the new firm, for instance an entrepreneur from industry, it is often called an *entrepreneur-based spin-off* firm. Sometimes, this person is called an external entrepreneur or, with a somewhat negative connotation, they are called a surrogate entrepreneur (Radosevich, 1995; Franklin *et al.*, 2001). Most likely, students will start a new company based on the spin-off technology or the knowledge they gained during their course. These companies are referred to as *student-based spin-offs*. For instance, a student follows a course on writing a business plan or is involved in one of the courses on photovoltaic cells. The student acquires the knowledge and gets inspired, which may stimulate them to start a company.

> Example: There are cases of student-based start-ups that use photovoltaic cells in roof tiles or build net-based, concentrated photovoltaic systems that can alter position and track the sun in order to obtain greater efficiency.

Finally, it can also be the case that external entrepreneurs like to exploit a scientific finding when they were neither taking part in the research nor were they students. In the latter case, the founder is using academic knowledge, and we would refer to this company as a *spin-off company*. The various technology transfer routes are given in Figure 7.1.

Reason academic start-ups can exist

Traditionally, universities are involved in teaching students and focus on more fundamental research. The further development of new technology and knowledge into products and services was mostly the province of other institutions, such as TNO in the Netherlands or the polytechnics and universities of applied sciences. However, the increased interest in commercializing the potential value of basic research and the need to exploit it sooner has led governments to use tax money, not only to conduct basic research, but also to speed up the innovation process and gain returns on invested tax money more quickly. A third generation of universities has emerged (Wissema, 2009), with the goal, not only to educate students and conduct fundamental research, but also to articulate the latest technology into

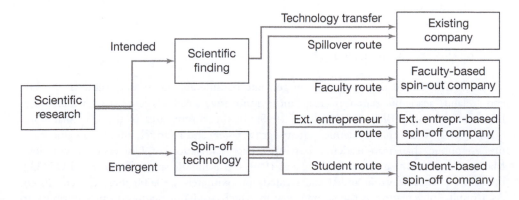

Figure 7.1 Technology transfer and academic spin-offs

applications that benefit society. Governments are seeking a more prominent role for universities to contribute to the knowledge economy and strengthen the competitiveness of the country and, more directly, the regions where these universities are located.

The transfer of academic knowledge and technology to the business sector can take place via three basic mechanisms:

1   The traditional mechanism is the education of students, who are employed after graduation and make use of their scientific training.
2   A second mechanism is that of consulting, contracting research and licensing academic knowledge to established industries.
3   The third mechanism is the academic start-up route, by which knowledge is exploited through the founding of a new venture.

Technology findings that are very new to the market are often characterized by a high degree of uncertainty about the technological outcome and market demands. Only a few pioneering firms that have little to lose, such as new start-ups, are willing to take the risks associated with early-stage innovations.

Economic value of academic start-ups

The interest in academic start-ups stems from the success of Silicon Valley. Silicon Valley is the region south of San Francisco that is considered by many policymakers and entrepreneurs to be the place where the latest technology and most influential companies are located. The GDP per capita is measured as ranking third globally,[1] and the region has more than 225,000 high-tech jobs. Many of the companies that contribute to these figures are spin-offs from Stanford University or have strong links with its research programmes. In Europe, too, examples exist of academic start-up success. Silicon Fen near Cambridge University is a high-tech region founded in 1970 through a Cambridge University initiative. It is home to high-tech software, electronics and biotechnology companies, with known examples such as ARM, Autonomy Corporation and AVEVA. In 2003, the region accommodated about 3,500 firms and 55,000 employees, contributing approximately £7.6 billion to the English gross value added.

Academic start-ups can create economic growth in four different areas:

1   economic value;
2   job growth;
3   innovative region;
4   firm diversity in the region.

First, it is believed that spin-outs can generate considerable economic value. In the UK and Ireland, academic start-ups create more innovative products and services than other high-tech start-ups (Blair and Hitchens, 1998). In the Boston area of the US, Shane and Stuart (2002) found that academic start-ups grow faster, and relatively more academic start-ups go public than non-academic start-ups. The Association of University Technology Managers reported that, between 1980 and 1999, US academic spin-offs generated US$33.5 billion in economic value added and created approximately 280,000 jobs (Cohen, 2000). As a result, job creation is the second way in which academic start-ups can contribute to economic growth. The third way is by their contribution to local economic development.

Box 7.1 Silicon Valley

In the late nineteenth century, it was predominantly oranges and other agricultural products that were grown in the Silicon Valley area. In 1885, Stanford University was founded, and its research was aimed at helping the local firms in the West to become more self-sustaining. Frederick Terman was the dean of engineering at Stanford during the Second World War. He actively recruited the best students across the US to come to his faculty and encouraged them, as well as his faculty, to start their own companies. William Shockley was one of the people Frederick Terman supported, and, in 1956, Shockley founded the Shockley Transistor Laboratory, based on his invention of the transistor. Soon after, a dispute between Shockley and his employees over his decision not to continue research on silicon-based semiconductors led to the departure of the 'traitorous eight',[2] who, together with Sherman Fairchild, formed Fairchild Semiconductor. This company is known for its 'Fairchildren': it was the birthplace of some sixty-five other start-ups in the field of electronics and semiconductors, among which Intel and AMD are well known. The success of Silicon Valley continued, not only in the field of semiconductors, but also in that of computers (Xerox, Apple), software (Adobe, Lotus, Oracle), Internet (Yahoo, Google), biotech (Genentech) and, more recently, the automotive sector (Tesla).

Academic start-ups apply recent technological findings and assist the creation and growth of knowledge-intensive, innovation-based industry in a region. Research has shown that, in the Boston area and in Silicon Valley, academic start-ups were more important in the early stages of development of scientific complexes than were firms that relocated to the region (Mahar and Coddington, 1965). Roberts (1991) indicated that most start-ups from MIT settled near the laboratories they emerged from and continued their relationship with them. The fourth contribution is that academic start-ups contribute to the diversity of industry sectors in a particular region. More diverse industries in a region make the region economically more stable. If, in one sector, sales or investments decline, the region is economically less affected compared with a region that is highly dependent on a single industry. Similarly, more small, entrepreneurial companies in a region also make the region more robust. In a region that is highly dependent on a single, large firm that is facing losses, the repercussions for employment will be larger compared with those in a region where the economy is built on many small, diverse firms.

Research on academic start-ups

Research on academic start-ups has emerged in a variety of streams since its introduction in the United States in the 1960s and 1970s. Research groups led by Edward Roberts (Roberts, 1991; Roberts and Malone, 1996), Arnold Cooper (1972) and, later, by Rogers (Rogers and Larsen, 1984, p. 189; Steffensen *et al.*, 1999) and Scott Shane (2004) took the first steps in comprehending these types of start-up. In Europe, research in academic start-up activities took off with researchers such as Philippe Mustar (1997) in France, Mike Wright (Wright *et al.*, 2004) in the UK, and Einar Rasmussen (Rasmussen *et al.*, 2006) in Norway. Many of these research programmes used an explorative or descriptive approach to identify types of academic start-up and study their characteristics. Today, three main research streams can be distinguished that deal with understanding the phenomenon of spin-offs at the level of (1) the national or regional economy, (2) the academic institution and (3) the start-up firm.

The economic perspective investigates the role of academic start-ups in creating economic growth by commercializing research findings that are funded by public research programmes. This research stream compares academic start-ups with other (technological) start-ups. The major findings are that, compared with non-academic start-ups, academic start-ups create more innovative products and services (Blair and Hitchens, 1998), grow faster and create more jobs (Cohen, 2000) and go public faster (Shane and Stuart, 2002).

The second research stream investigates how academic start-ups can contribute to the academic institution where they originated. It is shown that academic start-ups can commercialize early inventions the potential of which is yet unclear (Shane, 2004). Furthermore, they are believed to induce larger investments in academic research programmes, and the opportunity for faculty staff to take part in the start-up can be a financial mechanism to retain and attract well-qualified staff members.

At the firm level, studies have investigated, for instance, the definitions and typologies of academic start-ups, the motivation for founding these firms, the phases of growth, the role of the academic institution in the start-up's growth, and the factors that influence the success of academic start-ups. The main typologies are based on the objectives of the start-up and the relation between the academic spin-out and the academic institution and other network contacts (Roberts and Malone, 1996). Furthermore, this research stream investigates the motivation for scientists to start a spin-out, such as the conditions that bring the individual to change his/her career and become self-employed. However, most often, researchers have investigated the role of incubation centres during the growth of spin-offs (Allen and McCluskey, 1990; Roberts and Malone, 1996). Recently, research has focused on identifying the factors that can explain early spin-off success (Scholten *et al.*, 2015). Using case studies, Vohora *et al.* (2004) investigated the development of academic spin-offs and found several critical junctures that spin-offs need to overcome if they are to succeed.

Stakeholders in academic start-up success

Indicators of academic start-up success can be various. Although academic start-ups can be founded for a variety of reasons, one would expect that the revenue stream and profit ratios are the best indicators for success. However, academic start-ups are often very young companies that need to develop their products and services further before they can bring them to the market and, as a result, they are often in need of investment. To attract investment, the academic start-up needs to be able to show promising figures with regards to return on investment or a promising exit deal for investors when they sell their share of the company when it is more mature or when they go for initial public offering on the stock market.

1   *Founders*: The main stakeholders of the new company are the founders. They often have a strong self-interest in terms of freedom or self-direction. Furthermore, they like to see to it that the technology they worked so hard at is being implemented in practice. Or, in the case of social entrepreneurs, they like to see certain societal problems being solved and, therefore, start the new firm. However, they often have financial interest and like to increase their reputation or build themselves an image.

2   *Shareholders and investors*: The second group of stakeholders comprises the shareholders or investors. They primarily have a financial interest, which is often the upside potential of the exit deal. In some cases, investors have an interest in learning about new markets for further investments. The latter is often the case when existing firms invest in the start-up in order to tap into new technology or experiment in new markets.

3   *Academe*: The third group consists of academe (research group or academic institution), which is more interested in the extent to which the start-up will use the scientific finding that is being transferred. If the start-up is selling products based on a scientific finding, and the research group has negotiated a licensing deal, it may receive royalties and, therefore, it has an interest in the number of products being sold based on the IPR that was transferred to the start-up. In addition, it might be interested in collaborating with the start-up in follow-up research activities. For instance, when applying for research grants, a research group often needs to include a private company to make sure the knowledge being developed in the research activities has commercial value. When applying for a research grant, a research group can benefit from the connections it has with a start-up. It often makes negotiating easier and faster, and both can show in the application that they have worked together before. Of lesser importance is the reputation effect. Successful start-ups can attract considerable media attention, which has a positive effect on the economic and social value of the research group and academic institution.

4   *Regional public organizations*: The fourth group of stakeholders is regional public organizations, e.g. the local municipality and regional authorities. They are interested in job creation and in attracting highly skilled employment to their region. They also prefer stability in the region in periods of economic turmoil and, therefore, like to see start-ups contributing to industry diversity, making the region more versatile in case of economic shocks.

Success indicators

Various groups of stakeholders emphasize different performance indicators of academic start-ups. It would be helpful to discuss a number of success indicators in detail. In general, we can make a distinction between objective and subjective measures of start-up success. Objective success measures are hard data about the success of the new firm, such as traditional growth-rate measures. Subjective measures are 'softer' and express the success of the new firm based on the perceptions of individuals. The extent to which a performance

Table 7.1 Spin-out performance indicators that various stakeholders tend to emphasize

1 Founders	Financial: sales growth & profit ratio, exit deal
	Technology implementation in the market
	Personal: freedom, research interest
	Various: reputation
2 Shareholders & investors	Financial: sales growth & profit ratio, exit deal
	Various: learn new markets
3 Academe	Financial: licensing revenues, equity stake
	Research: additional research assignments
	Various: reputation
4 Regional public authorities	Economic: growth, sales, job creation, employment stability
	Various: diversity in industry

measure is appropriate depends on the extent to which it is reliable and valid. Reliability reflects whether it measures the object systematically and repeatedly with the same outcome. Thus, for various entrepreneurs, it should provide similar answers. Validity refers to the extent it measures what it is supposed to measure. This often depends on whether the entrepreneur understands the question in the way you want him to and provides you with the right information.

With regards to newly established firms, two renowned scholars, Covin and Slevin (1989) argue that objective measures show difficulties in terms of their cross-comparison, sensitivity and completeness. The cross-comparison of standard growth measures among multiple new ventures is often blurred. New ventures may have a variety of growth objectives, which makes the interpretation of data difficult. For example, Figure 7.2 shows that a typical consultancy start-up serving clients on a personal basis has a linear growth model, whereas, for instance, a scalable product start-up, such as an IT start-up developing mobile phone apps, has a scalable product and may not grow substantially in terms of employee numbers, but its cash-flow will follow more of a hockey-stick curve and have more nonlinear growth. For a linear-growth start-up, employee growth might be a good indicator of success, but, for a start-up with a scalable product, it might not reflect its true growth. Furthermore, the employee growth ratio does not always indicate success but could even be an indicator of inefficiency, in particular when we consider the definition of Stevenson and Gumpert (1985) that entrepreneurship is the acting upon an opportunity, regardless of the resources controlled. Therefore, it would be better for a start-up to have an organization that can change its focus and activities as new opportunities are identified. Flexibility is key, and large numbers of employees and assets will make the start-up inert and make it more difficult for the entrepreneurs to engage in emerging opportunities. Entrepreneurs would rather have access to certain resources through outsourcing activities and engaging in collaborations. As a result, the number of employees as a performance measure has some complications for understanding the true entrepreneurial position of a firm and could be, as such, an indicator of inefficient organization when it comes to dynamic environments and responsiveness to newly identified opportunities.

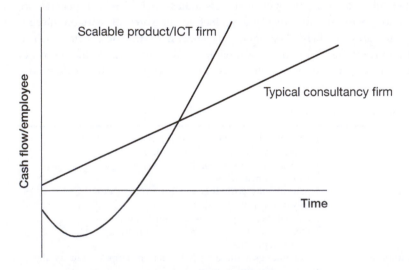

Figure 7.2 Growth comparison between scalable- and linear-growth start-ups

Furthermore, the growth measures of small and new firms are very sensitive to the smallness of the start-up, and relatively small changes may have a large effect on the measurement of growth. In new firms, the percentile growth-rate can differ enormously, for instance if a start-up grows from one to four persons compared with a start-up that grows from fifty to fifty-four persons. At the same time, if absolute growth rates were used, then that would be a wrong presentation as well. Growing with four people in a start-up is more challenging than growing with four people in a large firm.

Objective measures also bring difficulties with regard to their completeness, for example depending on the respondent's willingness to provide financial or employee data. New start-ups are not obliged to publish their financial status. Another objective measure that governmental organizations often use to measure new start-up success is survival rate, indicating the number of firms that still exist after a number of years. One problem with this measure is getting information about the firms that have ceased to exist. The reasons for stopping can vary: perhaps it is owing to failure, or maybe because the start-up is sold to another company. Also, some argue that a large number of start-ups survive the initial years because they are pampered too much. These start-ups may still exist owing to support they received, which may undo natural selection, whereas they should have been liquidated under the fierce markets conditions.

Problems with objective measures such as cash flow, revenues, employees and sales include:

- the problem of comparisons between nonlinear (scalable) and linear growth models;
- the problem of cross-comparing small start-ups with larger start-ups;
- the problem of incompleteness and the willingness of entrepreneurs to share information.

Subjective measures, on the other hand, reflect the respondent's opinion of operational activities, such as satisfaction with the progress of opportunities identified, technology development or collaboration. These subjective measures are self-reported by the entrepreneur and can have potential limitations as well. Relatively small issues that recently occurred may influence the respondent's opinion on a subjective measure. For example, satisfaction about a business relationship could have been harmed owing to shipment problems over the last week and may negatively influence the satisfaction level, although overall the collaboration is fruitful and going well. Also, stagnation of technological progress may be influenced by sudden setbacks. Levels of satisfaction are associated with a priori expectations. Subsequently, low satisfaction levels may result from high expectations before starting a technological development or be due to some miscalculated time frame. Thus, recent events may affect the validity and reliability of subjective measures.

The main issue with subjective measures is whether they measure a perception or behaviour. Subjective measures that are based on the entrepreneur's perception, such as 'Compared with competition, we are more innovative', can be very biased with the opportunistic entrepreneur. A behavioural measure, such as 'How much time do you spend on developing new product?', might be better, and better still is a behaviour measure based on factual data – for instance, 'Over the last 3 years we have launched three new products'.

Subjective measures may also rely on retrospective reports – for instance, the success of presenting a business proposal to potential investors. The time it takes to convince investors could be an indicator of success. The entrepreneur has to remember the process and how successful it was. Although the data being collected are self-reported, founder-reported measures can be considered reliable, especially in cases when questions are asked about simple facts and events, rather than past opinions or beliefs. In the case above, it would be good to ask about the number of meetings and the number of follow-up reports and questions that the investors posed to the founder. Again, however, it is difficult to make inferences from the number of meetings: does it reflect positive and fruitful progress, or is there a major problem to be solved?

Problems with subjective measures include:

- the problem of perception and bias from recent events;
- the problem of retrospective reporting;
- the problem of behavioural measures informing on what really happens.

Although the discussion above may give the feeling that measuring the success of academic start-ups is beset by many problems, the message is more about understanding the limitations of each measure and knowing the exact inferences about performance that can be derived from particular performance measures. On top of that, knowing the exact meaning of a performance measure is very important, as good performance measures might vary across different firms. Compared with start-ups in life sciences, ICT start-ups may grow quickly, as they can bring their product to market faster, with relatively low investments. Life sciences start-ups, on the other hand, need more time to conduct research or apply for patents and comply with safety regulations, such as the FDA. In addition, indicators of success in the early stage of the start-up may be far different from indicators of success in later stages of growth. In the early stage, success indicators could be the number of business ideas identified, or venture plan competitions won. At later stages, the filing of patents or agreements with launching or early customers might be important indicators, and, for a more mature start-up, indicators such as cash flow, sales or employee numbers might be more relevant. As a result, we acknowledge that indicators of success may not only be perceived differently by different stakeholders, but also are different during early growth stages compared with later growth stages. During the early stages of growth the focus is on opportunity identification, while in later stages the focus is on efficiency to become a sustainable firm.

The entrepreneurial ecosystem

Academic start-ups and the transfer of knowledge and technology from academe to industry have received much attention, and various studies have tried to better understand what the triggers are that spark off entrepreneurial behaviour in a region. These research streams often refer to the so-called entrepreneurial ecosystem that represents the elements that should be present in a region to help entrepreneurship flourish. The entrepreneurial ecosystem is related to a large variety of studies, such as the research stream on national innovation systems (e.g. Nelson, 1993; Freeman, 1995) and the research stream on innovative milieux and regional competitiveness (Maillat, 1998). With respect to the entrepreneurial ecosystem, Bahrami and Evans (1995) discuss the Silicon Valley ecosystem (see Figure 7.3). They discuss six components of this system that support the focal firm and make the region attractive and competitive:

1   Universities and research institutes contribute to the focal firm by providing technical knowledge and training young engineers. These institutions also play an important role in the networking and exchange of technology and knowledge between researchers and firms.

2   Venture capital provides the seed funding, specific industry knowledge and networking contacts that help to position and grow the new firm in the market. This is also often referred to as 'smart capital', because it helps the new firm to scale up and get ready for initial public offering or acquisition by an existing large corporate firm.

3   Support infrastructure reflects the necessary services that new firms need during the early stage of development. For instance, these include law firms, recruitment firms, design firms or specific tooling firms; see Box 7.2.

4   Entrepreneurial spirit is more intangible and relates to the culture or mindset of the people in the region. It reflects the willingness of people to accept risk and to engage more proactively in new developments. People with entrepreneurial spirit tend to question the status quo and feel comfortable when uncertainty is relatively high or when change is occurring more often.

5   Lead users are demanding customers that request the latest technology and new business models to implement in their organization. The US Ministry of Defense is mentioned as an important lead user for technology development and new firm development in Silicon Valley. Examples are radar development and the request for fast computing, which led to the development of semiconductors.

6   The talent pool is the flow of professionals who are available and remain in the area. They are the students who leave university, but also the experts who worked temporarily at a specific job in a start-up – for instance, a designer or marketer who has much expertise with launching customers.

Apart from the components of the ecosystem as suggested by Bahrami and Evans, some other elements are considered vital to the emergence of new technology-based start-ups as well. In the US, the Bayh–Dole Act in 1980[3] provided important incentives for commercial activities by universities. This Act gave universities property rights to inventions and technologies that originated from federally funded research. Since this Act, the number of universities in the US that have been involved in knowledge transfer has increased eightfold,

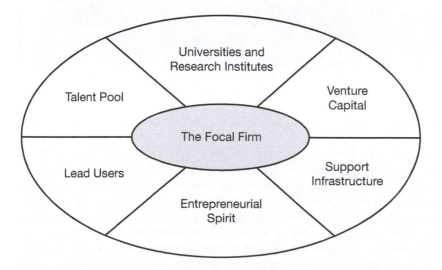

Figure 7.3 Constituents of an entrepreneurial ecosystem (Bahrami and Evans, 1995)

Box 7.2 IDEO design company

The IDEO Company is a design and consultancy company that has helped a large number of existing firms and start-ups to develop their product. The CEO of IDEO, Tim Brown, explains the vision of the company as follows: 'Design thinking is a human-centered approach to innovation that draws from the designer's toolkit to integrate the needs of people, the possibilities of technology, and the requirements for business success'. This approach brings together what is desirable from a human point of view with what is technologically feasible and economically viable. One of the known designs that the company was involved in was the development of the Palm V for 3com.

Image 7.1 Palm V

Source: © Heidi Pollock

and the number of patents filed by universities has increased fourfold. So, the Act clearly created a focus on technology transfer in the US. In Europe, we witness a similar trend, where the emergence of new firms is stimulated by various new regulations, as well as support programmes. These programmes include, for instance, activities aimed at increasing awareness of the possibilities to start a company, stimulating starters through providing them with business coaches, masterclasses and networking events that help to establish a culture in which the entrepreneurial spirit is promoted within universities and among students. However, these programmes also provide more tangible assets, such as accommodation and first-stage grants that support starters in translating their scientific findings into business plans.

Support programmes for academic spin-outs

The examples of Silicon Valley and others have inspired policymakers at regional levels and within universities to set up programmes to support the emergence and growth of academic spin-outs. Since the late 1990s, various programmes have started to create more firms. These programmes are built on raising awareness among students and faculty staff about the possibilities of starting a new firm and providing services and accommodation to help them during their start-up. The support programmes are developed by universities, regional author-ities and private organizations. Whereas regional authorities often provide accommodation and services at lower costs, the university often provides the start-up with specific technological expertise, laboratory space or specific equipment, and the private organizations assist with their networks of contacts and expertise in managing start-ups. The regional authorities and private organizations are often more active in support of the business model development. They help identify and evaluate a business idea and provide access to resources that are necessary during the start-up process.

Despite these support programmes, however, studies have identified that, although a lot of spin-offs are founded, only a very small proportion grow and succeed (Lambert, 2003). Although universities are keen to create spin-out companies, far too few of these become successful companies. It seems that universities are more focused on creating businesses rather than on creating wealth or successful start-ups.

Technology transfer offices and incubation

Beyond the direct support programmes is the entrepreneurial ecosystem, which includes a variety of organizations that can support the academic spin-out. Although they are all relevant to the discussion, technology transfer offices (TTOs) and incubation centres are more important during the early stage of the emergence of the start-up. TTOs work on behalf of a university or research institute to make a bridge between the academic environment and industry. They often initiate and coordinate research projects with industry and negotiate the terms of the contract, the licensing agreement or the transfer of IPR. The main objective of the TTO is to defend the interests of the university by marketing the academic experience and attracting funding for further research. They also articulate the needs of industry and act as broker between the research department and the industrial partner.

We discussed earlier that the deeper interest lies in making the university more valuable to society and providing an opportunity for academe to gain direct industry experience. When a new start-up emerges from the academic institution and uses intellectual property from the academic institution, the TTOs are often also involved in helping the formation and emergence of the start-up, and sometimes they even may take a share in the newly formed start-up. This is often arranged through a holding organization that manages the portfolio of shares in private companies held by the academic institution.

Some of the main challenges that TTOs have to deal with are related to conflicting academic and business incentives. This manifests predominantly in an academic interest in disclosing research findings through academic publications, whereas the business interest lies in not disclosing scientific findings, as they are a source of competitive advantage, and protection is key to staying competitive. Another challenge is the willingness of research groups, but also of TTOs, to transfer scientific findings to larger companies, because this may generate more direct and larger royalty income and may provide opportunities to conduct further contract research for the larger company (Temel *et al.*, 2013).

Some TTOs are very active in disclosing research findings, which cannot be solely attributed to their focus on business interests or on larger organizations. It is also dependent on the effort a TTO puts into the search in academe to find technology that can be disclosed. Scientists tend to focus on research activities and often do not have an incentive to disclose, other than publishing in scientific journals. An active search by the TTO is often required to identify technology that can be protected and licensed to industry. The extent to which the TTO is able to conduct such a search influences the disclosure rate. Also, the TTO's ability to justify the money that is needed for the complex patenting processes and to clarify the potential returns of patenting influences the disclosure rate. Markman *et al.* (2005) have further investigated the variety of roles that TTOs have played with regard to academic spin-outs. Based on interviews with 128 university TTO directors, they identified three different models:

1   The first is the traditional university structure, where the TTO is an integrated part of the traditional administration of the university. The officers are employed by the university, which also provides the funding for its activities. The focus is on generating income through licensing for cash, which makes management of the TTO relatively simple, although it may respond slowly because it is operating within the complex decision cycles of the university.
2   The second model is the non-profit research foundation. In this role, the TTO is a separate entity outside the university structure, with its own independent board. This TTO can be considered as a holding company, with its own budget and a revolving fund to manage and reinvest in the portfolio of spin-outs. The university can have a financial interest in it, but, with this construction, it is not immediately liable for the actions of the TTO. This construction gives more responsibility and incentives to the management of the TTO.
3   The third model is the for-profit model, in which the TTO is more like a private venture extension, and it has an independent CEO who has extensive experience in VC activities and raising capital for start-ups. The TTO has an arm's-length relationship with the university and thus provides the least liability for the university, while the flexibility for the TTO is large. Although the latter model has many advantages for spin-out companies, it may experience more of the problems of incongruence between the various incentive systems and goals that exist in the academic environment compared with industry.

Business incubation and support

Based on the type of support they provide, their objectives and the involvement they have in the start-ups, four main groups of business incubators can be distinguished:

1   The publicly funded business incubator aims to contribute to regional development and create new jobs; this type often has a non-profit model for managing the incubator and is sponsored either by the government or by different institutions and associations.
2   The university-funded incubator has a special focus on the commercialization of academic knowledge, the employment of graduates and the creation of spin-out ventures. It often engages more actively in seeking faculty–industry cooperation. This type of incubator often focuses on technology development and, because it often concerns technologies that are unproven and have high risk, they tend to be referred to as high-tech incubators.

3   The privately funded incubator has a goal to seek a return on invested capital. It can have a similar business model to that of VC funds, investing in a portfolio of start-ups and develop a revolving fund that generates income for the investors. These start-ups are often similar to those in the university incubator, but they are more risky and need further development before an existing firm will incorporate them. Some of the privately funded incubators have more of a real-estate appreciation and have a business model to provide office space to tenants. This is also referred to as the property incubator.

4   The fourth incubator is the corporate incubator. This incubator focuses mainly on investing in technology R&D and new markets that the corporation will eventually integrate into its main operation, either through the creation of new subsidiaries or inclusion within existing business units.

5   The fifth model is more a hybrid incubator that is based on a private–public partnership and has a mixture of goals and funding schemes.

The benefit of start-up support

Start-ups have some major disadvantages related to their newness and smallness. The problem of newness can refer to the novelty of technology itself, the novelty of the product or service and even the newness of the firm to the market or the new working conditions for the start-up team.

•   When the technology is very new, then the basic principles may not have been proven to work well, and problems such as the robustness of the technology in the operating environment or the scalability of the technology may lead to delays in market introduction and increase the costs of development. In particular, when the start-up operates at the edge of new knowledge development, there are few technology experts and little reference they can rely upon.

•   The liability of 'newness' is even more relevant when the knowledge to be transferred is new to the market and the start-up needs to convince partners and future clients in the market about the feasibility and added value of the new technology. The novelty of the products and services to the market makes it difficult for the start-up to explain the benefit, quality or robustness to the users. The users may also need to change the way they use the product or service, which requires them to learn new ways of doing things or unlearn the old way of doing things and, thereby, increases the switching costs. When switching costs on the clients' side are high, it is less likely that they will take up the new technology. This is even more the case when the new technology is associated with higher levels of risk. Either new technology that has not been proven or a new company that is lacking a track record of past success may induce these higher levels of risk.

•   This brings us to the newness of the start-up as a new organization, which makes it difficult to convince customers and business partners of its credibility as a firm capable of carrying out the tasks it promises, but also that it is financially stable enough and credible to sign contracts with. The start-up not only lacks a track record of customers, which makes it difficult for potential business partners to assess a new firm's credibility, but the end-users may also question the quality of the new firm's products or services and its organizational stability. Will the start-up be able to provide service updates or spare parts in future, or will it cease to exist and go bankrupt? The implications may even be broader, and the start-up may be involved in activities that lack social approval. One example is Herman the Bull, in the Netherlands; see Box 7.3.

- In addition, start-up entrepreneurs often find themselves in new roles and different working conditions. They have been researchers before and now need to change their mindset from a research focus towards a commercial focus. A strong focus on transferring the scientific finding to a commercial goal is needed, which requires a shift to market and start-up activities, and academic entrepreneurs increasingly find themselves in new roles.

Box 7.3 Herman the Bull

Herman the Bull was the first genetically modified bull in the world and lived between 16 December 1990 and 2 April 2004. The bull was named after its scientific creator, Herman Ziegeler, and was an experiment by the Dutch start-up Gene Pharming (today named Pharming). The bull was modified with human gene coding (DNA) to produce offspring among which were cows that could produce a specific multifunctional protein (lactoferrin). The idea was that the cows would produce specific baby milk that could help cure or relieve patients with specific diseases. This proposition raised great opposition in society, and several stakeholder groups opposed the idea and further development. As a result, the project was terminated by Dutch law, and it was demanded by law that the bull be slaughtered. However, the Dutch agriculture minister provided an amnesty, under the condition that Herman did not have any offspring, and he survived until his death at the site of the Dutch National Museum of Natural History, where he is still on display today.

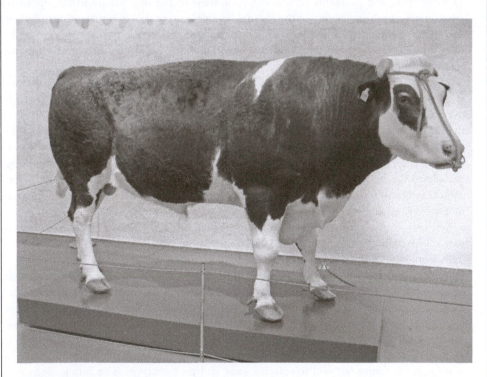

Image 7.2 Herman the Bull
Source: © Peter Maas

Besides problems related to newness, high-tech start-ups also experience liabilities of smallness due to a lack of resources. These can manifest in the absence of slack resources or economies of scale.

- The absence of slack resources is a result of the relatively small number of assets and thin financial base. Start-ups often lack the slack resources that are needed to be flexible and tap into opportunities that emerge. New opportunities often need immediate action and investments, which are often not available for start-ups. Also, to be able to take advantage of new opportunities, start-ups cannot rely on their current employees, who are either needed to carry out current operations or lack specific knowledge. They cannot, like incumbent companies do, make internal people available through rearranging tasks or attracting external people.
- Furthermore, because of the smallness of the start-up, it cannot benefit from the advantages that economies of scale would provide. Small production numbers or more tailored services make individual products and service agreements more expensive compared with those of large, existing organizations that produce larger quantities and service more clients. Also, the start-up may not have access to efficient production facilities or efficient distribution channels. The smallness of the start-up will put it in an unfavourable negotiation position.

Added value of support

Support activities provided by facilitating organizations such as incubators, technology transfer offices, entrepreneurship centres and regional authorities, can help start-ups to over-come the liabilities of newness and smallness. The support can manifest in various ways. We can conceptualize the support in terms of tangible and intangible assets. Tangible assets refer to all assets that can be physically observed, such as the provision of explicit resources, e.g. finance or accommodation, whereas intangible assets are the assets that cannot be physic-ally touched, such as expertise and coaching. Most often, it is practical to define support in terms of physical resources, networking, expert advice and moral support:

- Physical resources can vary from accommodation and reception support to equipment for product development. The latter includes lab facilities and specific tools, which may be very expensive for start-ups, and they often need these resources for a limited time. Spin-out companies generally lack a strong financial position to acquire these resources. Paying the market price would be too costly, and therefore support facilities may provide these resources to share or to use for a period of time. Incubators can lower these costs or be more flexible in providing the assets when needed.
- Networking support provides access to certain contacts. Alliance partners can directly provide information and knowledge that can improve the start-up's learning curve. As the source of entrepreneurial opportunities depends, in part, on the distribution of information in society, it is important for start-ups to interact with people and get exposed to new information, the lack of which can inhibit potential opportunities. Consequently, the extensive academic and industry network can help the academic entrepreneur in the process of identification of entrepreneurial opportunities. Furthermore, a strong relationship with the university makes it easier to attract finance from university funds, but, at the same time, investors such as informal or 'angel' investors may not always be enthusiastic about a university involvement in the start-up. It may slow down decision-making, and university officials are often not considered industry experts.

- Expert advice is the provision of expertise and coaching, such as guidance and advice. In some cases, this can also involve direct help to relieve the start-up of administrative and legal tasks and help it focus on its major activities. Furthermore, the expert advice can assist the spin-off in negotiations when setting up business contracts, and technological expertise can help spin-offs to translate research findings into commercial products.

These supportive functions can be found at a variety of institutions. Often, a single institution fulfils multiple support functions; however, some institutions have more expertise. For instance, the investors in the start-up firm can be a valuable source of capital, knowledge and networks of industry contacts. The government is often a provider of subsidies that can help start-ups with the means to carry out research and development. Universities often provide start-ups with expert knowledge, access to equipment and students who can work for the start-up. Incubator organizations give access to flexible accommodation, a network of start-ups and coaches who help develop the business plans and identify opportunities.

Rebound effects of support

Although the incubator may provide the start-up with support, a criticism is that, if it is not well organized, support doesn't help much and may even have a negative effect on the success and survival of the start-up in the end. This argument is rooted in the fact that university and incubation centres do not directly operate in the industry the spin-off is active in or is trying to enter and, therefore, can offer little help to increase the competitive edge of the spin-off.

Although accommodation can lower the cost function of the start-up, at the same time it removes start-up firms from the harsh commercial environment where economic rationality and price-based decision-making dominate. More important is the argument that support only pays off if it helps the start-up to focus on the commercialization of the scientific finding. Staying in the research group where the spin-off originated may influence its tendency to focus on further scientific research and technology development. Also, staying close to the research group may offer easy access to networks of academic colleagues and friends. However, discussions with ex-colleagues are most likely to involve the improvement of core technologies and research publications. The products that are eventually developed may achieve quality and performance levels beyond what commercial partners demand. Furthermore, relationships with existing academic contacts can hinder the development of new relationships that start-ups need to build with customers, suppliers and competitors. Even if the spin-out focuses on commercialization, when investment in a patent is made too early, it may induce a myopic mindset focused on exploiting the patent and getting returns on the investment. The patent, however, may not offer the full protection for the product that the market needs. As a result, a new investment in an updated patent may be needed, or the spin-out may try to exploit the present patent, precluding the possibility of further technological development for more appropriate market opportunities. When we look at support more in terms of what the benefit is, then we can distinguish a variety of support functions:

- The first support function for start-ups is *cost reductions*. These are focused on the cost structure of the company. Examples here are the availability of accommodation for start-ups, sharing office space or equipment, tax reductions, and subsidies that often take a long period before they are obtained or there is little chance of obtaining them, such as those provided by research councils, tax refunds or research subsidies. The idea is that, when the cost structure is lower for the start-up, it is easier for the start-up to make money available for its operations. Also, it makes the founding of the firm easier by taking away a lot of negotiation on location costs, arranging the standard equipment and facilities such as furniture, Internet connection, etc.

- *Network access* can be a second support function. This involves getting access to knowledgeable people, who share experience and provide role models, or incentives for those start-ups that are not yet that mature. Through this type of support, the start-up gets access to specific technological expertise or equipment. Also, network contacts in the business environment, such as coaches and investment managers, for instance, can help identify and evaluate a business idea and indirectly, through referrals, provide access to resources that are necessary during the start-up process. In principle, this type of support is not directly involved with the start-up and is more at arm's length. It provides the start-up with directions and incentives, and the start-up can decide how to benefit from them.

- *Competitive agility* is a type of support that is directly aimed at helping the start-up with its competitive position in the market. This often involves directly interfering with the start-up's activities and a closer relationship between the supporting organization and the start-up in order to understand how the competitive strength of the start-up can be improved. It can be experts who are directly involved in the business activities and help the start-up in certain fields of expertise, e.g. technology development and marketing activities – for instance, supporting the start-up in its access to important stakeholders and clients and taking part in the negotiations. Supporting the competitive agility of the start-up can also be achieved without direct involvement of the supporting organization. For instance, it may involve helping the start-up with certain equipment (specific tools and a laboratory) that the start-up urgently needs for its core activities. These resources improve the competitive position of the spin-off and fundamentally contribute to companies' competitive advantage. In other words, the support that is provided helps the start-up to build and develop resources and capabilities that are valuable, rare, imperfectly imitable and non-substitutable, according to what Barney *et al.* (2001) argue contributes the competitive advantage of the firm.

As a result, the support of spin-offs needs to be carefully balanced and focused on activities that help the commercialization of the scientific finding and cautious in helping the spin-off in lowering the cost function. Moreover, the detrimental effect of the parent support and the incubator as a buffer to the rugged landscape of the external market may eventually affect the spin-off. The university incubator provides a cushion against the commercial reality of the competitive marketplace. This can cause severe problems for the firm when it leaves the incubator. This raises the question of whether the university parent may also be a hindrance.

Chapter summary

In this chapter, we have discussed what academic spin-outs are, how they contribute to society, and what the main difficulties are that they face in their early development. These insights help entrepreneurs to better understand what it takes to start a spin-out company, but also, for policymakers in regional or university institutes, they show the role these companies play. This also helps to fulfil the goals those regions and universities have, such as regional growth and technology transfer. University–industry relations in the context of regional innovation systems and knowledge exchange are of growing importance. Role models such as Silicon Valley are often studied and act as examples for various regions to support entrepreneurship. In particular, the interaction between SMEs and universities has tremendous potential for regional economic growth and job creation. Local SMEs and universities can benefit from their geographical, social and cultural proximity, which is considered important to facilitate knowledge transfer, and knowledge spillovers, which in turn augment learning processes, innovation output and, eventually, regional competitive advantage. Universities and regional policymakers have recognized the benefits and increasingly initiate small-firm support programmes and set up incubator practices for new start-ups to flourish. These programmes have evolved differently, and their best practices have been discussed in this chapter as well.

Study questions

1   Explain the various ways scientific findings are brought to the market.
2   Discuss what the (dis-)advantages are of technology transfer to spin-outs for research groups.
3   Imagine you have to defend your business plan against a jury of corporate investors: what do you think they will consider relevant before making an investment in your company?
4   In your near region, what are the main components of the entrepreneurial ecosystem that you can identify?
5   For a university that has little experience in stimulating entrepreneurship and supporting spin-offs, what role would you advise for the technology transfer office?

Notes

1   See www.siliconbeat.com/2015/01/21/silicon-valley-ranks-3rd-globally-in-gdp-per-capita/?doing_wp_cron=1424770873.7157011032104492187500 (accessed 12 August 2015).
2   The traitorous eight are Julius Blank, Victor Grinich, Jean Hoerni, Eugene Kleiner, Jay Last, Gordon Moore, Robert Noyce and Sheldon Roberts.
3   'Patent ownership and federal research and development (R&D): A discussion on the Bayh–Dole Act and the Stevenson–Wydler Act', United States Congressional Research Service, 11 December 2000.

References

Allen, D. N. and McCluskey, R. (1990). Structure, policy, services and performance in the business incubator industry. *Entrepreneurship Theory & Practice*. 15(2): 61–77.

Bahrami, H. and Evans, S. (1995). Flexible recycling and high-technology entrepreneurship. *California Management Review*. 37(3): 62–89.

Barney, J., Wright, M. and Ketchen, D. J. (2001). The resource-based view of the firm: Ten years after 1991. *Journal of Management*. 27(6): 625–41.

Blair, D. and Hitchens, D. (1998). *Campus Companies – UK and Ireland*. Aldershot, UK: Ashgate.

Cohen, W. (2000). Taking care of business. *ASEE Prism Online*. January: 1–5.

Cooper, A. C. (1972). Spin-off companies and technical entrepreneurship. *IEEE Transactions on Engineering*. 1: EM-18.

Covin, J. G. and Slevin, D. P. (1989). Strategic management of small firms in hostile and benign environments. *Strategic Management Journal*. 10(1): 75–87.

Franklin, S., Lockett, A. and Wright, M. (2001). Academic and surrogate entrepreneurs in university spin-out companies. *Journal of Technology Transfer*. 26(1/2): 127–41.

Freeman, C. (1995). The national system of innovation in historical perspective. *Cambridge Journal of Economics*. 19: 5–24.

Lambert, R. (2003). *Lambert review of business–university collaboration: Final report*. University of Illinois at Urbana-Champaign's Academy for Entrepreneurial Leadership Historical Research Reference in Entrepreneurship. Available at: http://ssrn.com/abstract=1509981 (accessed 12 August 2015).

Mahar, J. F. and Coddington, D. C. (1965). The scientific complex – proceed with caution. *Harvard Business Review*. 43: 140–55.

Maillat, D. (1998). Innovative milieux and new generations of regional policies. *Entrepreneurship and Regional Development*. 10: 1–16.

Markman, G. D., Phan, P. H., Balkin, D. B. and Gianiodis, P. T. (2005). Entrepreneurship and university-based technology transfer. *Journal of Business Venturing*. 20(2): 241–63.

Mustar, P. (1997). Spin-off enterprises – How French academics create high-tech companies: Conditions for success and failure. *Science & Public Policy*. 24(1): 37–43.

Nelson, R. (1993). *National Innovation Systems: A comparative analysis*. Oxford, UK: Oxford University Press.

Pirnay, F., Surlemont, B. and Nlemvo, F. (2003). Toward a typology of university spin-offs. *Small Business Economics*. 21: 355–69.

Radosevich, R. (1995). A model for entrepreneurial spin-offs from public technology sources. *International Journal of Technology Management*. 10(7/8): 879–93.

Rasmussen, E, Moen, Ø. and Gulbrandsen, M. (2006). Initiatives to promote commercialization of university knowledge. *Technovation*. 26(4): 518–33.

Roberts, E. B. (1991). *Entrepreneurs in High Technology – Lessons from MIT and beyond*. New York: Oxford University Press.

Roberts, E. B. and Malone, D. E. (1996). Policies and structures for spinning off new companies from research and development organizations. *R&D Management*. 26(1): 17–48.

Rogers, M. E. and Larsen, J. K. (1984). *Silicon Valley Fever: Growth of high-technology culture*. New York: Basic Books.

Shane, S. A. (2004). *Academic Entrepreneurship: University spin-offs and wealth creation*. Northampton, MA: Edward Elgar.

Shane, S. A. and Stuart, T. (2002). Organizational endowments and the performance of university start-ups. *Management Science*. 48(1): 154–70.

Steffensen, M., Rogers, E. M. and Speakman, K. (1999). Spin-offs from research centers at a research university. *Journal of Business Venturing*. 15: 93–111.

Stevenson, H. H. and Gumpert, D. E. (1985). The heart of entrepreneurship. *Harvard Business Review*. March–April: 85–94.

Temel, S., Scholten, V.E., Akdeniz, R. C., Fortuin, F., Omta, S.W.F. (2013). University–industry collaboration in Turkish SMEs: Investigation of a U-shaped relationship. *The International Journal of Entrepreneurship and Innovation*, 14: 103–115.

Vohora, A., Wright, M. and Lockett, A. (2004). Critical junctures in the development of university high-tech spin-out companies. *Research Policy*. 33: 147–75.

Wissema, J. G. (2009). *Towards the Third Generation University: Managing the university in transition*. Cheltenham, UK: Edward Elgar.

Wright, M., Vohora, A. and Lockett, A. (2004). The formation of high-tech university spin-outs through joint ventures. *Journal of Technology Transfer*. 29(3–4): 287–310.

Further reading

Edquist, C. (1997). *Systems of Innovation: Technologies, institutions, and organizations*. London: Pinter.

Nelson, R. (ed.) (1993). *National Innovation Systems: A comparative analysis*. New York/Oxford, UK: Oxford University Press.

8   Lead users for market entry

Successful products

With a long line of highly successful products, it seems that anything Apple brings to the market virtually sells itself. Even minor product improvements create the hype of a brand new product that it appears everybody must have. When the iPhone 5 was introduced in September 2012, people queued up in long lines in front of Apple stores worldwide, just so they would be the first ones to own the latest model of that gadget. Supplies were low during the first week, encouraging impatient people to wait in line for a long time or else miss out on getting their hands on the new iPhone before the majority of buyers. After a few weeks, the hype had passed by, and things returned to normal. Apple has perfected its marketing strategy to the point of actually abusing its loyal customers. When the iPad 2 went on sale, on 11 March 2011, the Apple store in Palo Alto, CA, was open for business as usual. Inside the store, the iPad 2 was on display, and people could play around with it as much as they liked. However, they could not buy one yet, because the sale of the new iPad would start only later that day, at 5 p.m. sharp. That is why people had been queueing up all day in front of the store, patiently waiting until it was 5 p.m., and they could finally buy an iPad 2. The line stretched for many blocks, across intersections and around corners. It was a warm, sunny day, and people had been in line for many hours. This crazy phenomenon triggered the interest of the media, who came to take pictures and shoot videos for the local and national newspapers and news stations. In this way, Apple generates free publicity at the expense of its customers. Analysts look at the length of the line on the first day of sales as an indication of the expected success of the new product. Following that reasoning, the relatively short lines for the introduction of the iPad Mini (2 November 2012) predicted that this new device would not be as successful as its full-sized sister. That prediction turned out to be wrong, because the iPad Mini was not merely a *smaller* iPad but, more importantly, it was a *cheaper* iPad that was now affordable to more people.

Figure 8.1 shows how various products and services contributed to Apple's revenue from 2009 to 2013. Clearly, the iPhone is Apple's best-selling product, followed by the iPad and the Macintosh (in almost equal amounts). Notice how the introduction of a new model iPhone and iPad gives a huge boost to the sales of these products in the next quarter, only for sales to decline again in the following quarter. However, there is a continuous net growth in sales over time, which is one of the reasons why, as of 2014, Apple was the most valuable brand in the world (US$118.9 billion, up 21 per cent from 2013; Interbrand, 2014). In January 2015, Apple announced its financial results for the first fiscal quarter 2015 and posted a record quarterly revenue of US$74.6 billion and a record quarterly net profit of US$18 billion, overtaking ExxonMobil's 2012 record of US$17.9 billion as the highest quarterly profit ever attained.

Diffusion of innovations

Exactly how do innovations diffuse into the market? Where do the customers come from, and how do they decide to adopt the innovation (buy the product)? Intuitively, you imagine that the process probably starts hesitantly. Then, at some magic point in time, it takes off, and sales increase dramatically. However, as sales cannot increase indefinitely, there will come the inevitable point where sales must slow down, then decrease, and finally stop entirely. Unlike common goods, such as potatoes, toothpaste and socks, which consumers buy throughout their entire lives, innovative products have a finite life cycle. Everett Rogers (1931–2004) wrote the definitive and groundbreaking textbook on how innovations diffuse into the market, *Diffusion of Innovations*, the first edition of which was published in 1962. The pioneering work in diffusion theory was the 1943 study by Iowa State University professor Bryce Ryan and his graduate student Neil Gross on the adoption of hybrid seed corn by farmers in two Iowa communities (Ryan and Gross, 1943). Hybrid seed was an

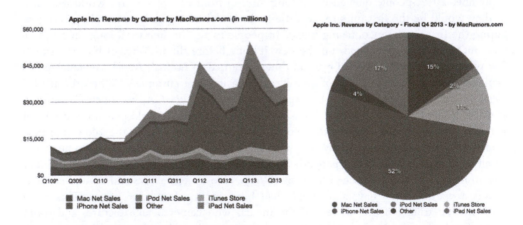

Figure 8.1 How Apple products and services contribute to its quarterly revenues (2009–13). The iPhone (150 million units sold in 2013) is responsible for 52% of Apple's fourth-quarter revenues in 2013, whereas the iPod contributed only 2%. Note that, in the first quarter of 2009, the iPod and the iPhone generated comparable revenues. The introduction of new models of the iPhone and iPad boosts the sales of these products in the next quarter

Source: MacRumors, 2013

Box 8.1 Failed Apple products

Image 8.1 Failed Apple products: Lisa
(1983)

Source: © Matthew Pearce

Image 8.2 Failed Apple products: G4
Cube (2000)

Source: © Carl Berkeley

Image 8.3 Failed Apple products: Portable
Mac (1989)

Source: © Álvaro Ibáñez

Image 8.4 Failed Apple products: Newton
(1993)

Source: © Ralf Pfeifer

With a seemingly endless stream of highly successful Apple products, it is easy to forget that the company has had its fair share of failing products as well. In 1983, Apple introduced the Lisa computer. The original sticker price was US$9,995, which roughly equates to US$21,000 today. Although the Lisa was a spectacular step forward in personal computing, the price tag was simply too high to make it a success. In 2000, Apple marketed the G4 Cube, a full-powered Mac in an extremely small, 8 × 8 × 8-inch cube, created by design guru Jonathan Ive. The first portable Macintosh computer was as big as a briefcase and weighed 16 lb. It had 1 MB of RAM, a black-and-white LCD screen and a full-sized keyboard. As with the Lisa, the hefty price tag (US$6,500) was the main reason the first portable Mac was not a commercial success. It was discontinued in 1991, barely 17 months after its release. Then there was the ill-fated Newton Personal Digital Assistant, introduced in 1993. A stylish, handheld organizer, it was far ahead of its time and could perform handwriting recognition of notes that you scribbled on to the screen with a stylus. According to John Sculley, CEO of Apple from 1983 to 1993, Apple spent US$100 million on the development of the Newton. It was a spectacular gadget, but, unfortunately, the handwriting recognition was flawed. Because of this inaccuracy, the Newton became known as a dud – a reputation that it never recovered from. The decisive death blow may well have been delivered by Gary Trudeau's Doonesbury cartoon from August 1993, in which Mike uses 'a digital assistant' that resembles the Apple Newton. When he scribbles, 'Hello, J.J., how are you?', the device recognizes his handwriting as 'Hell jars, noward, yoyo?', to which J.J. reacts with the deadly response, 'First generation, is it?'.

agricultural innovation developed by scientists at Iowa State University. It had several important benefits over existing corn seed, such as a 20 per cent increased harvest and better drought resistance. It was also attractive from a commercial point of view, as farmers had to buy new hybrid seed every year, because the harvested corn did not possess the hybrid characteristics. It was made available to Iowa farmers in 1928. In 1941, Ryan and Gross set out to investigate precisely how this innovation had been adopted by the farmers. Through personal interviews, they traced when each farmer had first adopted the hybrid seed corn, and how he had learned about it. Figure 8.2 shows the original graph from the 1943 paper by Ryan and Gross, in which the number of new adopters per year and the cumulative number of adopters since 1927 are plotted. The number of new adopters has roughly a Gaussian distribution, whereas the cumulative number of adopters has a distinct S-shape. The sample consisted of 259 farmers, and the data show that the hybrid seed corn innovation reached 99 per cent adoption after only 14 years.

The S-shaped curve is characteristic of the diffusion pattern of innovations: a slow start (only a few new hybrid seed adopters in each of the first 5 years), followed by a sharp increase, where as many as sixty-one farmers adopted the new seed in 1937 (24 per cent of all farmers in the sample), and finally a tapering off as the market becomes saturated. When all the farmers use the new seed, there can be no more new adopters, by definition. In this case, not all farmers adopted the hybrid corn seed: two out of the total of 259 farmers did not convert. Thousands of similar studies have been carried out for a wide range of innovations, and the adoption rate always has an S-curve shape. Figure 8.3 shows the diffusion rates of various technological innovations. Although each case follows an

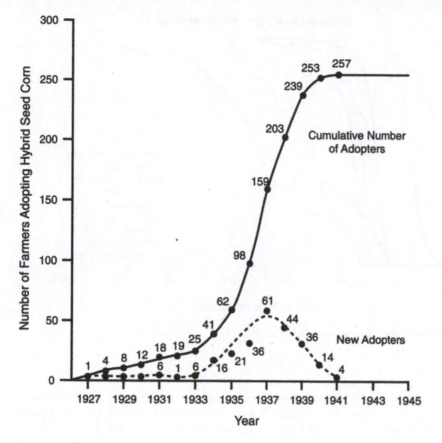

Figure 8.2 The number of new adopters per year and the cumulative number of adopters of hybrid seed corn by farmers in two Iowa communities since 1927

Source: Ryan and Gross, 1943

S-curve, there are distinct differences in the speed of the adoption (the steepness of the curve and the length of the leading tail). For example, it took 80 years from the introduction of the automobile before a 50 per cent ownership level was reached. Compare that with the diffusion of the PC, which required merely 20 years to reach that same penetration. More recent innovations such as the mobile phone and the Internet (not plotted in this graph) diffused even faster. Some innovations, such as the video cassette recorder (VCR), took a long time before the adoption suddenly increased sharply. This can be attributed to the invention of the integrated circuit (IC, or 'chip'), which lowered prices dramatically so that many more people could afford a VCR. Sometimes, the diffusion of one innovation depends on another innovative technology that allows for a quantum leap in price or performance. The first mobile phones were big and heavy, had a poor battery life and were very expensive. Microchips and mass production improved the performance (smaller devices that required less energy), and improved battery technology allowed for smaller, more powerful batteries. The combination of these improvements made mobile phones smaller, lighter, longer lasting, more user-friendly and cheaper. At that point in time, some 20 years after the initial market introduction, the diffusion of the mobile phone entered the fast-rising vertical part of the S-shape.

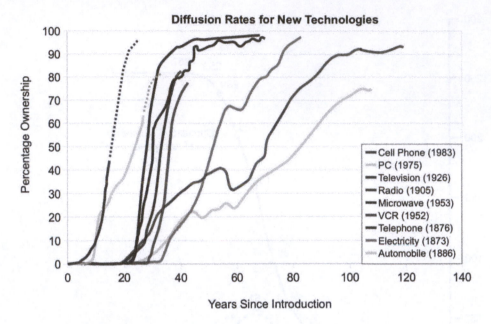

Figure 8.3 Diffusion rates of new technologies in the USA
Source: Brimelow, 1997

Diffusion of Innovations is one of the best textbooks in the field of innovation and entrepreneurship. Rogers discusses at length all the factors that influence the (rate of) adoption or rejection of an innovation. He defines five categories of 'variables determining the rate of adoption'. The most relevant category for the present discussion is his Category I: 'Perceived attributes of innovations'. Table 8.1 lists the five attributes in this category.

Customer segments

The observed pattern of diffusion – the S-curve – has its origin in the underlying Gaussian distribution of the number of new adopters over time. As was already evident from the relatively small sample of Iowa farmers, there are only a few people who adopt an innovation right away, and there are some people who are the very last ones to adopt it or even never adopt it at all. The motives and (personal) characteristics of these two customer segments

Table 8.1 The five perceived attributes of innovations (Category I of the variables determining the rate of adoption of innovations; Rogers, 1995)

Attribute	Description
1 Relative advantage	Competitive advantage over existing and competitive products
2 Compatibility	How well does it match (fulfil) customer needs?
3 Complexity	Innovations that are perceived as complex are more slowly adopted
4 Trialability	Innovations that can be tried before buying are adopted faster
5 Observability	Innovations that are more visible to others will be adopted faster

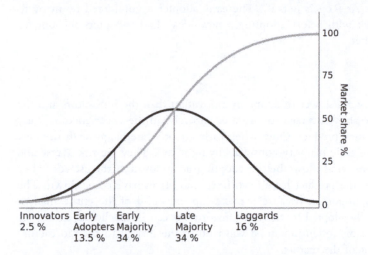

Figure 8.4 The diffusion of innovations according to Rogers (2003). When successive groups of consumers adopt an innovation (black curve), the market share (grey curve) will eventually reach the saturation level

Source: Wikipedia

are quite different. In between these extremes, we find the majority of customers. Assuming that the (theoretical) diffusion pattern for innovations is a perfect Gaussian distribution, Rogers subdivided the bell-shaped curve into five segments (see Figure 8.4), which he labelled as five customer segments: innovators, early adopters, early majority, late majority and laggards. Each segment makes up a specific percentage of the total population, and the individuals in each segment share a number of behavioural characteristics.

Innovators

At the leading end of the Gaussian distribution, we find the innovators: people who are the first ones to adopt an innovation. Although 'innovators' is a somewhat misleading name (after all, they did not *create* the innovation), it refers to their role of being essential in getting an innovation to the (mass) market. Innovators do not wait for other people to try the new product first so that they may learn from their experiences. They are willing to accept the risk of small imperfections that occur in many first-generation innovations. Generally, innovators are young people with sufficient financial liquidity, they interact with other innovators and they have a high tolerance for initial glitches in the product. Innovators are skilful in overcoming or solving these problems and are capable of using a new product without a manual, through experience, educated guesses and, if all else fails, trial and error. Innovators make up only 2.5 per cent of the total market.

Early adopters

This group too is generally made up of the young, well educated and financially well-to-do. Early adopters play an important role as opinion leaders. For an innovation to reach the early and late majority segments of the market, it is of crucial importance what the early adopters think of it. As Rogers puts it, 'The early adopter is considered by many to be the individual to check with before adopting a new idea'. Early adopters account for 13.5 per cent of the market.

Early majority

Individuals in this category are slower to adopt an innovation than the innovators and the early adopters. They have above-average social status and rely on the experiences of early adopters before buying a new product. Only when early adopters are happy with the new product will people in the early majority consider buying it too. They are risk averse and like to see which way the wind blows before adopting an innovation themselves. They wait until early glitches in the product have been fixed and prices have come down. The early majority category is important because it makes up one-third of the entire market. When an innovation is fully adopted by the early majority, it can be labelled as successful. As a result, many competitors (often imitators) will rush to the market to try and capture the remaining 50 per cent of the market.

Late majority

The people in this group are more hesitant to adopt an innovation than the early majority. They are sceptical and cautious and have fewer financial resources than the people in the previous categories. Often, peer pressure is a powerful mechanism that persuades them to adopt an innovation that has been around for several years already ('What? You don't have a smartphone yet? How on earth can you survive?'). The moment of adoption by the late majority usually coincides with considerably lower prices, because many competitors have entered the market. Like the early majority, the late majority makes up 34 per cent of the total market. At this stage of the product life cycle, real innovative companies are already targeting innovators and early adopters for the next generation of their product. For example, the Apple iPad was introduced in April 2010. Less than one year later, in March 2011, Apple released the iPad 2. New models followed in rapid succession: the iPad 3, in March 2012; the iPad 4 and iPad Mini, in November 2012; the iPad Air and iPad Mini 2, in November 2013; and the iPad Air 2 and iPad Mini 3, in October 2014.

Laggards

There are always people who are the last to embrace a new idea. In some cases, this is motivated by a fear of 'something new' – 'Things are good the way they are; why change?' – but often it is a rather irrational stubbornness. Laggards often resist change and postpone the inevitable as long as possible. Eventually, the system will defeat them, as the old way of doing things will disappear. In most of the Western world, you can no longer send a telex or a fax, get TV reception using an analogue aerial or pay with a paper cheque. In these cases, laggards are forced to upgrade their technology base to the Internet, digital or cable TV and debit cards. Laggards account for 16 per cent of the market.

In Figure 8.4, the Gaussian distribution covering the five categories is plotted, together with the accumulated percentage of the market share they constitute. The maximum market share is 100 per cent (by definition), but it is not always immediately clear what that encompasses. For example, when television sets were introduced, 100 per cent of the market was understood as one TV in every household. However, when TVs got cheaper and smaller, many households bought additional sets for the bedroom, the kitchen or the kids' rooms. Suddenly, the size of the market doubled or tripled. Nowadays, it is rare to find just one TV set in a household. This is a common phenomenon that should not be overlooked when estimating the size of the market. As soon as the price of an innovation drops significantly, the potential to sell more items increases dramatically, even for very expensive products such as cars. This market expansion usually occurs in the late majority stage of the diffusion process. In 2011, the number of mobile phones in the US (328 million) exceeded the US population (315 million; Kang, 2011), and the average US household (of 2.6 people) had an average of twenty-four electronic gadgets.

Crossing the chasm

The five consumer segments that make up the Gaussian distribution and cumulative S-curve shown in Figure 8.4 appear to be continuous and smoothly transition from one segment to the next. Is the distinction between these segments really well defined, and are the transitions truly smooth? Figure 8.3 indicated that the diffusion curves created from real data are not always perfectly continuous and smooth. Some S-curves, such as the cumulative adoption rate of the telephone, even show a dip in the percentage of ownership. In this case, that can be traced back to the Second World War. Apart from such dramatic incidents, there appear to be no flat segments in the S-curve that would indicate that sales have stopped. Only at the very beginning (no sales yet, the product has just been introduced) and at the very end of the life cycle (no more sales, the market is saturated) is the S-curve flat. Other than that, sales progress more or less continuously (give or take a few bumps along the way), which indicates a gradual transition from one consumer segment to the next. However, we note that these graphs depict highly successful products. Many products fail, and their diffusion patterns resemble incomplete S-curves, sometimes barely progressing from flat to rising. What went wrong? What distinguishes failed products from successful products? The short answer is that failed products did not succeed in selling to the majority of the customers in that market. That begs the question whether there are mechanisms at work that frustrate the transition from the early adopter stage into the early majority phase.

Geoffrey Moore (1991/2014) was the first to point out that high-tech products face a potentially fatal discontinuity in the adoption curve between the early adopters and the early majority. There are fundamental differences between innovators and early adopters on the one hand and the early majority on the other hand. Their expectations are different, and their resilience to deal with a less than perfect product creates a discontinuity (which Moore coined a 'chasm') between the two consumer groups (see Figure 8.5). The main difference between the two populations is that innovators and early adopters are technology enthusiasts who are interested in performance and generally self-reliant in dealing with new products, whereas the early majority and beyond want foolproof solutions that increase convenience. As an example, consider a sophisticated piece of innovative software that is developed by a start-up company. Innovators will jump on the new product the minute it hits the market. The early majority waits a little longer, but eventually they too are convinced of the added value that this new software offers. However, to reach the next group of customers, the early majority, requires a lot more effort from the start-up than the earlier adopters needed. The software has to be nearly flawless, as the early majority is generally unable to cope with a buggy product. There should be clear user manuals that deal with everything from installation to problem-solving. Whereas innovators and early adopters often intuitively find out how a new product works, the early majority and beyond

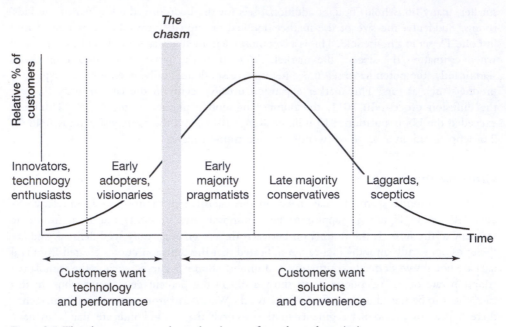

Figure 8.5 The chasm separates the early adopters from the early majority

Source: www.leighdrogen.com

require tutorials and step-by-step instruction. They also require ample customer support, with informative websites and telephone help desks that can be reached 24/7 to answer questions and solve problems. The majority segment wants practical solutions and enhanced convenience, not puzzles and challenges.

In his book *Crossing the Chasm* (1991/2014), Moore analyses the characteristics of the populations on either side of the chasm and describes strategies to overcome this barrier, including choosing the right target market (vertical), the most suitable distribution channel and optimal pricing. Although Moore makes a good case for the existence of a chasm in high-tech markets, Rogers does not agree that there is a discontinuity between the early adopters and the early majority. He therefore rejects the concept of the chasm:

> Pronounced breaks in the innovativeness continuum do not occur between each of the five categories [. . .] On the contrary, innovativeness, if measured properly, is a continuous variable and there are no sharp breaks or discontinuities between adjacent adopter categories (although there are important differences between them).
>
> (Rogers, 2003, pp. 263, 282)

Obviously, Rogers is right when it concerns successful products for which the S-shaped diffusion curves contain no flat segments. However, that merely indicates that the companies behind these products overcame the chasm, which is the precise reason that they were successful products. For many unsuccessful products, existence of the chasm is a likely explanation for their failure in the mass market. Recognizing that the chasm is a real threat to the success of a new product (especially a high-tech product) should be an essential part of the marketing strategy in the early phases of market penetration.

Sources of innovation

The theory of the diffusion of innovations provides a solid explanation of how an innovation is gradually adopted by subsequent customer segments, each with their own characteristics in terms of demands and expectations. But what happens at the very beginning of this process? How does an innovation start its life? Who are the very first people to buy a brand new product that has not proven itself in the market yet? For some innovations, specifically system innovations that require several concurrent innovations, this problem is aggravated. For example, who bought the first fax machine? And you first need an electricity grid before you can sell any light bulbs. Edison was well aware of this dependency and put a lot of effort into convincing the local government to replace gaslight technology and infrastructure with an electricity network. The first central electrical power plant in the US became operational in 1882. At the start, it provided the electricity for 400 lamps, distributed over eighty-five customers. More than 130 years later, we face a similar enigma with the introduction of electric vehicles. These network effects complicate matters enormously, and, for the sake of clarity, we will only focus on innovations that do not require other concurrent innovations.

Lead users

In his book *The Sources of Innovation* (1988), Eric von Hippel investigates the origin of innovations by raising the question: Who are the innovators? He argues that the traditional view that manufacturers are the main innovators needs to be replaced (or at least modified) by his findings from (then) 12 years of research on this subject, namely that innovations come from users, manufacturers, suppliers and others. For example, he presents data that show that innovations in scientific instruments predominantly come from users (77 per cent) and not from manufacturers (23 per cent), whereas the main sources of innovations in plastic additives are manufacturers (92 per cent) and not users (8 per cent). Suppliers are found to be the main innovators in wire termination equipment (56 per cent), ahead of manufacturers (33 per cent) and users (11 per cent). Unfortunately, Hippel does not distinguish between radical innovations and incremental innovations. Trott *et al.* (2013) convincingly argue that the overwhelming majority of radical innovations did not originate from users, simply because they had neither the vision nor the resources to make them happen. In 2005, CNN published a list of twenty-five widely used, non-medical innovations that had appeared since 1980 (CNN, 2005). Ranging from mobile phones, fibre optics and radio-frequency identification (RFID) tags to the Internet, GPS and the Space Shuttle, it is obvious that none of these innovations came from users who modified an existing product to suit their needs. From the cases that von Hippel presents, it is obvious that the user innovations are typically modifications and improvements to existing products. In that sense, the statistics on users as sources of innovations are strongly biased towards incremental innovations. Nevertheless, it is an interesting and important observation that some users are inclined to modify an existing product so that it better suits their needs. It may be indicative of a much larger customer base of people who are also not satisfied with the current product but do not modify it themselves. Unmet customer needs are an important target for aspiring entrepreneurs. Users who start modifying scientific instruments are usually knowledgeable, if not experts in the field, and they have the skills and resources to do so. Such user-driven improvements are less likely to occur in other industries, such as plastics manufacturing, aviation and semiconductors. Nonetheless, the important lesson is that users are not always entirely happy with existing products. Recognizing this market need creates opportunities for entrepreneurs.

Hippel (1986) defines lead users as users who possess the following characteristics:

1   Lead users face needs that will be general in a marketplace, but they face them months or even years before the bulk of that marketplace encounters them.
2   Lead users are positioned to benefit significantly by obtaining a solution to those needs.

Both of these characteristics are essential. Lead users must be representative of the majority of the market, otherwise they merely make up a niche in that market. Although some niches may be very attractive (expensive, high-end sports cars, for example), for most innovative products it is essential that there are sufficient customers in the early and late majority segments. The large investments involved in developing an innovative product must be earned back by exponentially increasing sales. In 2013, Apple spent US$4.5 billion on R&D and achieved net sales of US$170.9 billion. The majority of these earnings came from iPhone sales (150 million units sold in 2013). Even though US$4.5 billion seems like a huge R&D budget, it amounts to only 2.6 per cent of Apple's net sales. This ratio of R&D expenditure to net sales is called the R&D intensity, and, in 2013, Apple had the lowest R&D intensity of the top fifty companies (ranked by their annual R&D expenditure) listed in the annual scoreboard compiled by the European Union (2014). Among the companies with the highest R&D intensities were Huawei (25.6 per cent), Eli Lilly (23.9 per cent) and Intel (20.1 per cent). Figure 8.6 shows Apple's R&D expenditure from 1995 to 2013, both as an absolute amount (millions of dollars) and as R&D intensity. It is striking to see how, over the past decade, Apple increased its R&D expenditure by almost a factor of 10 from 2003 (US$471 million) to 2013 (US$4.5 billion), whereas its R&D intensity decreased by almost 70 per cent.[1] This implies that the money that Apple spends on R&D is an excellent investment, because it leads to progressively higher revenues.

Lead users are located at the extreme leading edge of the Gaussian distribution of the customer segmentation of the diffusion model, as a tiny subgroup leading the innovator category (see Figure 8.7). Purists may argue that lead users fall outside the distribution curve because the product (innovation) is not finalized and cannot be purchased yet. However, it is safe to assume that, once the innovation is marketed, lead users will be the first to

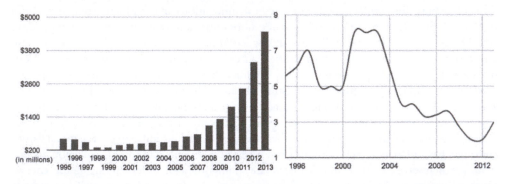

Figure 8.6 Apple's R&D expenditures from 1995 to 2013. Although the absolute expenditure (left) shows an exponential increase, the expenditure as a percentage of the net sales (right) actually decreases, indicating that the sales more than compensate for the R&D investments

Source: Heisler, 2014

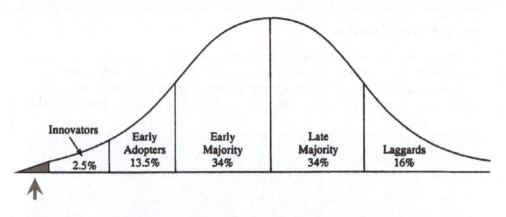

Figure 8.7 Lead users are found at the extreme leading tail of the Gaussian distribution of the customer segmentation of the diffusion model

adopt it. And, although lead users are by definition launching customers, the reverse is not necessarily true. Launching customers may or may not have been lead users, depending on their active involvement in the development of the innovation.

Although we follow von Hippel's definition of lead users, we do not regard lead users as people who create entirely new products or users who modify existing products themselves. Instead, we focus on the distinguishing characteristics that von Hippel attributes to this class of customer, namely that lead users have needs that are representative of the large majority of customers, but they have them much earlier, and they benefit substantially from an innovation that satisfies those needs. Early on in the product development process, entrepreneurs should identify such lead users and involve them in their product development. Because it can be difficult to find lead users, von Hippel has outlined a three-step strategy to identify potential lead users: (1) identify current trends in the field, (2) generate sources of lead users, and (3) network to find specific lead users. This identification process is followed by a fourth step in which the entrepreneur and the lead users collaborate to develop ideas for innovative new products.

Step 1: Identify trends

This is a logical first step, because, by definition, lead users have needs that are ahead of the majority of the market, and that makes them trendsetters. By studying the literature in the field of the proposed innovation, an entrepreneur can identify important trends and find out which experts are involved. He will learn a great deal more by interviewing these experts, who have a good overview of the industry and the development of these trends. These experts are also familiar with specific needs that have not been met yet.

Step 2: Generate sources of lead users

Within the companies that were identified as potential lead users in Step 1, the entrepreneur must find individuals who have a high incentive to innovate because of their leading-edge needs. To help identify lead users, the entrepreneur lists all the key attributes that these lead users have in common and determines which attributes represent the most important needs.

Box 8.2 The CamelBak

In 1988, Michael Edison participated in the Hotter'n Hell Hundred bicycle race in Texas (www.hh100.org). The temperatures during this 100-mile race exceeded 38°C, and water was supplied infrequently. In addition to those problems, Michael noticed that reaching for a water bottle when cycling can be dangerous. After the race, he started

Image 8.5 Artist impression of the CamelBak prototype
Source: www.camelbak.com

Image 8.6 CamelBak Classic with a 2-litre reservoir, aimed at road cyclists
Source: www.camelbak.com

thinking about a solution to these problems. What he came up with was a hydration pack, basically a flexible hose attached to a plastic bag filled with water. He found his inspiration in intravenous (IV) bags, with which he was familiar as a paramedic. His first prototype consisted of an IV bag contained in a sock, which he sewed to the back of his shirt. Because of the obvious similarity, he named it the CamelBak. After using it during a test ride, he was convinced that there was a market for his innovation.

In 1989, Edison started a company that produced CamelBaks. Six years later, he sold the company for US$4 million to businessman and art collector John G. Bowes. In 2003, Bowes sold Camelbak to the Bear Stearns investment bank for a whopping US$210 million. Presently, Camelbak Products, LLC produces a wide range of hydration products tailored to specific outdoor-sport markets, including cycling, climbing, skiing, hiking, triathlon and cross-country. The CamelBak company is also the supplier of hydration packs and protective gear to the US military and various law enforcement agencies.

Step 3: Network to find lead users

The process to find lead users can be described as 'snowballing': rolling a snowball makes it grow in size, thereby increasing the impact. The entrepreneur can interview experts and ask them whether they know other people who are even more expert in the field and whose needs are in line with the solution that the entrepreneur has to offer. In this way, the entrepreneur networks him/herself up to leading-edge users who have breadth of expertise and experience. This direct approach is much more effective than questionnaires or email enquiries. In general, the entrepreneur should look for people who can offer new and unexpected information.

Step 4: Develop ideas for innovative new products

Together with the lead users, the entrepreneur should develop concepts for practical solutions to the lead users' needs. It is an iterative and interactive search process that attempts to match the technological competencies of the company with the needs of the lead users. It is important to keep a clear focus on the fit with the (hopefully to follow later) majority market and not tailor the solution specifically to the niche of specific lead users. Furthermore, the entrepreneur must constantly try to quantify the value to the lead users of the solution under development, as this will enable them to come up with an appropriate pricing strategy. The price for an innovation should be determined by the value of the pain it removes, not by the price of manufacturing the innovation.

As an example of applying this methodology, one of the videos that Hippel hosts on his website shows how lead users were identified for Nortel Networks in its search for experts in need of the types of mobile web application for voice, video and data that the company was developing. First, the Nortel team studied the literature (scientific and trade journals) and talked to many experts in the field who had need of accurate, up-to-date information while on the road. These experts included military specialists, paramedics, police officers, animal trackers and professional tornado chasers. Their common characteristics were: a strong need for high mobility, a need for both voice and data communications, and a critical need for real-time, location-based data that are linked to them at all times. Using the four-step methodology, the Nortel Networks team identified more than twenty lead users who made important contributions to the development of real-time mobile web applications.

This structured approach is particularly useful in situations where finding lead users is difficult. A more opportunistic approach can also be used, as long as the main principles of the structured approach are obeyed. As an example, consider the case of Taniq, a TU Delft start-up that was founded in 2005. Initially, the company was called Straw Rising Technologies, because it applied a fibre-braiding technology developed in the faculty of aerospace engineering to make risers for the offshore oil industry.[2] Straw Rising Technologies soon discovered that the oil industry is one of the most conservative industries when it

---

Box 8.3 The Homer

In episode 7F16 of Matt Groening's animated TV series *The Simpsons* (Season 2, Episode 15; first aired on 16 February 1991), titled 'Oh brother, where art thou?', Homer Simpson is asked by his brother Herb, founder of Powell Motors, to design a car that appeals to the average American. Herb felt that his marketing division was out of touch with the needs of the average American (the mass market) and complained to his head of marketing: 'Instead of *listening* to what people want, you're *telling* them what they want'. That is why Herb asks Homer, whom he regards as the prototypical average American: 'I want you to help me design a car for all the Homer Simpsons out there'. Homer is given complete freedom in designing his ideal car (the *Homer*), much to the chagrin of the Powell Motor design team. When the prototype of the Homer is unveiled, Herb falls to his knees and cries out, 'What have I done? I'm ruined!' The development of the car had cost a fortune, and there was no market for it because of the enormous price tag (US$82,000). More importantly, Homer's needs in a car (tail fins, a bubble dome, three horns that play 'La Cucaracha', a separate soundproof bubble dome for the kids with optional restraints and nozzles) did not reflect those of the mass market at all. That clearly disqualified Homer as a lead user. He may have had the need for that kind of car long before everyone else, but there was no 'everyone else' – his needs did not reflect the needs of the early and late majority. Shortly after this disastrous experiment, Powell Motors went out of business, and the plant was bought by Komatsu Motors (Wikia, 2014).

Even though this is clearly an exaggeration of reality, it does illustrate how, in the 1980s, the American car industry lost its dominant market share to Japanese car manufacturers, who proved to be much more in touch with the needs of the average American car buyer. After the Second World War, the US produced 75 per cent of all passenger cars in the world. In 2010, this market share dropped to an all-time low of 4.7 per cent. In the 2010 world ranking of the number of cars produced (not including commercial vehicles), the US occupied sixth place, behind China, Japan, Germany, South Korea and India. Recently, the American automotive industry has reinvented itself and started producing smaller, more fuel-efficient cars. In the 2013 world ranking of the number of cars produced, the US was in second place, behind China (www.oica.net/category/production-statistics/2013-statistics).

comes to innovation, because the stakes are extremely high: safety regulations are very strict, and the risk of losing valuable days of production is unacceptable. That means that the time to market for such innovative risers could easily be 10 years. How can a start-up company survive such a long time without revenues? The answer in this case was: find an application for the fibre-braiding technology that is closer to market. One of the ideas Taniq came up with was air springs for cars. Taniq designed a concept for a braided air spring, as a lightweight alternative to steel springs or hydraulic systems, and talked to market leaders in car springs to see if they were interested in this solution. Instead of the enthusiastic reception it had hoped for, Taniq's concepts were met with great scepticism by Company X.[3] Company X did not consider air springs as the solution to a problem, because it did not have any problems with its spring systems. However, Company X was intrigued by the possibilities that this new technology offered and was quick to suggest that it might provide a solution to a real problem that it experienced with the turbo hoses it manufactured. A turbo hose must be able to withstand high pressures, and, occasionally, its turbo hoses malfunctioned and burst. Together with Taniq, Company X began developing stronger turbo hoses. This example shows the importance of talking to experts in the field who are aware of trends in the industry. The trend was not in spring systems, but the interview with Company X put Taniq in contact with experts who were aware of a real trend: the demand for stronger turbo hoses. This snowballing aspect of the networking approach to identifying lead users was very important in the case of Taniq.

Chapter summary

This chapter explained how innovations diffuse into the market. Understanding the mechanisms underlying this diffusion is of paramount importance, because it determines the failure or the success of any new product. Five different customer segments are identified, each with its own peculiarities. There are two crucial hurdles to clear. The first hurdle is how to enter the market in the first place. A successful market entry depends on a good product–customer fit. If the lead user concept is applied in a structured manner, this fit can be optimized iteratively. The second hurdle is how to reach the majority market. The early majority customer segment has needs that are distinctly different from the early adopter segment. Crossing this chasm is important, because the majority market is necessary to earn back the research costs involved in developing a new product.

Study questions

1   What is a system innovation? Give three examples of successful system innovations. Give one example of a system innovation that is currently still under development, and explain how you would try to market it.
2   Choose a high-tech gadget (mobile phone, tablet, etc.) and conduct a poll among your fellow students on when they first bought it. Bin the results as a function of time and plot a diffusion curve.
3   Suppose that you were developing a flying car. Describe at which stage in the development process you would try to find lead users and where you might find them.
4   Find someone whom you consider to be an innovator, as defined by Rogers' market segmentation. Ask this person about the last five electronic devices they acquired and write down the manufacturer. What can you say about these companies?

Notes

1 For 2014, Apple posted an R&D expenditure of US$6.0 billion and net sales of US$182.4 billion, which yields an R&D intensity of 3.3 per cent: still one of the lowest in the business.
2 'A drilling riser is a conduit that provides a temporary extension of a subsea oil well to a surface drilling facility' (http://en.wikipedia.org/wiki/Drilling_riser).
3 Obviously, Company X is an anonymization of a real company.

References

Brimelow, P. (1997). The silent boom. *Forbes*. 160 (1). Available at: www.forbes.com/forbes/1997/0707/6001170a.html (accessed 21 March 2014).

CNN. (2005). Top 25: Innovations. Cnn.com. Available at: http://edition.cnn.com/2005/TECH/01/03/cnn25.top25.innovations/ (accessed 5 January 2015).

European Union. (2014). *The 2014 EU Industrial R&D Investment Scoreboard*. Luxembourg: Publications Office of the European Union, 978–92–79–43860–8 (pdf), ISBN 978–92–79–43861–5 (print).

Heisler, Y. (2014). A look at Apple's R&D expenditures from 1995–2013. *The Unofficial Apple Weblog*. Available at: www.tuaw.com/2014/02/12/a-look-at-apples-randd-expenditures-from-1995-2013/ (accessed 5 January 2015).

Hippel, E. von (1986). Lead users: An important source of novel product concepts. *Management Science*. 32(7): 791–805.

Hippel, E. von (1988). *The Sources of Innovation*. Oxford, UK: Oxford University Press.

Interbrand. (2014). *The Best 100 Brands*. interbrand.com. Available at: http://bestglobalbrands.com/ (accessed 5 January 2015).

Kang, C. (2011). Number of cellphones exceeds U.S. population. *The Washington Post*. Available at: www.washingtonpost.com/blogs/post-tech/post/number-of-cell-phones-exceeds-us-population-ctia-trade-group/2011/10/11/gIQARNcEcL_blog.html (accessed 31 December 2014).

MacRumors. (2013). Apple Reports Q4 2013 Year-End Results: $7.5 Billion Profit on $37.5 Billion in Revenue. MacRumors.com. Available at: www.macrumors.com/2013/10/28/apple-reports-q4-2013-year-end-results-7-5-billion-profit-on-37-5-billion-in-revenue/ (accessed 5 January 2015).

Moore, G. A. (2014). *Crossing the Chasm: Marketing and selling disruptive products to mainstream customers* (3rd edn). New York: HarperBusiness. (Originally published 1991.)

Rogers, E. M. (1995) *Diffusion of Innovations* (4th edn). New York: Free Press.

Rogers, E. M. (2003). *Diffusion of Innovations* (5th edn). New York: Simon & Schuster.

Ryan, B. and Gross, N. C. (1943). The diffusion of hybrid seed corn in two Iowa communities. *Rural Sociology*. 8(1): 15–24.

Trott, P., Duin, P. van der and Hartmann, D. (2013). Users as innovators: Exploring the limitations of user-driven innovation. *Prometheus*, 31(2): 125–38.

Wikia. (2014). The Homer. Wikia.com. Available at: http://simpsons.wikia.com/wiki/The_Homer (accessed 31 December 2014).

Part III

Managing the entrepreneurial firm

Chapter 9 discusses what entrepreneurs can expect when introducing their product to the market. We will explain that another long and exciting journey is yet to start. Unfortunately, there is not yet a recipe that all start-ups can follow to achieve success, and so Chapter 10 explains that it is better to adopt a *contingency* or *contextual* approach that emphasizes the unique situation of each individual entrepreneur. In short, this means that every entrepreneur should determine the specific (business) context of his venture and adapt his way of doing business accordingly. Once the new business venture is up and running, further new products and services are required, and Chapter 11 looks at how businesses can develop new products and services. To grow the venture still further, entrepreneurs may have to consider alternative options for growth, and Chapter 12 examines niche strategies for entrepreneurs.

9 Niche strategies

Introduction

This chapter focuses on entrepreneurs who have just mastered a technological principle and are about to introduce a radically new high-tech product into the market on the basis of that principle. The current chapter describes the types of strategy they can adopt when introducing their product to the market.

What can entrepreneurs expect when they are about to introduce a radically new product? Traditional diffusion theory (Rogers, 2003) implies that a smooth, S-shaped diffusion curve can be expected after introduction. This smooth, S-shaped curve reflects the cumulative number of adopters over time, typically for a durable product. The curve reflects the notion that, at first, the number of adopters is small, but, once more customers communicate the benefits of the product and show the use of the product to other potential customers, more and more adopters will emerge, and the curve will bend upwards. Traditional diffusion theory perceives the diffusion process as a communication process. If each adopter communicates the benefits of the product to multiple peers, some of whom then also adopt the product, then an exponential development (the upwards-bending curve) can emerge. Later on, when the limits of the target group are approached, the curve will bend back again and asymptotically approach the maximum number of potential adopters. At this stage, adopters may still communicate the benefits of the product to peers, but by then most of the peers already know or have even adopted the product, meaning that the rate of new adopters will diminish. This idea is visualized in Figure 9.1(b), showing direct large-scale diffusion after introduction.

Chandrasekaran and Tellis (2006, 2007) claim that the S-curve diffusion model does not capture the early market evolution of a radically new high-tech product. Several other articles confirm that claim (Brown, 1992; Golder and Tellis, 1997; Ortt and Delgoshaie, 2008). In practice, the diffusion of these products starts more erratically. Niches are recognized as an important step when introducing radically new high-tech products (Moore, 1991,

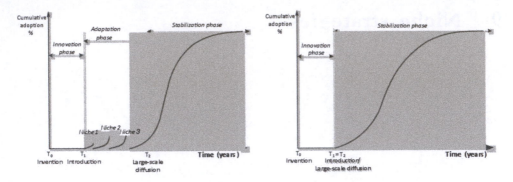

Figure 9.1 Two alternative patterns of development and diffusion of products

Source: Ortt and Suprapto, 2011

1995; Meldrum, 1995; Lynn *et al.*, 1996). Our empirical data confirm that the S-curve does not capture early market evolution. In contrast with Figure 9.1(b), we found that almost 80 per cent of radically new high-tech products show a pattern of development and diffusion that resembles Figure 9.1(a) (Ortt, 2010; Ortt and Suprapto, 2011). The main difference is that, in Figure 9.1(a), after the first introduction, an erratic phase occurs, referred to as the adaptation phase, in which the product is introduced in different market niches.

The emergence of a so-called adaptation phase implies that the basic conditions causing a smooth S-shaped diffusion curve do not hold. This smooth curve emerges in the case where one population of potential adopters communicates the benefits of one type of product to each other. If one or more conditions do not hold, a pattern such as in Figure 9.1(a) can be expected. For example, if the population of potential adopters is divided into subpopulations, or niches, that primarily communicate within rather than across their population, diffusion can die out temporarily or completely. Another cause of a more erratic diffusion process can be that, while diffusion is occurring, the technology, the product form and price (or other elements of the marketing mix) evolve. That is particularly likely for products that require an extensive system of complementary products and services. The investment in such a system requires a critical mass of users that is not available at the time of first introduction. It makes sense in these cases to introduce a simple version of the product first. As a result of changes in the product over time, the product will attract different subgroups of customers over time, and the potential market shifts over the life cycle. As a result of these conditions, the diffusion may become more erratic and may look like Figure 9.1(a) rather than (b).

In the current chapter, we focus on this adaptation phase and will describe what niche strategies can be distinguished during this phase and how an analysis of the market situation can reveal which of these niche strategies should be considered for introduction in a particular case. From a managerial or entrepreneurial perspective, the focus on this so-called adaptation phase makes sense: the management literature often describes niche strategies as an important step in creating a market for new high-tech products (DeBresson, 1995; Meldrum, 1995; Lynn *et al.*, 1996; Hultink *et al.*, 1997; Gerlagh *et al.*, 2004; Moore, 2014). Furthermore, the available case material that was described in the previous chapter illustrates how some well-known high-tech products diffused through several specific niche applications prior to large-scale diffusion in a mainstream market. Box 9.1 introduces niche applications of some cases from our own research.

Box 9.1 Niche applications for telephony, the contraceptive pill and the microwave oven

In the late nineteenth century, telephony was first used as a local burglar alarm in a bank, for intra-company communications and as a means to contact the nearby telegraph office and transfer telegrams (Dordick, 1990; Winston, 1998; Huurdeman, 2003). These niche applications differed fundamentally from the large-scale telephone application that emerged later. Similar differences can be found for other products as well. From the late 1920s on, the contraceptive pill was first introduced as a hormone preparation for complaints such as problem pregnancies, gynaecological cancers, menopausal complaints in women and hormonal disorders in men, before it became a regular contraceptive that diffused in a mass market from the 1960s (Junod and Marks, 2002). The microwave oven was first used to prepare food in trains and ships from 1947, before it became a standard cooking device in consumer households (Osepchuk, 1984, 2009). These cases have in common that they describe radically new high-tech products (at the time of their introduction), and that different niche applications preceded the large-scale diffusion of these products in a mass-market application.

Image 9.1 Old burglar alarm
Source: © Richie Diesterheft

Source: Ortt *et al.*, 2012, p. 1

> ### Box 9.2 Learning goals of the chapter
>
> After reading the chapter, you should be able to describe:
>
> - what a market niche is, and what types of niche can be discerned depending on the timing of their emergence;
> - twelve market factors, actors or functions necessary for large-scale diffusion of high-tech products;
> - how these twelve factors, actors or functions can be categorized in two groups, one group directly affecting large-scale diffusion and another group having a more indirect effect;
> - how market situations can be characterized using these factors, actors or functions;
> - ten different niche strategies;
> - when and in what market situation each niche strategy can be applied;
> - the assumptions of the approach introduced in this chapter.

From a scientific perspective, distinguishing specific niche strategies and being able to assess the market situation in order to select some of these strategies fill an important gap. A review of the extant literature reveals that only a limited number of very generic niche strategies are described in the literature (Ortt *et al.*, 2012). Furthermore, it is unknown in what market situations those strategies can be applied.

In the next section, we will start by defining *strategic niches* and proceed with summarizing information from our previous work on these niche applications for radically new high-tech products. In the section following that, we will describe specific niche strategies.

Some empirical findings on niches in the adaptation phase

A market niche is a relatively small group of customers with specific wants and demands regarding a product (Shani and Chalasani, 1993; Dalgic and Leeuw, 1994). Parrish *et al.* (2006) contrast niche and mass marketing in terms of the size of market (small or large) and product characteristics (specialized or generic functionalities). In this chapter, the focus is on market niches that emerge prior to large-scale applications, so-called *strategic niches*, rather than the niches that emerge in mature markets.

In previous work (Ortt and Suprapto, 2011; Ortt *et al.*, 2012), we explored how many strategic niches emerge typically, and whether or not this number differs per industry. Table 9.1 shows an overview of these findings. The first and second columns describe the industries and the number of cases, i.e. high-tech products, per industry. The third and fourth columns describe the total number of niches per industry and the average number of niches per case in that industry, respectively. The last four columns characterize the niches by indicating whether the high-tech product is used by the government in a civil or military function, and whether the product is used by business or consumer households.

The results in columns 3 and 4 indicate that the number of strategic niches differs per industry. Pharmaceutics has a relatively low number of strategic niches compared with the other industries. The results in the last row of columns 5–8 show that most of the strategic niches are 'business' niches (53 out of a total of 115 niches), and the remainder are 'consumer'

Table 9.1 Number of niches and their type per industry

Industry	No. of cases	No. of niches	Average no. of niches per case	Government, civil niches	Government, military niches	Business niches	Consumer niches
Chemicals, metals & materials	13	34	2.6	4	5	15	10
Pharmaceutics, healthcare equipment	13	5	0.4	–	–	–	5
Telecommuni cations equipment	11	39	3.5	8	10	13	8
Electronic equipment	12	37	3.1	2	5	25	5
Total	49	115	2,3	14	20	53	28

Source: Ortt *et al.*, 2012

niches (28 out of a total of 115 niches) and government niches (20 out of a total of 115 niches). So, almost half of the strategic niches are business niches, whereas both the government and consumer niche applications represent about a quarter of the strategic niches.

The other data in columns 5–8 show the types of niche found per industry. In Chemicals, all four types of strategic niche can be found, but the strategic niches with private customers (be they business or consumer customers) outnumber the government niches by far (be they public or military customers). Pharmaceutics not only has a very limited number of strategic niches, but also, if they appear, the customers for these niches are consumers, and other types of niche are not found in our sample. In Telecommunications, all four types of strategic niche do appear, and, in contrast with Chemicals, the distribution of the niches over the categories is more even. Finally, for Electronics, we also found all four types of strategic niche, and most of them are business niches (twenty-five out of thirty-seven niches). We conclude that the numbers and the types of strategic niche are industry specific. This notion confirms earlier findings (Ortt and Suprapto, 2011).

In the same article (Ortt *et al.*, 2012), we also explored the sequences of strategic niches for radically new high-tech products. Four different types of strategic niche are distinguished: Government civil, Government military, Business and Consumer niches. Using these types, we focused on subsequent strategic niches representing a transition between public and private niches, business and consumer niches and civil and military niches.

In the sample of radically new high-tech products, most strategic niches are business applications in the private sector, and the transition from business to business applications occurs most often. Transitions from business to consumer market are found more often than the reverse transition. The transition from a military to a civil niche happens as often as the reverse, from a civil to a military niche, but the number of transitions from and to military applications is relatively low compared with transitions within the civil sector.

These findings emphasize the importance of strategic niches in the early diffusion stages of radically new high-tech products. The number, classification and sequences of these niches do not yet reveal the niche *strategies*, nor do they indicate when (in what market conditions) these niche strategies can be adopted. The next section will address these issues.

Niche strategies to introduce high-tech products in specific market situations

Table 9.1 (Ortt and Suprapto, 2011; Ortt *et al.*, 2012) shows that different numbers and types of strategic niche appear per industry. This result is a first step in explaining the emergence of these niches. A second step is to distinguish the specific actors, factors and functions (henceforth referred to as factors) in the industry that play a role in the formation of these niches. Each of the industries represents a different configuration of factors that seems to influence the emergence of strategic niches. To explore whether and how this configuration causes niches, we adopt the following assumption: *Strategic niches appear when development, production or large-scale diffusion and use of a new high-tech product is hampered.* Following this line of reasoning, we look at factors in the market required for the development and large-scale diffusion of a new high-tech product.

To find the factors required for the *development* of new high-tech products, we look at factors in complete innovation systems and we combine the information from four descriptions of innovation systems (Malerba, 2002; Geels, 2004; Bergek *et al.*, 2008; Edquist, 2011). To find factors required for the *large-scale diffusion* of new high-tech products, we use factors that we found earlier in a multi-case study approach on strategic niches (Ortt and Suprapto, 2011) and factors that were found to influence the length of the adaptation phase (Ortt and Delgoshaie, 2008). All of the resulting factors are ordered and combined into twelve categories (see Table 9.2).

A problem with the factors described in Table 9.2 creates a barrier to large-scale diffusion. It is important to understand our assumptions: we not only assumed that barriers cause the emergence of strategic niches, but we also hoped to analyse these barriers to indicate what types of specific niche strategy can be adopted. In practice, that took a while. If, for example, the customers (Factor 5) are missing in the system, then large-scale diffusion is seriously hampered. However, the existence of this barrier does not reveal what type of niche strategy can be adopted. Later on, we found out that the twelve categories of factors have different roles. Some factors can directly block large-scale diffusion (such as the lack of customers), whereas other factors serve as an explanation for that barrier. Customers can be lacking, for example, because they don't have the knowledge required to understand and use a product, or they can be lacking because these customers cannot afford the product. In these cases, completely different niche strategies should be considered.

We assume that Factors 1–6 in Table 9.2 have a direct effect on the large-scale diffusion of the high-tech product, whereas Factors 7–12 have a more indirect effect, because they influence one or more of the first factors. If one or more of these factors is missing, or otherwise forms a barrier to large-scale diffusion, then large-scale diffusion becomes less likely, and a niche strategy might be a good choice (see Figure 9.2). Having distinguished six direct and six indirect factors with an effect on large-scale diffusion, we were able to formulate $6 \times 6 = 36$ conditions. These conditions can be seen as market situations. For each of these market situations, we studied historical cases with a similar situation. Our understanding of the cases and the market situation helped to distinguish between ten specific niche strategies.

The model in Figure 9.2 is built up in two layers. Factors 1–6 (middle part of Figure 9.2), referred to as core factors, represent the core technological and market system required for large-scale diffusion. Some of these core factors refer to technical components and subsystems such as the product itself, the production system and complementary product and services. Some other factors refer to actors such as suppliers and customers. The institutional aspects refer to the laws, rules, norms and values used to guide processes such

Table 9.2 Actors, factors and functions necessary for large-scale diffusion

Factors	Description
1 New high-tech product	The product can be defined and distinguished using three elements: the functionality provided by the product, the technological principle(s) used and the main components in the system (first tier of subsystems). The unavailability of (one or more components of) the product means that large-scale diffusion is not (yet) possible. The product needs to have a good price/quality compared with competitive products in the perception of customers before large-scale diffusion is possible
2 Production system	Availability of a good production system is required for large-scale diffusion. In some cases, a product can be created in small numbers as a kind of craftsmanship, but industrial production technologies are not yet available. In that case, large-scale diffusion is not possible
3 Complementary products and services	Complementary products and services refer to products and services required for the production, distribution, adoption and use. The product, together with complementary products and services, forms a socio-technological system. The unavailability of elements in that system means that large-scale diffusion is not (yet) possible
4 Suppliers (network of organizations)	The producers and suppliers refer to the actors involved in the supply of the product. Sometimes, multiple types of actor are required to supply the entire system. In that case, a kind of coordination (network) is required. Sometimes, actors with considerable resources are required, for example to provide an infrastructure. If one or more vital roles, resources or types of coordination are not present in the socio-technological system, large-scale diffusion is blocked
5 Customers	The availability of customers means that a market application for the product is identified, that customer segments for these applications exist, and that the customers are knowledgeable about the product and its use and are willing and able to pay for adoption. If applications are unknown or if customer groups do not exist, are not able to obtain the product or are unaware of the benefits of the product, large-scale diffusion is blocked
6 Institutional aspects (laws, rules and standards)	The regulatory and institutional environment refers to the laws and regulations that indicate how actors (on the supply and demand side of the market) deal with the socio-technological system. These laws and regulations can either stimulate the application of radically new high-tech products (such as subsidy that stimulates the use of sustainable energy) or completely block it (such as laws prohibiting something)
7 Knowledge of technology	The knowledge of the technology refers to the knowledge required to develop, produce, replicate and control the technological principles in a product. In many cases, a lack of knowledge blocks large-scale diffusion
8 Knowledge of application	Knowledge of the application can refer to knowing potential applications. If a technological principle is demonstrated but there is no clue about its practical application, large-scale diffusion is impossible. A lack of knowledge of the application can also refer to customers who do not know how to use a new product in a particular application. In that case, large-scale diffusion is not possible
9 Natural resources and labour	Natural resources and labour are required to produce and use a new high-tech product. These resources and labour can be required for the production system, for complementary products and services or for the product itself. In many cases, a lack of resources and labour blocks large-scale diffusion
10 Sociocultural aspects	Sociocultural aspects refer to the norms and values in a particular culture. These aspects might be less formalized than the laws and rules in the institutional aspects, but their effect might completely block large-scale diffusion
11 Macro-economic aspects	Macro-economic aspects refer to the economic situation. A recession can stifle the diffusion of a new high-tech product
12 Accidents or events	Accidents or events such as wars, accidents in production or accidents in the use of products can have a devastating effect on the diffusion of a new high-tech product

Source: Ortt *et al.*, 2013

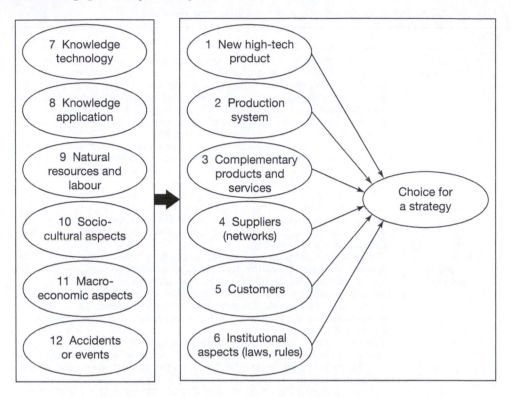

Figure 9.2 Factors important for the development and large-scale diffusion of new high-tech
        products and, hence, for the choice of introduction strategy

as production, supply, adoption and use. Each of these core factors needs to be in place to enable large-scale diffusion. The second layer of factors (left part of Figure 9.2), referred to as influencing factors, contains contextual factors that explain why problems emerge in the core system. Two of these influencing factors relate to knowledge: knowledge of the technology and knowledge of the application. One factor represents natural resources and labour. Two factors refer to the sociocultural aspects and macro-economic aspects that drive or hamper the core system. Finally, accidents and unexpected events are added to the model.

A goal of the model is to help an entrepreneurial company to choose specific niche strategies. We claim that, for this choice, a combination of the core factors (Factors 1–6 in Figure 9.2) and the influencing factors (Factors 7–12 in Figure 9.2) have to be considered. In the next section, we will describe the strategies and the conditions in which they might be considered.

Specific niche strategies

In Table 9.3, we summarize ten different niche strategies and describe the conditions in which these niche strategies can be considered.

If some, but not all, factors hamper large-scale diffusion, a scenario with a relatively long adaptation phase is likely. In that case, an entrepreneurial company can consider one of the niche strategies. In Table 9.3, different niche strategies are described. Each of these niche

Table 9.3 Specific niche strategies and the conditions in which they can be considered

Specific niche strategies	Description of the niche strategy	Conditions to consider specific niche strategy
1 Demo, experiment and develop niche strategy	A niche strategy can be adopted to demonstrate the product in public in a controlled way so the limited quality of performance is not a problem. As part of the strategy experimenting with the product is important to develop the product further, for example in a research environment	Knowledge of the technology is lacking and that affects the availability of the product itself, because the functionality is not provided with sufficient quality
2 Top niche strategy	A niche strategy can be adopted where handmade products can be made to order, in small numbers, for a specific top-end niche of the market	Knowledge of the technology is lacking and that affects the availability of the product for a reasonable price
	A skimming strategy can be adopted in which the top niche of customers is supplied first with a special product	Knowledge of the technology is lacking and that affects the production system with which controlled production of products with a constant and good enough quality and reasonable price is possible
		Resources for the product or the production are lacking or very expensive and that affects the product's price
3 Subsidized niche strategy	A niche strategy can be adopted where the product is subsidized if the use of the product by a particular segment of users is considered as societally relevant or important	Knowledge of the technology is lacking and that affects the availability of the product or the production system, and that in turn affects the availability of the product for a reasonable price
		Resources for the product or the production are lacking or very expensive and that affects the product's price
4 Redesign niche strategy	A niche strategy can be adopted where the product is introduced in a simpler version that can be produced with the existing knowledge, less use of resources and, therefore, for a lower price	Knowledge of the technology is lacking and that affects the availability of the product or the production system and that in turn affects the availability of the product for a reasonable price

continued . . .

Table 9.3 Continued

Specific niche strategies	Description of the niche strategy	Conditions to consider specific niche strategy
	A niche strategy can be to explore an application where institutional aspects are more favourable. Mostly leads to redesign	Resources for the product or the production are lacking or very expensive and that affects the product's price
	A niche strategy can be to explore an application where suppliers or customers have no resistance to produce and use it. Mostly leads to redesign	Knowledge of the application of the product is missing or sociocultural aspects affect the availability of appropriate institutional aspects (laws, rules and standards) and, thereby, hamper diffusion
		Sociocultural aspects affect the availability of suppliers or customers
5 Dedicated system or stand-alone niche strategy	A niche strategy can be adopted where the product is used in stand-alone mode or a dedicated system of complementary products and services is designed (e.g. a local network when an infrastructure is not available on a wider scale)	Knowledge of the technology is lacking and that affects the availability of complementary products and services
6 Hybridization or adaptor niche strategy	A niche strategy can be adopted by which the new product is used in combination with the old product and, thereby, all existing complementary products and services can be reused. Or an adaptor/convertor is provided to make the product compatible with existing complementary products and services	Knowledge of the technology is lacking and that affects the availability of complementary products and services
		Resources are lacking and that affects the availability of complementary products and services
7 Educate niche strategy	A niche strategy can be adopted aimed at transferring the knowledge to suppliers	Knowledge of the technology is lacking and that affects the availability of suppliers or customers
	An educate and experiment (pilot) niche strategy can be adopted aimed at increasing customer knowledge	

Strategy		
8 Geographic niche strategy	A niche strategy can be adopted where institutions (laws and rules) are relatively easy to arrange or are less strict	Knowledge of the technology or its application is lacking and that affects the availability of appropriate institutional aspects (laws, rules and standards)
	A niche strategy can be adopted in another geographic area where resources, suppliers or customers are available	Resources are lacking affecting the availability of the product or complementary products and services
	A niche strategy can be adopted in another geographic area where suppliers are available and not hampered by these unexpected events or accidents	Sociocultural aspects or macro-economic aspects affect the availability of suppliers, customers and appropriate institutional aspects
	Accidents and unexpected events affect the availability of appropriate institutional aspects	
9 Lead user niche strategy	A niche strategy can be adopted finding innovators or lead users. These lead users can co-develop the product, and innovators are willing to experiment with the product	Knowledge of the application of the product is missing and that affects a clear view on customer applications, specific product requirements and customer segments by suppliers
		Sociocultural aspects, macro-economic aspects or accidents and unexpected events affect the availability of suppliers or customers
10 Explore multiple markets niche strategy	A niche strategy can be adopted in which multiple customer applications can be explored	Knowledge of the application of the product is missing and that affects the availability of a clear view on applications, usage patterns and product benefits by customers
	Visibility of the first applications might stimulate explorative use in new applications	

strategies is most applicable when particular combinations of core factors and influencing factors (see Figure 9.2) are in place.

Discussion

On the basis of historical case analyses, we were able to distinguish ten different niche strategies to commercialize high-tech products. These strategies are described in the chapter. Entrepreneurs face significant uncertainties regarding market and technological developments, and a proper market and technology assessment can help reduce the risk by enabling them to choose the right niche strategy. In the chapter, we present a model to assess the market and technology consisting of twelve factors.

On the one hand, our approach, to assess the market and technology context and choose a niche strategy that fits the context, is a considerable improvement on the contemporary literature on niche strategies. On the other hand, our approach also has some weaknesses, and they become visible when we observe the assumptions in the approach. Several assumptions are important. First, we assume that companies want to produce and sell new products on a large scale. Strategic niches appear when development, production or large-scale diffusion and use of a new high-tech product are hampered. Second, we assume that the market can be assessed in terms of a set of barriers to large-scale diffusion, and that the proper niche strategy can be selected by means of such an assessment. Third, we assume that these barriers should be divided into factors blocking large-scale diffusion and factors causing this blockade. The combination of the blockade and its cause is required to select the proper niche strategy. All of these three assumptions can be challenged.

We have proposed a kind of static analysis of the market (with a focus on actors, factors and barriers that facilitate or block large-scale diffusion). The analysis helps to choose a strategy. This choice is good in that particular market situation. Market situations, however, change over time. Future research should, therefore, discuss sequences of strategies and mechanisms of change and thereby focus on dynamic analyses rather than static analyses.

Chapter summary

This chapter discusses the strategies that entrepreneurs can consider to commercialize their high-tech product. Ten specific niche strategies are distinguished, and we show how a more detailed market assessment can help the choice of specific niche strategies.

Study questions

1   Rogers' smooth, S-shaped diffusion curve assumes that product diffusion is the communication of an idea in a relatively homogeneous population. In practice, different aspects play an important role in the emergence of a more erratic start of the diffusion process. Some of these aspects will be addressed in the questions below:

  • If the new product has to compete with another version of the new product, a kind of design or standard competition can emerge. An example of this standard competition can be found during the development and early stages of the diffusion of the DVD. Different formats, DVD+, DVD-, were available at that time, and these versions competed because they were incompatible. What would be the effect of such a competition on the diffusion curve?

- If the new product has to compete with an old type of product, another type of competition emerges. An example of this competition is the competition between DVD and video cassettes. What would be the effect of such a competition on the diffusion curve?

- Sometimes an innovation starts to diffuse in a relatively closed subpopulation or niche. An example would be the diffusion of video telephony among people with a hearing impairment during the 1980s and 1990s, when Internet and Skype were not yet available. The niche of people with a relatively serious hearing impairment who depend on lip reading and gesture language for communication therefore could benefit from the addition of video signals to telephone contact. However, this group of people represents a relatively separate subpopulation who visit special schools and libraries, for example. What would be the effect of such a subpopulation on the start of the diffusion curve?

- Products, especially when their use requires an extensive system of complementary products and services, are different from ideas. Ideas can spread freely, whereas the use of these products requires investment in, and payment for, the complementary products and services. This difference implies that, for products, a critical mass of users is required before investment in the system makes sense. What would be the effect of such a critical mass on the start of the diffusion curve?

2 What type of strategy can be recommended when the new product has to compete with an old product from a large incumbent company? Why would a niche strategy make sense in this situation? What specific types of niche strategy would you consider in these situations?

- What types of specific niche strategy would you recommend when customers lack the knowledge to understand and use the product?

- What types of specific niche strategy would you recommend when customers lack the spending power to buy and use the product?

References

Bergek, A., Jacobsson, S., Carlsson, B., Lindmark, S. and Rickne, A. (2008). Analyzing the functional dynamics of technological innovation systems: A scheme of analysis. *Research Policy*. 37(3): 407–29.

Brown, R. (1992). Managing the 'S' curves of innovation. *Journal of Marketing Management*. 7(2): 189–202.

Chandrasekaran, D. and Tellis, G. J. (2006). A critical review of marketing research on diffusion of new products. *Review of Marketing Research*. 3: 39–80.

Chandrasekaran, D. and Tellis, G. J. (2007). Diffusion of new products: A critical review of models, drivers, and findings. *Review of Marketing*. 3: 39–80.

Dalgic, T. and Leeuw, M. (1994). Niche marketing revisited: Concept, applications and some European cases. *European Journal of Marketing*. 28(4): 39–55.

DeBresson, C. (1995). Predicting the most likely diffusion sequence of a new technology through the economy: The case of superconductivity. *Research Policy*. 24(5, September): 685–705.

Dordick, H. S. (1990). The origins of universal service: History as a determinant of telecommunications policy. *Telecommunications Policy*. 14(3, June): 223–31.

Edquist, C. (2011). Design of innovation policy through diagnostic analysis: Identification of systemic problems (or failures). *Industrial & Corporate Change*. 11: 1–29.

Geels, F. W. (2004). From sectoral systems of innovation to socio-technical systems: Insights about dynamics and change from sociology and institutional theory. *Research Policy*. 33(6–7): 897–920.

Gerlagh, R., Van der Zwaan, B., Hofkes, M. W. and Klaassen, G. (2004). Impacts of CO_2-taxes in an economy with niche markets and learning-by-doing. *Environmental & Resource Economics*. 28: 367–94.

Golder, P. N. and Tellis, G. J. (1997). Will it ever fly? Modeling the takeoff of really new consumer durables. *Marketing Science*. 16(3): 256–70.

Hultink, E. J., Griffin, A., Hart, S. and Robben, H. S. J. (1997). Industrial new product launch strategies and product development performance. *Journal of Product Innovation Management*. 14(4): 243–57.

Huurdeman, A. A. (2003). *The Worldwide History of Telecommunications*. Hoboken, NJ: Wiley-Interscience.

Junod, S. W. and Marks, L. (2002). Woman's trials: The approval of the first oral contraceptive pill in the United States and Great Britain. *Journal of the History of Medicine*. 57(April): 117–60.

Lynn, G. S., Morone, J. G. and Paulson, A. S. (1996). Marketing and discontinuous innovation: The probe and learn process. *California Management Review*. 38(3): 8–37.

Malerba, F. (2002). Sectoral systems of innovation and production. *Research Policy*. 31(2): 247–64.

Meldrum, M. J. (1995). Marketing high-tech products: The emerging themes. *European Journal of Marketing*. 29(10): 45–58.

Moore, G. A. (1991). *Crossing the Chasm*. New York: HarperBusiness.

Moore, G. A. (1995). *Inside the Tornado*. New York: HarperBusiness.

Moore, G. A. (2014). *Crossing the Chasm: Marketing and selling disruptive products to mainstream customers* (3rd edn). New York: HarperBusiness.

Ortt, J. R. (2010). 'Understanding the pre-diffusion phases', in J. Tidd (ed.), *Gaining Momentum: Managing the diffusion of innovations*. London: Imperial College Press, pp. 47–80.

Ortt, J. R. and Delgoshaie, N. (2008). Why does it take so long before the diffusion of new high-tech products takes off? *Proceedings of 17th International Conference on Management of Technology, International Association for Management of Technology (IAMOT)*, Dubai.

Ortt, J. R. and Suprapto, M. (2011). The role of strategic niches in creating large-scale applications for high-tech products. *Proceedings of 20th International Conference of the International Association for Management of Technology (IAMOT)*, Miami Beach, FL.

Ortt, J. R., Langley, D. J. and Pals, N. (2013). 'Ten niche strategies to commercialize new high-tech products', in S. Cunningham, J. R. Ortt, J. Rezaei and N. Salimi (eds), *2013 IEEE International Technology Management Conference & 19th ICE Conference*. The Hague, Netherlands, pp. 1–12.

Ortt, J. R., Trevino Barbosa, S. I. and Meijer, S. A. (2012). 'Sequences of niche applications prior to large-scale diffusion', in Y. Hosni, S.C. Hung and T. Khalil (eds), *Managing Technology–Service Convergences in the Post-Industrialized Society*. Taiwan, pp. 1–12.

Osepchuk, J. M. (1984). A history of mcrowave heating applications. *IEEE Transactions on Microwave Theory and Techniques MTT*. 32(9): 1200–24.

Osepchuk, J. M. (2009). The history of the microwave oven: A critical review. *Microwave Symposium Digest, 2009. MTT '09. IEEE MTT-S International*, pp. 1397–400.

Parrish, E. D., Cassill, N. L. and Oxenham, W. (2006). Niche market strategy for a mature marketplace. *Marketing Intelligence & Planning*. 24(7): 694–707.

Rogers, E. M. (2003). *Diffusion of Innovations*. New York: Free Press.

Shani, D. and Chalasani, S. (1993). Exploiting niches using relationship marketing. *Journal of Business & Industrial Marketing*. 8(4): 58–66.

Winston, B. (1998). *Media Technology and Society: A History: From the telegraph to the Internet*. New York: Routledge.

10 Entrepreneurship in context

Would it not be great if there were a unique way in which entrepreneurs could innovate successfully? It would be easy for every entrepreneur to become and stay innovative. Just follow the guidelines of the successful innovation recipe and eternal financial glory is within reach. In this chapter, we argue that things are not as easy as that, and that it is better to adopt a *contingency* or *contextual* approach that emphasizes the unique situation of each individual entrepreneur. In short, this means that every entrepreneur should determine the specific (business) context of their venture and adapt their way of doing business accordingly.

Introduction

It will hardly come as a surprise to learn that many scientific researchers and consultants are looking for the ultimate set of success factors. Known examples are *In Search of Excellence*, by McKinsey consultants Peters and Waterman (1982) and *Built to Last – Successful habits of visionary companies*, by Collins and Porras (2004). These two studies list several conditions that companies need to fulfil if they want to become and stay successful. For instance, Peters and Waterman emphasize the importance of staying close to the customer and minimizing the amount of staff at headquarters.

Scientists have been very active in this area as well. A famous piece of research into success factors in innovation was conducted by Keith Pavitt in the SAPPHO project (1984), with the aim of finding factors that would explain the success of innovation. However, the question is whether successful innovation can be reduced to a simple collection of golden rules.

To explain why success factors are not valid for entrepreneurs to set up their business, we need to take a step back and discuss the different types of knowledge in the natural and social sciences. To start with, we consider entrepreneurship as a subset of management, and, therefore, the management sciences (e.g. organizational science, marketing science, innovation management science) are quite relevant. For a social science such as management science (which, by way of economic science, is influenced by the natural sciences),[1] it is extremely tempting to start the quest for the ultimate success factors and to maintain that quest as long as possible.

However, management science is (unfortunately?) not a natural science but a social science, as management science deals with studying the behaviour and decisions of *people* and *organizations* in a managerial setting. Social reality (which comprises 'management reality') is more obstinate than natural reality. Social reality, together with its study, is not characterized by a closed system but by an open system. This means that it is not possible for management scientists to study their topic in isolation from factors that might possibly influence their study topic. For natural scientists, it is easier to carry out research within a closed system, as they can set up experiments in laboratories where they master the conditions in which they do their research.

Within management science, there are many factors that can play a role in determining what does and does not work. In addition, the types of factor, the number of factors and the interactions between them will change over time. This means that management science cannot be captured in fixed laws. Owing to the continuously changing, complex relationship between these factors, there are no universal principles that always apply. If there were, enormous wealth would make any kind of economic crisis obsolete, through eternal successful innovation based on knowing the success factors. After all, if you are so smart, why aren't you rich?

A short introduction to management

The next question is why techno-entrepreneurs need to develop insight in such a highly philosophical and non-practical area such as knowledge patterns. Why should an entrepreneur, who is busy translating a patent into a business plan and who is thinking day and night about technical matters, financial issues and building up his innovation network, need to know what knowledge pattern applies to his business? The best reason is that an entrepreneur needs to understand that his (future) business is different from his technological background and education. The educational environment in which he 'grew up' and was 'raised' is fundamentally different from the environment in which he will spend his working life.

The *techno*-entrepreneur was raised in accordance with the principles of the natural sciences, where every question has a unique, exact and correct answer. It is a world where the truth can be calculated, often in a very detailed way. Also, it is a world that regards the physical reality as the genuine reality and that assumes that technological developments are the most important developments. Logic is all-important, and rationality brings progress to man and society. In addition, this world is largely seen in objective terms, leaving little or no room for subjectivity. The world is as it reveals itself, documented by our infallible senses.

However, without wanting to pass judgement on this approach and perspective, it does not apply to the social (management) world, the world in which the entrepreneur has to conduct their business. This world is the subject of the social sciences, to which the management sciences belong. In this world, and with these kinds of science, man occupies a central position, individually and in coherence. In this world, truths are not fixed forever, but they change over time. Although many social phenomena are of all times, such as wars and economic crises, that does not mean that the same explanations are valid every time, which ultimately means that there are no fixed laws.

Box 10.1 Knowledge patterns

The social and natural sciences differ in their study object and how they generate scientific knowledge. Table 10.1 shows four kinds of *knowledge pattern*, including the differences between social sciences and natural sciences.

Table 10.1 Four different knowledge patterns

Domain	Period	
	Temporal	*Eternal*
Local	Contingency	'Climate zones'
Universal	Cohort effects	Scientific laws
	Age effects	

In Table 10.1, a distinction is made between the (physical) domains to which knowledge can refer. This domain can be universal, in any location, or local, in one location. Also, a distinction is drawn between the times in which the knowledge is valid: temporal versus eternal. On the bottom right, we find the 'classic' natural sciences, which concern themselves with identifying scientific laws: fixed regularities or correlations that always apply. One of the most famous examples is the law of gravity.

On the top right, we find scientific knowledge that is universal but local. This type of knowledge we call 'climate zones'. In fact, climate zones are a good example of this type of knowledge. Certain types of weather are always found in certain parts of the planet. Other, less physical examples of this type of knowledge pattern come from the cultural sciences, which have shown that certain customs, rituals and values are found in certain areas.

On the bottom left, we find the cohort and age effects. Here, we see knowledge that is valid universally but is temporal. We call them cohort and age effects because they are good examples of this type of knowledge. For example, people tend to go to college between the ages of 18 and 26 (an age effect), and when, in a certain period, many babies are born, that will affect the number of people retiring 65 years later (cohort effect).

On the top left, finally, we find the contingency or contextual knowledge pattern. Later, we will discuss this pattern in greater detail and explain why this approach is important to entrepreneurs. For now, suffice it to say that, according to this approach, all knowledge is bound to a unique place and time. That means that we cannot and must not assume in advance that there are fixed relationships between variables of the kind that we find in the natural sciences. On the other hand, it also does not mean that the variables are in no way related. According to this approach, *fixed* relationships between variables are possible, but they will change continuously, and so there is no dependency between them, but rather a (required) mutual 'fit'.

Box 10.2 Science and falsification

The criticism that the social sciences, and thus management science, are not scientific because they do not produce fixed laws is not justified, because knowledge can only be said to be scientific when it is arrived at in a *scientific* way (process). This means that science is primarily a process. Of course, this also means that the content of a statement *as such* can be described as being scientific or unscientific, although it needs to be associated with a scientific process. Karl Popper, the famous science philosopher, pointed out that statements need to be falsifiable to be characterized as scientific. The statement 'Everything has become twice as big last night' is a statement that cannot be verified and cannot, therefore, be the subject of a scientific research process. Similarly, the statement 'All human behaviour originates from selfish motives' (in which even altruistic actions are seen as serving one's own interests) cannot be subjected to a critical scientific process. The term 'selfishness' is defined in such broad terms as to include everything, leaving no room for (possible) alternative explanations and making it impossible to determine when people are not being selfish.[2] Well-known examples of such a broadening of meaning are Sigmund Freud's 'subconscious' and Karl Marx's 'class struggle'. According to Freud, all human behaviour could be reduced to processes in the subconscious (which is hard to examine), and Marx argued that every social change was the outcome of the struggle between different social (economic) classes. So, in addition to the question of how a certain claim has come about (process), it is also important to formulate knowledge in such a way as to indicate when it does not apply (content).

Image 10.1 Portrait of Karl Marx
Source: © Friedrich Karl Wunder

Truths in the management sciences are subjective and temporary, then. Of course, the subjectivity has to do with the fact that people and organizations shape the social world, and that the behaviour of people and organizations is hard to capture in natural laws. In fact, it is the people and organizations that shape the social world in the first place. Every management theory needs to take this into account. The social world is not a world that is characterized by natural laws that can be discovered piece by piece, but one that is instead characterized by a close interaction between the object being investigated and the subject conducting the research. In the next section, about success factors, we will see a good example of how management gurus bombard the world with alleged success factors, and how they affect the management of companies. The chapter on futures research and entrepreneurship, Chapter 2, also contained an example of how people's expectations and predictions regarding the future influence that very future. Because the social world is 'made' by people and organizations, their view of that world almost coincides with that actual world. This is why we repeat the statement made by W. I. Thomas that was quoted in that same chapter: 'If men consider things as real, they are real in their consequences'.

Thus, objective truths do not necessarily have to coincide in the social world. In concrete terms, this means that an entrepreneur needs to be aware that, for instance, the best product from a technical point of view is not always the most successful product. What matters is the perception of the product among consumers or decision-makers within a company, which is often not based on the supposed technical qualities of the innovation.

Because management sciences focus on the subjective world of business and society, they make up the domain of the entrepreneur, who needs to use scientific theories, models and frameworks to understand, interpret and explain this world, in order to make the right decisions for his enterprise. When we look at Table 10.1, the knowledge pattern that is most suitable to the techno-entrepreneur is the contextual (or contingency) approach, followed by the 'climate zones' and the cohort and age effects. Traditional natural sciences are considerably less relevant to the techno-entrepreneur when it comes to *organizing* and *managing* their company. Needless to say, they are relevant when it comes to the technical side of their product.

Why success factors are not successful

Many management scientists and consultants are (still) looking for the philosopher's stone of the management sciences: success factors. This section contains a brief, critical discussion of two studies that examined a number of studies into success factors.

A famous, and later infamous, study of what makes *businesses* successful is *In Search of Excellence: Lessons from America's best-run companies*, by Peters and Waterman (1982). Based on a survey among forty-three *Fortune*-500 companies, the authors identified the following 'eight attributes that emerged to characterize most nearly the distinction of the excellent, innovative companies':

1   a bias for action and active decision-making; facilitating quick decision-making and problem-solving tends to avoid bureaucratic control;
2   close to the customer – learning from the people served by the business;
3   autonomy and entrepreneurship – fostering innovation and nurturing 'champions';
4   productivity through people – treating rank-and-file employees as a source of quality;
5   hands-on, value-driven – management philosophy that guides everyday practice – management showing its commitment;

6   stick to the knitting – stay with the business that you know;

7   simple form, lean staff – some of the best companies have minimal HQ staff;

8   simultaneous loose–tight properties – autonomy in shop-floor activities plus centralized values.

Later, this study became infamous, because it turned out that a lot of the information had been made up by the authors. However, what is also interesting is that the forty-three companies, which were initially very successful (such as Atari, IBM and Xerox), turned out to be less successful a few years later. Apparently, these companies had been unable to adapt to the business 'laws' of a new era.

Many attempts have also been made to identify the success factors of successful *innovation*. One of the first studies in this area was the Sappho research conducted by Keith Pavitt *et al.* An example of a more recent study in this field is the one by Van der Panne *et al.* (2004), who conducted a meta-analysis of scientific articles aimed at identifying the success factors of innovation. They came up with the following list:

1   a firm's culture that is open to innovation;

2   experience with innovation;

3   multidisciplinarity of R&D;

4   clear innovation strategy and a management style suited to that;

5   compatibility with the firm's core competences;

6   product quality and price relative to those of substitutes;

7   adequate timing of market introduction.

Although a full discussion of all the success factors mentioned in this list goes beyond the scope of this chapter, we want to comment briefly on the list:

• The first success factor sounds nice and clashes somewhat with the 'hard thinking' on innovation in which R&D and patents occupy a central position. The problem is, however, that it is hard to distinguish cause from effect with this success factor. An innovative company will have no trouble understanding that being innovative is good for business, and its culture will therefore be open to innovation. Or, does a business culture that finds innovation important lead to more innovative behaviour? The same mutuality applies to the fourth success factor: which comes first, the innovation strategy or the management style?

• As far as the third success factor, 'multidisciplinarity of R&D', is concerned, we want to remark that it is not tautological in nature, nor does it suffer from an unclear cause–effect relationship. However, in our opinion, this success factor does not apply in all cases. In a highly technological sector, R&D does not have to be multidisciplinary in nature: focusing on technical R&D can be smarter. And, the development of an incremental innovation requires no highly technological knowledge initially, but especially requires knowledge about market developments.

• The fifth item on the list, 'compatibility with the firm's core competences', is hard to reconcile with the innovative nature of innovation. It may apply to companies that mainly innovate incrementally, but companies that are looking for radical innovations will need to have new core competences.

• The sixth success factor, 'product quality and price relative to those of substitutes', is tautological in nature. The hallmark of successful innovation is that it is better than existing, competing products, processes or services. The quality and price levels of the innovation are important success factors relative to other products, processes or services.

- Factor seven, 'adequate timing of market introduction', is also tautological in nature, as becomes clear from the use of the word 'adequate'. The question is, of course, what timing is adequate? That can depend, among other things, on the type of innovation, the company's innovation strategy and the sector in which the company operates.

To summarize, the success factors identified by Van der Panne *et al.* are insufficiently informative, because they are circular or tautological in nature, perhaps because many studies into success factors are quantitative in nature and predominantly use questionnaires to ascertain the success factors, adding a subjective element to the research and the risk of obtaining contradictory results. In addition, any broad meta-analysis that includes a large number of studies is likely to result in a large list of success factors, with an increased likelihood of contradictory results. To provide some sort of coherent outcome almost necessarily involves coming up with generalizing statements about what is good for innovation. The question is whether having a lack of unanimity is a bad thing. In the first section of this chapter, we stated that the social sciences allow room for multiple 'best practices'. The only success factor that remains intact is that a successful company is able to select the success factors that will increase its success.

Contingency and contextual innovation management

We have stated that the nature and principles of management are different from those that apply in the natural sciences. Although finding success factors (which can be viewed as a natural-science approach to management) is in itself interesting, the factors do not help explain how businesses can improve their performance. In this section, we discuss the concept of contingency and contextual (innovation) management, which emphasizes various situations in which companies find themselves and discards the idea that there is such a thing as a universal 'business recipe'.

We want to make it clear from the outset that the contingency (and contextual) approach is not the same as 'anything goes'. It is not based on the notion that everything is connected and, therefore, too complex to understand. The focus of the contextual approach is on finding relationships between variables that need to be reconciled, that need to 'fit'. According to Donaldson (2001), who wrote a comprehensive book on contingency theory, 'the essence of contingency theory is that organizational effectiveness results from fitting characteristics of the organizations, such as its structure, to contingencies that reflect the situation of the organization' (p. 1). He sees a contingency as 'any variable that moderates the effect of an organizational characteristic on organizational performance' (p. 7). The so-called contingency (or contextual) factors can be diverse in nature. The traditional versions are environment, size and strategy. The organizational structure needs to adapt to these contingency factors to operate optimally. Because this has to do with optimizing the organizational structure, it is also known as 'structural contingency theory'. We do not focus here exclusively on the organizational structure, but more on innovation- and entrepreneurship-related contingency factors. The examples presented below are related to that.

There are two aspects of contingency that need to be emphasized:

1   First, contingency factors are often considered to be 'environmental'. Sometimes, the term environment is used literally, in the sense of the organization's environment, for

instance the industry in which it operates. However, environment can also refer to a factor that is not immediately under the control of the business, such as the state of the technology.

2   Another aspect is that the contingency factors are subject to change, so that the organizational aspects need to change accordingly. Donaldson (2001, p. 2) puts it as follows:

> Organizations are seen as adapting over time to fit their changing contingencies so that effectiveness is maintained. Thus contingency theory contains the concept of a fit that affects performance, which in turn, impels adaptive organizational change. This results in organizations moving into fit with their contingencies, creating an association between contingencies and organizational characteristics.

So the contingency (contextual) factors are not fixed but can change over time. This is sometimes referred to as *reactive contingency*, with misfits being temporary and decision-makers (managers) being able to restore the fit. Closely connected to this is *anticipatory contingency*, where the manager knows what the relationships should be and is able to intervene in time to restore and/or prevent a misfit. Table 10.2 is a small example of what we have discussed.

The point of Table 10.2 is that a non-diversified strategy needs to be linked to a functional structure. The moment the company adopts a diversified strategy, the organizational structure has to switch to a multidivisional structure. The two other combinations are seen as misfits.

The 'classic' example of the contingency approach is the relationship between organizational structure and size, task interdependence and task uncertainty, as shown in Table 10.3.

Table 10.3 shows that it is wise to match a larger size of the company with an increase in specialization, formalization, structural differentiation and decentralization. This allows a company to fine-tune its own organization. In Figure 10.1, we see the specific relationship

Table 10.2 Fitting organizational structures and strategies

	Undiversified strategy	*Diversified strategy*
Multidivisional structure	Misfit	Fit
Functional structure	Fit	Misfit

Source: Donaldson, 2001, p. 14

Table 10.3 The relationships between organizational structure and size, task interdependency and task uncertainty

Contingencies	*Organizational structure*		
	Specialization formalization	*Structural differentiation*	*Decentralization*
Size	+	+	+
Task interdependence	−	−	−
Task uncertainty	−		+

Source: Donaldson, 2001, p. 30

Structural differentiation

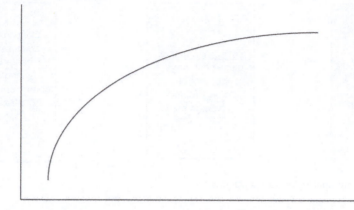

Size = total number of employees

Figure 10.1 The relationship between size and structural differentiation
Source: Donaldson, 2001, p. 70

Table 10.4 The relationship between the nature of technology and the type of organization

| | Contingency of technology | | | | | |
	Routine					Non-routine
Organic	5	−4	−3	−2	−1	0
	4	−3	−2	−1	0	−1
	3	−2	−1	0	−1	−2
	2	−1	0	−1	−2	−3
	1	0	−1	−2	−3	−4
Mechanistic	0	1	2	3	4	5

Source: Donaldson, 2001, p. 211

between size and structural differentiation, which is the core of the 'classic' structural contingency theory.

The relationship between the organization factor and the contingency factor does not have to linear in nature and can also be continuous (see Figure 10.1). In Table 10.4, we present an example that relates to the relationship between the nature of the technology and the type of organization.

Table 10.4 shows that a specific value can be assigned to every combination. The optimal score is 0, and the lesser scores are all negative. It turns out that the combinations (1,1), (2,2), (3,3), (4,4) and (5,5), which in this case follow a linear pattern, are the right scores (combinations). The other combinations are all to greater or lesser extent misfits and need to be corrected to improve the company's performance.

Strictly speaking, it is difficult to speak of 'the' contingency theory. Various contingency factors are distinguished for different management-related subjects. The 'classic' contingency

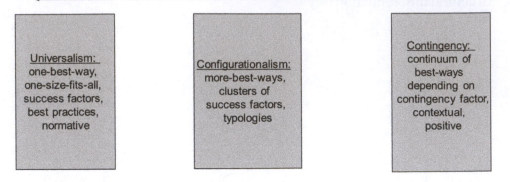

Figure 10.2 Various approaches to management

factors came from studies into organizational structure and focused above all on size and complexity. As we will see shortly, applying the contingency approach to the subject of *innovation* yields different contingency factors.

In addition to the specific content of a contingency factor (size, complexity, uncertainty, etc.), we can also look at how strictly the contingency approach is applied. There are management scientists who argue that the performance of a company depends entirely on its match with the contingency factor, whereas others are less strict about this relationship. Figure 10.2 shows these different approaches, including the 'success factor' approach.

Figure 10.2 presents three approaches on a continuum, from a unique success factor (universalism), via a combined cluster of success factors (configurationalism), to a series of contingency factors that have a unique combination (match) with the organizational factor. Universalism explains the success of a company by following one or more success factors. Configurationalism argues that success factors can be combined into meaningful clusters ('configurations'). In principle, companies that find themselves in one of those clusters are successful, whereas other companies have a wrong cocktail of (inconsistent) success factors. Well-known examples of clusters are the organization typology proposed by Henry Mintzberg (1994) and the various strategies of Michael Porter (1985).

So, universalism assumes that there is a (unique) optimum that applies to every company, whereas configurationalism argues that there are various, local optimums that are discrete, which means that the choice of optimum is less important, as long as the choice is made with conviction, and the company does not attempt to formulate a compromise between the various local optimums. Finally, there is the contingency approach that is matched to the contingency factor on the basis of the status of the independent variable (in this case, a characteristic of the organization, such as the way it innovates or the level of technological uncertainty).

A contextual approach to innovation management

In this section, we explore the configurationalism approach for which we use the term *contextual*. The contextual approach is based on the contingency approach, but does not assume the existence of a single factor, and instead argues there are several factors. The contextual approach is also based on configurationalism, but, in this approach, the various clusters are not discrete but placed in a continuum. The various *contexual* factors have a continuously changing value. The advantage of this intermediate combination is that it does justice to the complexity of (successfully) managing an organization by taking more than one contingency factor into account. In addition, this intermediate approach offers a wider choice than configurationalism with regard to the number of successful combinations (clusters) and does more justice to the continuous nature of the variables related to the aspects of the organization and its functioning. Below, we discuss a number of studies that are more or less based on the contextual approach.

First of all, we look at the relationship between technological and market-related uncertainty, and the type of innovation strategy: see Figure 10.3.

Figure 10.3 shows that the level of market-related and technological uncertainty influences the choice of innovation strategy. When the level of uncertainty is low, it is wise (and possible) to adopt an innovation strategy that is highly process-oriented and uses quantitative data. This case primarily involves incremental data, and the success factor has little to do with, for example, the uniqueness of the idea (the 'what' of the innovation) but more with how the idea is being developed (the process). Also, in the case of incremental innovation, there is usually enough information available about (future) markets and technology, making it possible to approach the innovation from a quantitative perspective. On the other hand, when uncertainty levels are high, it is difficult to plan the 'innovation journey', turning the innovation process into a learning process with regard to the innovation as such, as well as the question as to how it should be developed. This innovation process that is predominantly a learning process, the outcome of which is not certain in advance, will have to be adjusted throughout the development process. This study is contextual, because the variables on the two axes are not discrete but continuous, and the clusters merge into

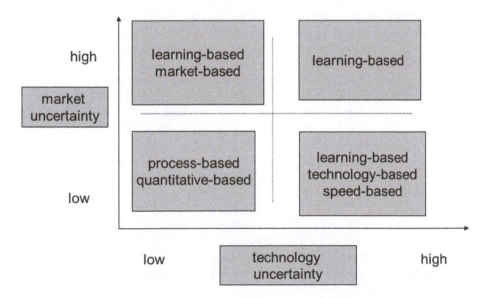

Figure 10.3 The relationship between market-related and technological uncertainty, and innovation strategies

Source: Based on Ansoff, 1999, Moriarty and Kosnik, 1989, and Lynn and Akgün, 1998

Table 10.5 Differences in innovation between government and the private sector

Characteristics of innovation in government organizations	Characteristics of innovation in the private sector
One time (example infrastructure)	As often as possible
Not much diffusion	As much diffusion as possible
Sociopolitical context is very important	Sociopolitical context is less important
More often non-technical	More often technical
External cooperation is difficult	External cooperation is important
Monopolistic motives	From competition
Primarily risk-avoiding	Not averse to risk
Complex (various interests)	Less complex (fewer interests)

each other. In this study, both axes are part of the company's environment, and the four different innovation strategies are the subject of choice for the companies.

Another contingency factor that can be important for the approach to innovation is the organizational background and context. Here, we apply it to the differences between public and private organizations. Based on that, we have identified the following differences when it comes to innovation: see Table 10.5.

Table 10.5 shows that, when it comes to innovation, there are considerable differences between government and the private sector in a number of areas. For example, research into innovation at the Dutch Transport Ministry (Duin *et al.*, 2011) shows that many innovation projects are (just) a one-time affair, whereas, in the private sector, commercial interests ensure that innovation is much more an ongoing activity. Also, the private sector tends to be less risk-averse compared with the public sector. The question is whether this contextual factor (organizational context) will remain in place for much longer with regard to public versus private. With public–private collaborations on the increase, the public sector is starting to behave more and more like a commercial organization (think of the increasing trend to measure performance indicators in education), and the private sector increasingly takes broader social interests into account (think of the emergence of sustainable entrepreneurship). Again, the distinction that is drawn here between the public and the private sectors should be seen not as a radical difference but as a gradual one.

The kinds of innovation system that are described in Chapter 6 is heavily inspired by literature on the relationship between technology and society. However, management sciences have also paid attention to the collaboration between the public and private sectors in the area of innovation. One of the most popular recent developments in this area is 'open innovation' by Henry Chesbrough (2003; see also Chapter 6). His 'open innovation' concept is based on the following principles:

- The vast majority of the required knowledge and skills are located outside the organization.
- Share, license, sell and buy patents and other forms of knowledge.
- An organization does not have to take part in the entire innovation process, but can step in or leave along the way.
- The success of many innovations can be explained by having the right business model. It is important to choose the right business model early on in the innovation process.

Table 10.6 The conditions for closed and open innovation (Chesbrough, 2003)

Closed innovation	Open innovation
Largely internal ideas	Many external ideas
Low labour mobility	High labour mobility
Little VC	Active VC
Few, weak start-ups	Numerous start-ups
Universities unimportant	Universities important
Examples: nuclear reactors, mainframe computers	Examples: PCs, movies

As we support the adoption of a contextual approach, it is interesting to see under what circumstances 'open innovation' is the smart approach. Chesbrough himself, in the first pages of his book, indicates that open innovation is not a cure-all, and that it is only a successful innovation strategy under certain circumstances. Not all cases meet the conditions that make open innovation a worthwhile strategy: see Table 10.6.

Table 10.6 shows under what conditions an organization should opt in favour of closed or open innovation. The conditions in question are largely environmental (context) aspects (i.e. the sector). However, the fact that it is not always easy to identify the context, never mind making a selection, is illustrated by an example of innovation at the Dutch Military Intelligence and Security Service (MIVD; Duin *et al.*, 2010). Needless to say, this organization is involved in highly classified activities and has a natural preference for closed innovation. However, this sector is also becoming more open and, since 9/11, it even has a 'duty to share'. In addition, the MIVD's core business is the processing of information, which is increasing an ICT issue, an essentially open industry, which means that the organization will also have to become more open. However, not all the information the organization gathers, or other information, can be shared or gathered and analysed together. Figure 10.4 shows that this can create a problematic situation. A closed environment requires a closed innovation process, and an open environment requires an open innovation process. For the MIVD, that means that it is important to make its innovation more open (because it is operating in a more and more open environment), while, at the same time, protecting its innovation process to prevent information falling into the wrong hands.

For the MIVD, the problem is that, unlike commercial organizations, it cannot simply switch from a closed environment to an open environment. An important issue with regard to applying a contextual approach is that businesses need to be able to adjust their organization (in the broad sense of the word, so beyond the organizational structure) to the contingency factor, which, one may assume, is easier for a commercial business than it is for an organization such as the MIVD. It also shows that adapting an organization to its environment, a core concept of the contingency approach, does not mean that that organization is a slave to its environment, but that the organization has enough power and independence to change. That is certainly good news for techno-starters and other kinds of entrepreneurs, because the size of an organization need not be as important to the way it is functioning. The classic contingency factor 'size' is less important to innovation in general and to 'open innovation' in particular.

With regard to Figure 10.2 (the continuum with the approaches), again, the four cluster types are ideals, and the continuous character of the variables on the two axes can provide a host of intermediates. Organizations can even operate in different clusters. Large(r) organizations are especially likely to combine different kinds of innovation management.

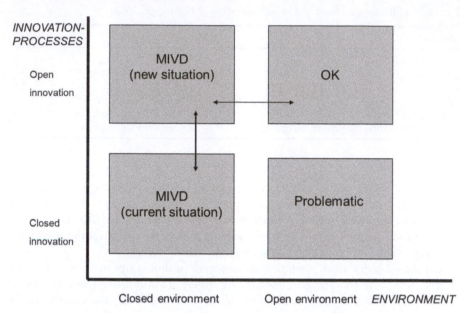

Figure 10.4 Open and closed innovation combined with open and closed environments

In the section on the relativity of success factors, we referred to so-called 'contextual innovation', which assumes that the type of innovation process depends on the organization's context (Ortt and Duin, 2008), which puts it close to the contingency approach. Contextual factors include:

- the type of innovation (radical versus incremental);
- the type of sector;
- the type of culture;
- the type of organization.

Based on these factors, four types (generation) of innovation process can be determined:

1 technology push (first generation: circa 1950–65);
2 market pull (second generation: circa 1965–80);
3 parallel processes (combination of technology push and market pull; third generation: circa 1980–95);
4 network innovation (fourth generation: circa 1995 to present).

  Although these four types have a strong historical component, which is why they are referred to as generations, they do exist side by side now. In fact, different generations can coexist within individual companies. For instance, the consumer division of Philips has a market-pull approach, whereas its medical system division bases its innovation approach on parallel innovation processes (Van den Elst *et al.*, 2006). Shell, to name another example, bases its innovation approach on the type of innovation: incremental innovations are funded by the business units, whereas more radical innovations are supported by the company's headquarters (Verloop, 2006). Although the diversity of approaches is in itself a good thing, both internally and between companies, problems may arise when different approaches clash. Companies from different sectors that innovate together may have excellent arguments for doing so (complementary knowledge, risk-sharing, etc.), but they need to be aware that the fact that they have different ideas does not make their collaboration any easier. In our view, this is one of the reasons why innovation networks, no matter how necessary and popular they may be, do not always succeed in speeding up innovation.

Closing remarks

Although including a philosophical subject such as contingency in a practical book on entrepreneurship may seem a little strange, we feel that it is relevant, because the technological background of many entrepreneurs can bring them into conflict with the 'laws' of the market and society, two factors that are increasingly relevant to successful entrepreneurship. The content of this chapter is not meant to be put into practice immediately, but it has to be in the mind of every entrepreneur, which means the following:

- Be aware that social and business realities are different and have to be experienced differently from the 'hard' scientific reality.
- Knowledge of the market and society is often a subjective affair, and tends to be highly transient.
- Success factors need to be considered very carefully. It is good to learn from business successes, but one should not copy them blindly and simply project them on to one's own organization.
- Business successes need to be interpreted as a case or case studies – examples or studies that show intensively how companies operate and why they are or are not successful. Case research is an excellent research strategy when it comes to entrepreneurship.
- Change is the only constant. If there is one success factor that has to be mentioned, it is the fact that companies need to adapt continuously to their (the) environment. Contingency factors change all the time, as, consequently, do successful ways to conduct business. In that sense, entrepreneurship equals change.

Chapter summary

Given that technology-based entrepreneurship often originates at technical universities, it is important to know that entrepreneurship is part of the management sciences, as, in contrast to the natural sciences, the research output of management sciences is often much less straightforward. The context variable is decisive in research into entrepreneurship. Therefore, there are no golden rules for becoming a successful entrepreneur: those golden rules will differ for every context in which the entrepreneur operates, and these success factors also differ over time.

Study questions

1   What are the main differences between the natural sciences and the management sciences?
2   Why is it futile to look for success factors for entrepreneurship and innovation?
3   Describe contextual innovation management in your own words.
4   Determine the contextual factors of your own business.

Notes

1   The distinction between the natural sciences and the social sciences does not have to be maintained at any cost. Inter- and multidisciplinarity can help bridge the gap between C. P. Snow's 'two cultures'.
2   Strictly speaking, this also means that laws in the natural sciences are not falsifiable (and thus not scientific), because it is hard to indicate when they are not valid.

References

Ansoff, H. I. (ed.) (1969). *Business Strategy: Selected readings*, Vol. 72. London: Penguin.

Chesbrough, H. (2003). *Open Innovation*. Boston, MA: Harvard Business School Press.

Collins, J. and Porras, J. I. (2004). *Built to Last: Successful habits of visionary companies*. New York: HarperBusiness.

Donaldson, L. (2001). *The Contingency Theory of Organizations*. Thousand Oaks, CA: Sage.

Duin, P. van der, Sule, M. and Bruggeman, W. (2011). Deltas for the future: Lessons learned from a water innovation programme. *Irrigation & Drainage*. 60(S1), 122–8.

Duin, P. van der, Dirven, J., Hazeu, C., Linde, E. van de and Rademaker, P. (2010). On the use of studies of the future for organizational change in Dutch government ministries. *Foresight*. 12(4): 23–36.

Lynn, G. S. and Akgün, A. E. (1998). Innovation strategies under uncertainty: A contingency approach for new product development. *Engineering Management Journal*. 10(3): 11–17.

Mintzberg, H. (1994). The fall and rise of strategic planning. *Harvard Business Review*. 72(1): 107–14.

Moriarty, R. T., and Kosnik, T. J. (1989). High-tech marketing: Concepts, continuity, and change. *Sloan Management Review*. 30(4): 7–17.

Ortt, J. R. and Duin, P. A. van der (2008). The evolution of innovation management towards a contextual approach. *European Journal of Innovation Management*. 11(4): 522–38.

Pavitt, K. (1984). Sectoral patterns of technical change: Towards a taxonomy and a theory. *Research Policy*. 13: 343–73.

Peters, T. J. and Waterman, R. H. (1982). *In Search of Excellence: Lessons from America's best-run companies*. New York: HarperBusiness.

Porter, M. E. (1985). Technology and competitive advantage. *Journal of Business Strategy*. 5(3): 60–78.

Van den Elst, J., Tol, R. and Smits, R. (2006). Innovation in practice – Philips Applied Technologies. *International Journal of Technology Management*. 34(3–4): 217–31.

Van der Panne, G., Beers, C. van and Kleinknecht, A. (2004). Success and failure of innovation: A literature review. *International Journal of Innovation Management*. 7(3): 1–30.

Verloop, J. (2006). The Shell way to innovate. *International Journal of Technology Management*. 34(3–4): 243–59.

Further reading

Drejer, A. (2002). Situations for innovation management: Towards a contingency model. *European Journal of Innovation Management*. 5(1): 4–17.

Miller, R. and Blais, R. A. (1993). Modes of innovation in six industrial sectors. *IEEE Transactions on Engineering Management*. 40(3): 264–73.

Ortt, J. R. and Duin, P.A. van der (forthcoming). *Contextual Innovation Management*. Routledge.

Tidd, J. (2001). Innovation management in context: Environment, organization and performance. *International Journal of Management Reviews*. 3(3): 169–83.

11 Developing new products in the new venture

The potential rewards of new product development (NPD) are enormous. One only has to consider the rapid growth of companies such as Samsung and HTC in the mobile-phone industry. Prior to this, similar success was achieved by Nokia and Motorola in the early development of the same industry. This example illustrates an important point, that success in one year does not ensure success in the next. Both Motorola and Nokia have experienced severe difficulties since 2012.

Research by Cooper and Edgett (2008) has suggested that, on average, new products (defined here as those less than 5 years old) are increasingly taking a larger slice of company sales. For 3M, for example, new products contributed to 30 per cent of sales in 2014, for Johnson and Johnson, the figure was 25 per cent of sales in 2014, and, for DuPont, a staggering 39 per cent of sales came from new products. The life cycles of products are becoming increasingly short. This is clearly evident in the mobile phone-handset business, where virtually all of Samsung's and Apple's sales are from products that are less than 3 years old. The implications for the new venture starting out with a new product are clear: further new products will be required in the very near future, if the firm wants to survive beyond 1 or 2 years. As the firm launches its initial product, it needs also to be planning future new-product ideas.

Product development as a series of decisions

The existing literature on product development is vast. This is largely because many different positions can be taken to view the process, such as engineering design, marketing, operations management and R&D management. Arguably, the review of the NPD literature by Krishnan and Ulrich (2001) remains one of very few that attempt to pull this wide and vast literature together. This review examines product development as a series of decisions. Within the product development project, they divide the decisions into four categories: concept development, supply chain design, product design and production ramp-up/launch. This is a useful way to consider the issues in NPD for the new venture.

Within concept development there are five basic decisions to be made:

1   What are the target values of the product attributes?
2   What will the product concept be?
3   What variants of the product will be offered?
4   What is the product architecture?
5   Finally, what will be the overall physical form and industrial design of the product?

Within the decisions surrounding supply chain design, Krishnan and Ulrich (2001) argue that the following questions are key:

1   Which components will be designed specifically for the product?
2   Who will design and produce the product?
3   What is the configuration of the physical supply chain?
4   What type of process will be used to assemble the product?
5   Who will develop and supply the process equipment?

Marketing's role in NPD

Marketing can provide the necessary information and knowledge required by the firm to ensure the successful development of innovative new products and the successful acceptance and diffusion of new products. In both cases, it is usually the insights with respect to understanding potential customers that marketing supplies. Uncovering and understanding these insights is where effective marketing is extremely valuable. The acquisition of the deep insights necessary for truly innovative products requires great skill, as much of the information gained from customers for such products needs to be ignored (Veryzer, 2003). Research within marketing has shown for many years that gaining valuable insight from consumers about innovative new market offerings, especially discontinuous new products, is extremely difficult and can sometimes lead to misleading information (Hamel and Prahalad, 1994). Indeed, frequent responses from consumers are along the lines of, 'I want the same product only cheaper and better'. Von Hippel (2007) has suggested that consumers have difficulty in understanding and articulating their needs and has described this phenomenon as 'sticky information' – that is, information that is difficult to transfer (similar to the notion of tacit knowledge). Recently, 'user toolkits' have been shown to facilitate the transfer of so-called sticky information and have enabled firms to better understand the precise needs and desires of customers (Franke and Piller, 2004). The greater uncertainties involved in discontinuous innovations demand both insight and foresight from firms. Advanced technology presents significant technical and market uncertainty, especially when the technology is emerging and industry standards have yet to be established. Appreciating and understanding the potential new technology and uncovering what the market will and will not embrace are key challenges for marketing. Indeed, bridging the technology uncertainty and market need is critical for a commercially viable new product.

Highly innovative or discontinuous new products are particularly demanding in terms of early, timely information, if they are to avoid being judged harshly by the market later. It does not matter whether marketing personnel or R&D scientists and engineers provide the information and knowledge, but their input into the NPD process is essential. The product development team needs to determine the following: What are the potential applications of a technology as a product? Which application(s) should be pursued first? What benefits can the proposed product offer to potential customers? What is the potential market size, and is this sufficient? (Leifer *et al.*, 2000, p. 81).

Using the customer to develop new products

There has been much written in the NPD literature about the need to involve customers at an early stage in the process and to integrate them into the process in order to capture ideas fully (von Hippel, 1986; Henard and McFadyen, 2012; and Khan *et al.*, 2012). Despite this, outside consumer-product industries, customer involvement in NPD has been limited and largely passive in most industries. There are many reasons for this limited utilization of consumers in NPD, and we have touched on some above, but perhaps the most limiting factor is the disconnection between customers and producers. Nowadays, technology enables an innovative way of involving and integrating customers into the product development process. In this context, it is here that new technologies, most notably in the form of toolkits, offer considerable scope for improving connection between consumers and producers. Franke and Piller's (2004) study analysed the value created by so-called 'toolkits for user innovation and design'. This was a method of integrating customers into NPD and design. The so-called toolkits allow customers to create their own product, which in turn is produced by the manufacturer. An example of a toolkit in its simplest form is the development of personalized products obtained by uploading digital family photographs via the Internet and having these printed on to products such as clothing or cups, etc., thereby allowing consumers to create personalized, individual products for themselves. User toolkits for innovation are specific to a given product or service type and to a specified production system. Within those general constraints, they give users real freedom to innovate, allowing them to develop their custom product via iterative trial and error (Von Hippel, 2001; Franke and Piller, 2004). Nambisan (2002) offers a theoretical lens through which to view these 'virtual customer environments'. He considers the underlying knowledge creation issues and the nature of the customer interactions to identify three roles: customer as resource, customer as co-creator and customer as user. These three distinct, but related, roles provide a useful classification with which to examine the process of NPD. This classification recognizes the considerably different management challenges for the firm if it is to utilize the customer in the NPD process.

A firm's capabilities, networks and product platforms

The company's core capabilities, and those that it can develop or acquire, bound what it can accomplish. This is particularly so for small start-up firms. However, a broader view brings in the notion of distinctive capabilities. This is wider than technical or operations competence. These broader capabilities include an organization's 'architecture', and this

Table 11.1 Product strategies

Product strategy	Firm	How?
Product proliferation	Honda	On entering the European motorcycle market, Honda offered an enormously wide range of engine sizes
	Procter & Gamble	When launching its disposable nappy, Proctor & Gamble offered a wide range of sizes and gender-specific products
Value	VW	VW offers a high-quality product with emphasis on reliability. It is not the most expensive and emphasis is on value for money
	Toyota	Similarly, Toyota uses the same product strategy in different market segments
Design (outward appearance)	Dyson, Apple	Both Dyson and Apple emphasize good design in all of their products, frequently pioneering unique styles and offering elegance and easy-to-use products
Innovation/ unique features	3M, Merck, Philips	3M and, more recently, Merck and Philips have developed reputations for product innovation. This is based on a strong technology culture. This is distinct from design in that, although the product may incorporate a new outward appearance, it is the use of new technology that is the focus of the strategy
Service	American Express, Tesco	Both American Express and Tesco continue to be at the forefront of service development. Historically, American Express pioneered many service offerings. More recently, Tesco (UK retail grocer) has competed by continually offering new and improved services to its customers. Its competitors always seem to be trying to catch up
Ease of use	Apple	Sometimes, technology advances do not deliver enhanced productivity, because of usability problems. This is increasingly a big challenge in an era when everything is integrated in a single device (mobile phone)
First to market	Fashion houses, Ubisoft computer games	This strategy provides a clear opportunity to build market share advantages; there is earlier market and customer experience, the ability to influence markets and standards, the possibility to build entry barriers, and innovation image benefits, often seen as a glamorous strategy. However, there are big risks! Also, this is somewhat problematic in ICT: as interconnectivity is the rule, market dominance can seldom be achieved
Fast follower	Sagem mobile phones	Wait until market is clarified: avoid market education costs. Nearer in time to eventual market: easier to predict; ability to use newer technology. The key here is to be fast, not slow, follower

embraces the network of relationships within, or around, the firm. These relationships might cover customers, suppliers, distributors or other firms engaged in related activities. This leads to the perspective that product development, and the competitive rivalry of which it is usually a part, can sometimes be better understood as undertaken by networks of partnerships and alliances, rather than by individual, isolated producers (Doyle, 1995).

Chapter 7 introduced the concept of networks and explained that their composition can vary widely. In some high-tech industries, a horizontal alliance of competitors or firms might dominate, and perhaps they form a consortium for the R&D of a technology. For example, Kodak, Fujifilm, Minolta, Nikon and Canon were allies in the development of the Advanced Photo System. In other industries, it might be a vertical arrangement between suppliers, manufacturers, distributors and possibly even customers. It can be a formal agreement, a loose collection of understandings or a system 'managed' by a powerful member.

Saying this of capabilities leads to complications. If networks are competing, rather than individual firms, then the activities across the network need to be coordinated. Sometimes, it is the manufacturer that is dominant and leads and controls the network, as in the motor industry, for example, where Toyota has used its suppliers to develop new products for many years. Sometimes it is a distributor that takes the lead and initiates new product categories, as in food retailing. On occasion, a large customer can dominate, show the need for a new product and encourage suppliers to innovate, as in the health services or defence industries. The effectiveness with which the leadership and coordination are undertaken substantially influences what products are developed and how they are developed. Another consideration is that the network members may have a collection of varied motives for being party to the relationship. Over time, they may come to place stress on other motives that result in their becoming less interested in the network's aims and less willing to cooperate. The network leader therefore needs to spend some time monitoring motives and encouraging, or inducing, full cooperation between all network members. If the network is established for the development of a technology, then the partners have other sets of problems once the technology is available. How do they share the results, and how do they each go on to establish distinctive, competitive products?

The abilities to choose appropriate partners for the network and keep them focused are important attributes for network leadership. Developing and refining the network's innovative ability are crucial, and this is not restricted to technical innovation, because innovation in business processes and in distribution can also have a large impact.

Capabilities change. Without continuous attention, they can become ineffectual or redundant, as the technology or the market requirement moves on. Alternatively, capabilities may be enhanced through internal development, through external acquisition and through the bringing together of new partnerships and alliances, so that the network's capability is deeper or wider. Most capabilities thrive through continuity: through continuous incremental enhancement around a technology or a set of related technologies.

Product platforms

Emphasis upon continuity in the development of capabilities is also consistent with the idea of an evolving product platform that a 'product family' shares. Muffatto and Roveda (2000) use the car industry as the classic example of this idea, where several individual models may share the same basic frame, suspension and transmission. As they say, 'a robust platform is the heart of a successful product family, serving as the foundation for a series of closely related products' (p. 618). The Sony Walkman gives another illustration, with its 160 variations and four major technical innovations between 1980 and 1990, all of which were based upon the initial platform. Black & Decker rationalized its hundreds of products into a set of product families, with consequent economies throughout the chain, from procurement to distribution and after-sales service. In all these cases, the evolution of the product platform, along with the evolution of the requisite capabilities, is central to the product development strategy.

This notion may have originated in engineering, but it can be applied widely. Mobile-phone handsets, food, cosmetics, clothing and furniture manufacturers can be seen to have product platforms and families. Johnson & Johnson and its development of Acuvue disposable contact lenses provides another example. Many people needing vision correction did not wear traditional hard or soft contact lenses because of the discomfort and the cleaning requirements. Acuvue uses high-quality soft contact lenses sold at a sufficiently low price to allow disposal after a week, without cleaning. This distinctive advantage, which was clearly relevant to many consumers, led to the successful launch that defined a new market segment. The original product became the basic platform for continuing innovation that is leading to other new offerings in Johnson & Johnson's vision care-product family.

Sometimes, entirely new platforms and entirely new capabilities are required. Step changes in the product or manufacturing technology, in the customer need or in what the competition offers, and how it offers it, can demand radical rather than incremental change. The risk is all the more if that means the adoption of new technologies, outside the firm's traditional arena.

If we look at the software industry, we see that, today, products are developed from multiple components. For example, Figure 11.1 shows how a product can begin with a range of derivative or fundamental technologies to which common applications are added and then specific applications for particular market segments. This shows one platform supporting several different products with very different strategic objectives. The objective with product platforms is to obtain commonality and benefits of scale within the company boundary. The basic idea is to differentiate all the components visible to the customer, while, at the same time, sharing components and production processes across product models (Gawer and Cusumano, 2014). The application of the product platform concept is causing concern for many industry analysts, who believe the search for commonality has gone too far at the expense of brand distinctiveness. According to Muffatto and Roveda (2000) and Mohr *et al.* (2010), the benefits gained through using product platforms are:

- reduced cost of production;
- shared components between models;

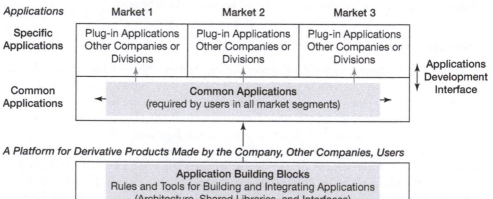

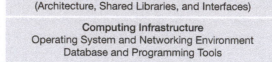

Figure 11.1 Platform strategy for software products

- reduced R&D lead times;
- reduced systemic complexity;
- better learning across projects; and
- improved ability to update products.

Use across firms and models presents many challenges. According to Kim and Chhajed (2000), in practice, it is difficult to achieve an optimum or best solution. Inevitably, compromises are sought between engineers and designers from the different brands, resulting in decisions that are not in the interest of either brand. Moreover, with inter-firm product platforms, some of the sought-after gains, such as shared components between models and reduced complexity, were not achievable, because of the constraint of factory sequencing or the architectural structure of the brand.

Opportunities in the competitive environment

Technologists are sometimes guilty of focusing their energies on their technology without due regard for the wider business environment. To avoid this criticism, start-ups need to examine the competitive environment in which their business will operate. The external environment constrains what can be done, for example within the bounds of current understanding of a technology. Sometimes, the external environment dictates what must be done – for example, following the introduction of a new piece of legislation protecting an aspect of the natural environment, such as vehicle emissions. It can present possibilities and opportunities, such as a breakthrough in an enabling technology or the new affluence of consumers that allows them to be prepared to pay more for products in a particular category. The external circumstances can also pose threats and problems, as when a competitor introduces a significant product advance, or when another rival closes access to materials or to distributors through its acquisition of companies in those activities.

Close analysis of the present situation in the market is fundamental, along with speculations about how it might progress, and, because of the potential importance of external events and conditions, some type of environmental monitoring, in a strategic sense, has become a key exercise in strategy search. Assessments of the present situation can be extended to conjectures about future environments, and, in some industries, such as aerospace or pharmaceuticals, this may require a very long-term view. A range of alternative future scenarios may be built around these conjectures, indicating guesses about what the organization sees to be the aspects of its environment carrying the most stress. These speculations might deal with some of the following issues:

1   Estimates would be needed about the way the technology will change, and these could be more or less rigorous. They could involve some brainstorming within the organization, and it could seek various forms of external advice from government agencies, research centres, consultants and universities.

2   Estimates might also be made about how the industry's competitive structure may alter. Are the same competitors likely to be contending in the market in the future? Are there any indications that any are preparing some kind of strategic shift? Will any withdraw or reduce their activities within the industry? Will there be changes in how companies compete and the positioning they seek in the market? Will there be any new entrants from other industries, or from other countries? Unexpected arrivals in the industry, especially if they are well funded, well managed and come with a significant

innovation, can be particularly troublesome. That was the case when Mars entered the ice-cream business and quickly secured a significant market share.

3   Another area of concern could be how any regulatory framework may evolve, and this could include the extent to which it would limit activities in the future or open new possibilities.

4   Customer needs may be a further area on which to speculate. Will they become more demanding and require better materials and better performance in the products they use? Will they perceive some emerging technology as a substitute? Will they have new kinds of need, and will there be new kinds of customer?

Taking various combinations of these factors could yield a series of scenarios, and the investigation of the implications for the organization of each of them could indicate important issues requiring attention. Such future scenarios may throw up attractive or unattractive situations, and the organization may then attempt to do what it can to prepare itself and to increase the likelihood of the former, while inhibiting the latter. This will help to shape ideas about the potential role for new products and the scope of the problems and opportunities that they are intended to address.

Differentiating and positioning the product/service

Product strategy will express how the organization seeks to differentiate itself, and distance itself, from its competitors and it will be the bedrock of its market positioning. It is axiomatic that, for new products to be successful in the market, they need to be perceived to be beneficial by prospective buyers. The benefit needs to stand out, to be distinctive and attractive. This distinction needs to be relevant to buyers, and it needs to be seen to be relevant by them. It is pointless being distinctive in a way that consumers believe to be irrelevant or incomprehensible.

Differentiation

Broadly, the differentiation sought by competitors could be based upon cost, with a value-for-money proposition, or it could be based upon superior quality, which might encompass better materials, better performance, new features, uncommon availability or better service. A useful perspective on product differentiation is provided by Levitt's idea of product augmentation (Levitt, 1986). He suggests that there are four levels on which products can be considered:

1   *The core product* comprises the essential basics needed to compete in a product market: a car needs wheels, transmission, engine and a rudimentary chassis.
2   *The expected product* adds in what customers have become accustomed to as normal in the product market: for a car, this would be a reasonably comfortable interior and a range of accessories.
3   *The augmented product* offers features, services or benefits that go beyond normal expectations.
4   *The potential product* would include all the features and services that could be envisaged as being beneficial to customers.

An interesting implication of this categorization is that it can demonstrate that the position is dynamic, because customer expectations change. In the example of the car, where would air conditioning be placed in these categories? Until recently, it would have been an augmentation for mass-market vehicles, but it has now become a standard expectation in new cars. Competition drives up consumer expectations. One rival introduces something new, and, if it meets customer acceptance, other rivals follow. In consequence, augmentations become expectations, and this ratchet effect means there is no equilibrium until the full potential has been realized. Even then, changes to the technology, or to another technology, might release an entirely new kind of potential, so that the process continues.

Another implication is that, as firms migrate upwards in this process, they leave market opportunities for others to exploit. There may be niche markets left for 'unbundled' products or services making low-cost, basic offers with no frills. Airlines are an example.

The choice of differentiation strategy is pivotal. It reaches back to core capabilities and forwards to positioning strategy. The differentiation will not be effective unless it is rooted firmly in the organization's capabilities, or in the capabilities of the network delivering the new product. Similarly, the positioning of the product in the market needs to be built upon, and consistent with, the differentiation strategy.

Product positioning

Product positioning refers to the perceptions customers have about the product. It is a relative term that describes customer perceptions of the product's position in the market relative to rival products. It is founded upon understanding how customers discriminate between alternative products and it considers the factors customers use in making judgements or choices between products in the market being investigated. These are referred to as the customer's evaluative criteria, and they may be the product's physical attributes, but they can also include customer assessments about whom the product is meant for, when, where and how it is used, and aspects of the brand's 'personality' (e.g. innovative, functional, old-fashioned, exclusive, frivolous, fun).

Positioning studies begin by determining a relevant set of products. The criterion for inclusion is that they must be perceived by customers to be choice alternatives. Then, a list of determinant attributes is generated: that is, a list of attributes that are salient or the most important to customers in discriminating between the alternatives. With this framework, customers' perceptions and preferences are then collected. This could be by survey, using a structured questionnaire. Respondents would be asked to scale their feelings about each product on each attribute. They could also be asked their preferred level for each attribute. The output can be portrayed in a diagram (sometimes called a brand map or perceptual map) showing the locations of each product against the attributes (the dimensions) and relative to the preferred level (the ideal point). This is most readily understood if the analysis is restricted to two dimensions. For example, for a food product, the dimensions might be nourishment and calorie count, and respondents could rate all the brands they know in the category from high to low on these. Some brands may be seen to be highly nourishing, with a high calorie count, and some not so nourishing, with a low calorie count. Illustrations can be found in Mohr *et al.* (2010).

Such a study would show the proximity of, or the distance between, the perceived positions of the products considered. This might show the positions to be crowded in one area, or well spaced. If an ideal point – that is, the customers' preferred position – is introduced, then the relative distance of each product from this ideal can be measured. If these relative distances accord reasonably with the relative market shares of the products, then it could be assumed that the dimensions chosen are a fair representation of the way customers choose in this market. Generally, it would be expected that the higher market shares would be won by products nearer to the ideal point.

Customers may be far from unanimous about these perceptions and preferences. If the observations were widely scattered, then further research would be needed to understand how customers make their evaluations, and perhaps other dimensions might be tried. If there were several clusters of preferences, each in a different part of the map, this might indicate different market segments. In the food example above, there could be one group preferring a very nourishing product with a low calorie count and another group wanting something nourishing with a high calorie count. Mapping product positions against these two ideal points might then reveal one segment to be well served, with many products, but an opening for a new product near the other ideal point, where there may be no major existing brands.

Positioning strategy depends upon the choice of an appropriate base. This base must be relevant and important to customers and related to how they make choices in that product field. It should also attempt to distance the brand from the positions of rivals. Wind (1982) offers six bases: product feature, benefits, use occasion, user category, position against another product or dissociation from all other products. Crawford (1997) adds parentage (where it comes from), manufacture (how it is made) and endorsement (people you respect say it is good).

Selecting an appropriate position can make the difference between success and failure. It determines what the organization tells the market about the product, whom it tells and how it tells it. Motorcycle producers take various positions. Piaggio's Vespa scooter is aimed at young riders and, latterly, at women. Suzuki is also now targeting women as a distinctive segment. Some of the most expensive machines are now aimed at older men with a revived interest in motorcycling and higher discretionary income. For most products, there may be a host of features, benefits and applications; few, if any, products have a single feature, a singular benefit and one narrow application. Choosing from among the possibilities can lead to creative and unique solutions and, consequentially, to a highly differentiated strategy. For example, Procter & Gamble (P&G) position two products, identical in terms of specification, very differently. 'Sure' is targeted in the US at young males between 18 and 25, whereas 'Secret' is targeted at young females between 12 and 24. The brands clearly have different packaging and marketing communications to reflect their target market and positioning. This simple example illustrates the significance of positioning in modern marketing, especially in fast-moving consumer goods. Positioning can also result in costly mistakes, with products being positioned in strange ways that consumers neither understand nor find credible. As the market grows and matures, it may become necessary to consider repositioning. The original differentiation could become less effective as competitors crowd in, or as new types of buyer, with different expectations, adopt the product. A repositioning exercise could focus upon some reformulation of the product, some change to the image projected, a realignment of the segments targeted or a change to the distribution channels employed.

Competing with other products

In a famous, best-selling book, called *Product Juggernauts: How companies mobilize to generate a stream of winners*, Deschamps and Nayak (1995) argued that, even in basic industries such as chemicals and minerals, suppliers always found ways of differentiating their products from those of their competitors. There have been additional strategies since, but these have been variations on the original five. A typology of different product strategies that firms have used

Table 11.2 Product performance criteria

1 Performance in operation	10 Ease of maintenance
2 Reliability	11 Parts availability and cost
3 Sale price	12 Attractive appearance/shape
4 Efficient delivery	13 Flexibility and adaptability in use
5 Technical sophistication	14 Advertising and promotion
6 Quality of after-sales service	15 Operator comfort
7 Durability	16 Design
8 Ease of use	17 Environmental impact
9 Safety in use	

in competition is shown in Table 11.1. Even some of the new business models that were discussed in Chapter 5 adopt one or more of the product strategies shown in Table 11.1.

As products compete with one another, they are thus compared with one another. This leads to selection criteria and buyer behaviour. The latter is a subject and textbook in its own right and beyond the scope of this book. It is necessary to note, however, that most models of buyer behaviour recognize two kinds of factor – objective and subjective. Objective factors may or may not be tangible, but they must be quantifiable and measurable. By contrast, subjective factors are intangible and are influenced by attitudes, beliefs, experience and associations that the decision-maker holds towards the product. If we leave the subjective criteria to the behavioural sciences and turn our attention to the objective criteria, it soon becomes clear that, to discriminate between products, performance criteria are required. Many of us would recognize a list of factors, for we have probably drawn up such a list when going to purchase a tablet computer or a car. For the most part, however, such performance criteria do not play a large part in our buying decisions. In industrial markets, the reverse is the case, and such criteria are the norm. Indeed, in many instances, buyers will forward their performance criteria to a list of suppliers and await a quote detailing price, warranties, delivery, etc. Table 11.2 shows typical product performance criteria commonly used by buyers in assessing a product.

Objective product characteristics enable firms to be grouped together so that the whole economy can be classified. The Standard Industrial Classification (SIC) manual was first published in the United States in 1945. SIC codes now form part of an international system, making it possible to make precise comparisons between products and services between countries.

Many products may appear objectively similar, such as washing machines. Products in this group are often made to a standard size (typically 600 mm wide, 500 mm deep and 1,000 mm high). Other performance criteria, such as load capacity and spin speed, can all be compared, but subjective information is supplied to the customer via branding. The process of branding can take many forms and is not restricted to physical products. Moreover, successful brands are not easily copied. For example, Dyson did not file for patents in the United States and yet, through branding, has been able to offer a unique product to consumers that competitors have struggled to imitate.

Managing the development of new products

The fuzzy front end

Within the NPD literature, the concept of the so-called 'fuzzy front end' is the messy, 'getting started' period of NPD processes. It is at the beginning of the process, or 'the front end', where the organization develops a concept of the product to be developed and decides whether or not to invest resources in the further development of an idea. It is the phase between first consideration of an opportunity and when it is judged ready to enter the structured development process (Koen *et al.*, 2001; Kim and Wilemon, 2002). It includes all activities, from the search for new opportunities through the formation of a germ of an idea to the development of a precise concept. The fuzzy front end disappears when an organization approves and begins formal development of the concept.

Although the fuzzy front end may not require expensive capital investment, it can consume 50 per cent of development time, and it is where major commitments are typically made involving time, money and the product's nature, thus setting the course for the entire project and final end product. Consequently, this phase should be considered an essential part of development, rather than something that happens 'before development', and its cycle time should be included in the total NPD cycle time.

Time to market

Time to market (TTM) is the length of time it takes from a product being conceived to its reaching the marketplace. TTM is important in industries where products become outdated quickly. A common assumption is that TTM matters most for innovative products, but actually the first mover often has the luxury of time, whereas the clock is clearly running for the followers. TTM can vary widely between industries: say 15 years for aircraft and 6 months for food products. Yet, in many ways, it is a firm's TTM capability relative to its direct competitors that is far more important than the naked figure. Although other industries may be much faster, they do not pose a direct threat – although one may be able to learn from them and adapt their techniques.

As usual, there are some other factors that need to be considered when analysing a firm's TTM. For example, rather than reaching the market as soon as possible, delivering on schedule may be more important: for example, to have the new product available for a trade show can be more valuable. Many managers argue that the shorter the project, the less it will cost, and so they attempt to use TTM as a means of cutting expenses. Unfortunately, a primary means of reducing TTM is to staff the project more heavily, and so a faster project may actually be more expensive. Finally, as we have seen throughout this chapter, the need for change often appears midstream in a project. Consequently, the ability to make changes during product development without being too disruptive can be valuable. For example, one's goal could be to satisfy customers, which could be achieved by adjusting product requirements during development in response to customer feedback. Then, TTM could be measured from the last change in requirements until the product is delivered. The pursuit of pure speed of TTM may harm the business (Cooper and Edgett, 2008).

Agile NPD

Flexible product development is the ability to make changes to the product being developed or in how it is developed, even relatively late in the development process, without being too disruptive. Consequently, the later one can make changes, the more flexible the process and the less disruptive the change, the greater the flexibility. Change can be expected in what the customer wants and how the customer might use the product, in how competitors might respond, and in the new technologies being applied in the product or in its manufacturing process. The more innovative a new product, the more likely that the development team will have to make changes during development.

In his book *Flexible Product Development* (2007), Preston Smith uses the software industry to show how having an agile NPD process enables a firm to adapt to changing markets. Many industrial NPD software projects apply agile methodologies these days, such as *Scrum*, *eXtreme Programming* and *feature-driven development*. Petri Kettunen from Siemens studied some of these systems and found that agility in embedded software product development can be further enhanced by the use of typical NPD principles (Kettunen, 2009).

New products as projects

Globalization is a major market trend today, characterized by both increased international competition and extensive opportunities for firms to expand their operations beyond current boundaries. Effectively dealing with this important change, however, makes the management of global NPD a major concern. To ensure success in this complex and competitive endeavour, companies must rely on global NPD teams that make use of the talents and knowledge available in different parts of the global organization. Thus, cohesive, well-functioning global NPD teams become a critical capability by which firms can effectively leverage this much more diverse set of perspectives, experiences and cultural sensitivities for the global NPD effort (Salomo *et al.*, 2010).

Recent research in this area by Sivasubramaniam *et al.* (2012) indicate that team leadership, team ability, external communication, goal clarity, and group cohesiveness are the critical determinants of NPD team performance. Unsurprisingly, the established literature on new product development (NPD) management recognises top management involvement (TMI) as one of the most critical success factors and this is confirmed in a recent comprehensive review of the literature by Felekoglu and Moultrie (2014).

We have seen that a product idea may arise from a variety of sources. We have also seen that, unlike some internal operations, NPD is not the preserve of one single department. It is because a variety of different functions and departments are involved that the process is said to be complicated and difficult to manage. Furthermore, although two separate new products may be similar generically, there will frequently be different product characteristics to be accommodated and different market and technology factors to be addressed. To be successful, NPD needs to occur with the participation of a variety of personnel drawn from across the organization. This introduces the notion of a group of people working as a team to develop an idea or project proposal into a final product suitable for sale. The vast majority of large firms create new project teams to work through this process. From initial idea to launch, the project will usually flow and iterate between marketing, technical and manufacturing groups and specialists. The role of the new project team is at the heart of managing new products and is the focus of the case study at the end of this chapter. Additionally, NPD has developed its own jargon, and Table 11.3 offers an overview of sources of the key terminology.

The link with the product innovation process

The link between R&D and NPD is often overlooked, or they are frequently treated as separate subjects. In practice, the two activities are interlinked. This can be simply shown by looking at the extended product life cycle. This well-known conceptual framework purports to capture some of the stages in a product's life cycle, from launch to final withdrawal. What is seldom shown is the series of activities prior to the first stage, *introduction*. For some products, most notably aircraft or pharmaceuticals, the lead time prior to launch

Table 11.3 NPD terminology

NPD terminology	Definition
The fuzzy front end	The messy 'getting started' period of NPD processes. It is the front end where the organization formulates a concept of the product to be developed and decides whether or not to invest resources in the further development of an idea
Business opportunity	A possible technical or commercial idea that may be transformed into a revenue-generating product
Product concept	A physical form or a technology plus a clear statement of benefit
Screening	A series of evaluations, including technical, commercial and business assessments of the concept
Specifications	Precise details about the product, including features, characteristics and standards
Prototype/pilot	A tentative physical product or system procedure, including features and benefits
Production	The product produced by the scale-up manufacturing process
Launch	The product actually marketed, in either market test or launch
Co-joint analysis	A method for deriving the utility values that consumers attach to varying levels of a product's attributes
Commercialization	A more descriptive label would be market introduction, the phase where the product is launched and hopefully begins to generate sales revenue
Commercial success	The end product that meets the goals set for it, usually profit

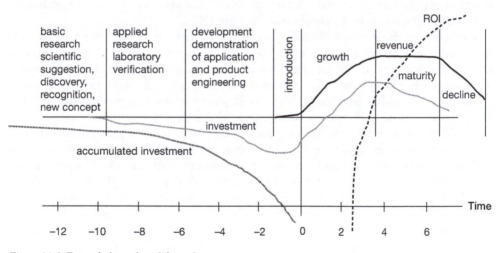

Figure 11.2 Extended product life cycle

can be 10 or even 15 years. Figure 11.2 shows the extended product life cycle with some of the key R&D activities incorporated. Mapped on top are the investment and expenditure curves showing the scale of upfront money required in some industries, most notably those with long lead times, as previously discussed.

It is important to bear in mind that an investment in R&D to develop an existing product further is not generally viewed by product managers as a high-risk activity. The following quote from the brand manager of the makers of one of the leading washing detergents in Europe reflects a commonly held view:

We know we can improve the product, our scientists can always improve the product. In fact the launch date for our new improved shampoo has been set but the research is still on-going! The only doubt is the extent of the improvement that our scientists will make.

A similar example could be drawn from the software industry, which is synonymous with new, improved versions of its software. The key point here is the way R&D investment is viewed. For many firms with years of experience in the management of R&D, an output is expected from their investment in R&D; the only doubt is the detail. Given this perspective on R&D, the following section analyses the range of effects that R&D investment can have on a product's profitability.

The effect of R&D investment on products

Analysis of the products that a company manages will reveal that these contribute in different ways to the overall profit and growth of the company. It is important to recognize that R&D activities can influence this profit contribution in several ways.

Development of existing products

The life cycle of most products lasts for several years. There are some products, especially in the food industry, that seem to have an eternal life cycle. Cadbury's Milk Tray and Coca-Cola are two examples of products that have been on the market for over 100 years. In virtually all other industry sectors, however, a product's market share will slowly fall, as competitors compete on price and product improvements. R&D's role is to extend the life of the product by continually searching for product improvements. The two most common approaches to extending the life of a product are capturing a larger market share and improving profit margins through lowering production costs. For example, the performance of zinc–carbon batteries has improved greatly, owing to the threat of alkaline batteries such as Duracell. This has helped to improve the market share for zinc–carbon batteries. Similarly, PC manufacturers such as Dell, Apple, Hewlett-Packard and IBM are continually lowering their production costs in order to ensure that their products compete successfully in the PC market.

Early introduction of a new product

Many companies strive to be technological leaders in their industry. Their aim is to introduce innovative products into the market before the competition to gain a competitive advantage. In some industries, such as pharmaceuticals, this approach is very successful. In other sectors, being first to market does not always ensure success.

Late introduction of a new product

Deliberately postponing entry into a new market until it has been shown by competitors to be valid reduces the risk and costs. This was the approach used by Amstrad in the UK consumer electronics market. Furthermore, by deliberately slowing down product launches into the market, it is possible to maximize profits. For example, software companies have been very successful in launching improved versions and upgrades every 6–9 months.

Long-term projects

Looking further into the future, R&D departments will also be developing products that the public does not yet realize it requires. This area also includes starting new initiatives and new areas of research. Technology-intensive companies such as Siemens, Microsoft, Airbus and 3M will be working on products for 2020 and beyond.

Evaluating R&D projects

It is not unusual for technology-intensive firms to have many more ideas than they are able to fund as research projects; the problem, as usual, is limited resources. Inevitably, choices have to be made about which ideas to support and convert to a funded project and which to drop. There have been many studies on this common problem faced by R&D managers (see Farrukh *et al.*, 2000; Cooper, 2001; Carbonell-Foulquie *et al.*, 2003). The decision as to which projects to select for further resources will inevitably result in others being dropped. Typically, in large firms, for every sixty technical ideas considered, approximately twelve will receive funding for further evaluation. Of these, about six will receive further funding for design and development; half of these will be developed into prototypes and may even go for market testing. However, only two will remain for product launch, and, in most cases, only one of these is successful. Figure 11.3 illustrates the dropout rate of project ideas. Dropping an R&D project is theatrically referred to as 'killing a project'. Unsurprisingly, it causes considerable anxiety among those involved, especially when one's fellow scientists have been involved with the project for many months or, in some cases, years. Evaluating research projects, then, is a critical issue.

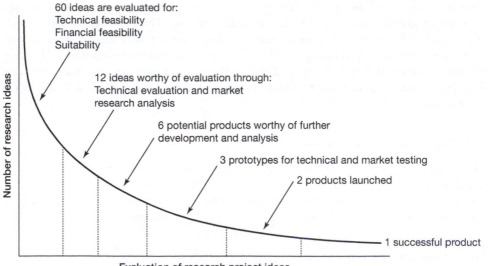

Figure 11.3 Dropout rates

Evaluation criteria

The evaluation criteria used by businesses vary considerably from industry to industry. There is a considerable body of research devoted to this single area of evaluating research projects. This is not surprising, given the long list of famous cases illustrating how many firms rejected projects that later turned into extremely successful products. To this list we must now add that the world's best-selling human drug – Pfizer's Viagra – was almost dropped because of the market-research findings (see Box 11.1).

It is important to recognize that, although many firms may state publicly that they adopt quantitative weighted scoring models or specially adapted software to evaluate all project ideas, inevitably, as with so many business decisions, there is an element of judgement. After all, that is what managers are in position to do – make decisions based on their experience and expertise. This is confirmed by a study of R&D decision-making in the electronic sensors industry by Liddle (2004). He argues that managers continue to rely on rules of thumb and heuristics for the evaluation of research projects.

Whether businesses use formal evaluation models or more informal methods, most will involve some or all of the checklist items shown in Table 11.4. This can be developed further using a weighted checklist or scoring model in which each factor is scored on a scale. A relative weight reflecting the importance of that factor is used as a multiple, and the weighted scores for all factors are added.

The NPD literature offers a plethora of screening and decision-making methods and techniques aimed at assisting managers in making this difficult evaluation. Cooper (2001) identifies three broad categories of screening methods:

1   benefit measurement models;
2   economic models; and
3   portfolio selection models.

Chapter summary

This chapter has discussed the challenge of developing further new products once a venture is established. Having a successful product is rarely sufficient to ensure long-term survival. Firms need to start planning the next generation of new products that will flow from the firm. This chapter has discussed many of the common approaches used by firms to create and manage the development of new products. It has also looked at some of the common problems faced by established firms in getting products to the marketplace.

Study questions

1   Apply the notion of product platform to a technology start-up firm you are familiar with. What are the issues that would need to be considered to ensure it would be successful?
2   Would you agree that product portfolio analysis is too simplistic to be of much value?
3   Trace the connections between differentiation strategy, core capabilities and positioning strategy. How are they relevant to new product planning?
4   Are brand extensions as relevant in industrial markets as in consumer markets? Do they have a strategic role, or are they short-term tactical exercises?

Box 11.1 Pfizer's Viagra almost slipped away!

Pfizer's Viagra is now part of business folklore as an example of a successful new product. Viagra is one of the most recognized brands in the world; it has become a social icon, with sales in excess of US$1.9 billion; and it has transformed Pfizer from a medium-sized pharmaceutical firm into the world's leader. However, Viagra was almost dismissed during clinical trials as interesting, but not clinically or financially significant.

The discovery of Viagra was unintended, in that it fell out of clinical trials for a new drug being developed for the treatment of angina (angina is defined as brief attacks of chest pain due to insufficient oxygenation of heart muscles). In 1992, following 7 years of research, a clinical trial was undertaken in Wales for a compound known as UK-92.480. The findings from the trial on healthy volunteers revealed disappointing results. The data on blood pressure, heart rate and blood flow were discouraging. The R&D project was in trouble. Some patients reported side effects of episodes of indigestion, some reported aches in their legs, and some reported penile erections. This final point was listed merely as an observation; at that moment, no one said 'Wow' or 'Great'. Indeed, the decision to undertake trials into erectile dysfunction was not an obvious one. This was partly because the prevailing view at the time was that most

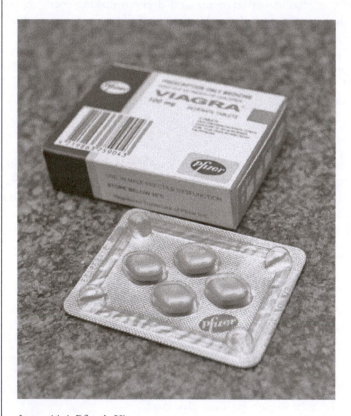

Image 11.1 Pfizer's Viagra
Source: © SElefant

erectile dysfunction was psychological and not treatable with drugs. Few people believed it was possible to produce an erection with an injection of drugs. Pfizer was preparing to drop the angina R&D project owing to its disappointing results. It was also considering dropping all studies on the compound, even as a possible drug for erectile dysfunction. This was partly because it was not clear that it would have a clinical use. Not all the healthy volunteers had reported erections. How would Pfizer be able to conduct trials for such a condition? Moreover, the market for such a drug was not clear. At that time, survey results revealed only 1 in 20 million men suffered from erectile dysfunction; hence, even if a medicine could be developed, the market would be very small. The R&D team involved in the project managed to gain 2 years of funding to develop the drug and undertake clinical trials. The rest is, as they say, history. Moreover, the actual market for this type of drug is now known to be far greater than the data had revealed. This is a cautionary tale of the need sometimes to encourage innovation and support scientific freedom in the face of evidence to stop the project.

Table 11.4 R&D project evaluation criteria

Criteria	Typical questions
1 Technical	Do we have experience of the technology? Do we have the skills and facilities? What is the probability of technical success?
2 Research direction and balance	Compatibility with research goals? Balance of risk in project portfolio?
3 Competitive rationale	How does this project compare with the competition? Is it necessary to defend an existing business? Is the product likely to be superior?
4 Patentability	Can we get patent protection? What will be the implication for defensive research?
5 Stability of the market	How stable is the technology? Is the market developed? Is there an industry standard?
6 Integration and synergy	What is the level of integration of this project relative to other products and raw materials? Will it stand alone?
7 Market	What is the size of the market? Is it a growing market? Is there an existing customer base? Is the potential big enough to warrant the resources?
8 Channel fit	Do we have existing customers who might be interested, or do we have to find new customers?
9 Manufacturing	Can we use existing resources? Will we require new equipment, skills, etc.?
10 Financial	Expected investment required and rate of return?
11 Strategic fit	Does it support our short-term and long-term plans for the business?

5   The software industry seems to have a very flexbile NPD process enabling changes to be made to the product at any time. Consider whether this approach could be applicable for other industries, such as mobile-phone handsets.

6   Explain why TTM may be less important than a flexible NPD process.

References

Babcock, D. L. (1996). *Managing Engineering Technology: An introduction to management for engineers* (2nd edn). London: Prentice Hall.

Brown, J. S. and Eisenhardt, K. M. (1998). *Competing on the Edge: Strategy as structured chaos*. Boston, MA: Harvard Business School.

Carbonell-Foulquie, P., Munuera-Aleman, J. L. and Rodriquez-Escudero, A. I. (2003). Criteria employed for go/no-go decisions when developing successful highly innovative products. *Industrial Marketing Management*. 33(4): 307–16.

Cooper, R. G. (2001). *Winning at New Products* (3rd edn). Cambridge, MA: Perseus.

Cooper, R. G. and Edgett, S. J. (2008). Maximizing productivity in product innovation. *Research Technology Management*. 51(2): 47–58.

Cooper R.G. and Edgett, S.J. (2008). Maximizing productivity in product innovation, *Research Technology Management*, March.

Crawford, C. M. (1997). *New Products Management* (4th edn). Burr Ridge, IL: Irwin.

Deschamps, J. P. and Nayak, P. R. (1995). *Product Juggernauts: How companies mobilize to generate a stream of winners*. Boston, MA: Harvard Business School Press.

Doyle, P. (1995). Marketing in the new millennium. *European Journal of Marketing*. 29(13): 23–41.

Farrukh, C., Phaal, R., Probert, D., Gregory, M. and Wright, J. (2000). Developing a process for the relative valuation of R&D programmes. *R&D Management*. 30(1): 43–53.

Felekoglu, B. and Moultrie, J. (2014). Top Management Involvement in New Product Development: A Review and Synthesis. *Journal of Product Innovation Management*, 31:159–175.

Franke, N. and Piller, F. (2004). Value creation by toolkits for user innovation and design: The case of the watch market. *Journal of Product Innovation Management*. 21(6): 401–16.

Hamel, G. and Prahalad, C. K. (1994). Competing for the future. *Harvard Business Review*. 72(4): 122–8.

Hippel, E. von (1986). Lead users: A source of novel product concepts. *Management Science*. 32(7): 791–805.

Hippel, E. von (2001). Perspective: User toolkits for innovation. *The Journal of Product Innovation Management*. 18: 247–57.

Hippel, E. von (2007). Horizontal innovation networks – By and for users. *Industrial and Corporate Change*. 16(2): 293–315.

Kettunen, P. (2009). Adopting key lessons from agile manufacturing to agile software product development – A comparative study. *Technovation*. 29(6–7): 408–22.

Kim, J. and Wilemon, D. (2002). Focusing the fuzzy front end in new product development. *R&D Management*. 32(4): 269–79.

Kim, K. and Chhajed, D. (2000). Commonality in product design: Cost saving, valuation change and cannabilisation. *European Journal of Operational Research*. 125(3): 602–21.

Koen, P., Ajamian, G., Burkart, R., Clamen, A., Davidson, J., Ámore, R. D., Elkins, C., Herald, K., Incorvia, M., Johnson, A., Karol, R., Seibert, R., Slavejkov, A. and Wagner, K. (2001). Providing clarity and a common language to the 'fuzzy front end'. *Research Technology Management*. March–April: 46–55.

Krishnan, V. and Ulrich, K. T. (2001). Product development decisions: A review of the literature. *Management Science*. 47(1): 1–21.

Leifer, R., McDermott, C. M., O'Connor, G. C., Peters, L. S., Rice, M. P. and Veryzer, R. W. (2000). *Radical Innovation: How mature companies can outsmart upstarts*. Boston, MA: Harvard Business School Press.

Levitt, T. (1986). *The Marketing Imagination*. New York: The Free Press.

Liddle, D. (2004). R&D 'Project selection at Danahar', MBA dissertation, University of Portsmouth.

McGrath, M. (2001). *Product Strategy for High-Technology Companies – Accelerating your business to web speed* (2nd edn). Blacklick, OH: McGraw-Hill.

Mohr, J., Sengupta, S. and Slater, S. (2010). *Marketing of High-Technology Products and Innovations* (3rd edn). Harlow, UK: Prentice Hall.

Muffatto, M. and Roveda, M. (2000). Developing product platforms: Analysis of the development process. *Technovation*. 20(11): 617–30.

Nambisan, S. (2002). Designing virtual customer environments for new product development: Toward a theory. *Academy of Management Review*. 27(3): 392–413.

Salomo, S., Keinschmidt, E. J. and De Brentani, U. (2010). Managing new product development teams in a globally dispersed NPD program. *Journal of Product Innovation Management*. 27(7): 955–71.

Sivasubramaniam, N., Liebowitz, S. J. and Lackman, C. L. (2012). Determinants of New Product Development Team Performance: A Meta-analytic Review. *Journal of Product Innovation Management*, 29: 803–20.

Smith, P. G. (2007). *Flexible Product Development: Building agility for changing markets*. San Francisco, CA: John Wiley.

Thomke, S. H. (2003). *Experimentation Matters: Unlocking the potential of new technologies for innovation*. Boston, MA: Harvard Business School Press.

Veryzer, R. (2003). 'Marketing and the development of innovative products', in L. Shavinina (ed.), *The International Handbook on Innovation*. Oxford: Elsevier, pp. 845–55.

Wheelwright, S. C. and Clark, K. B. (1992). *Revolutionising Product Development*. New York: The Free Press.

Wind, Y. (1982). *Product Policy*. Reading, MA: Addison-Wesley.

Further reading

For a more detailed review of the product and brand management literature, the following develop many of the issues raised in this chapter:

Biemans, W. G., Griffin, A. and Moenaert, R. K. (2007). Twenty Years of the *Journal of Product Innovation Management*: History, participants, and knowledge stocks and flows. *Journal of Product Innovation Management*. 24: 193–213.

Biemans, W., Griffin, A. and Moenaert, R. (2010). In search of the classics: A study of the impact of *JPIM* papers from 1984 to 2003. *Journal of Product Innovation Management*. 27: 461–84.

Gawer, A. and Cusumano, M. A. (2014). Industry Platforms and Ecosystem Innovation. *Journal of Product Innovation Management*, 31: 417–33.

Henard, D. H. and McFadyen, M. A. (2012). Resource Dedication and New Product Performance: A Resource-Based View. *Journal of Product Innovation Management*, 29: 193–204.

Kahn, K. B., Barczak, G., Nicholas, J., Ledwith, A. and Perks, H. (2012). An Examination of New Product Development Best Practice. *Journal of Product Innovation Management*, 29: 180–92.

Sivasubramaniam, N., Liebowitz, S. J. and Lackman, C. L. (2012). Determinants of New Product Development Team Performance: A Meta-analytic Review. *Journal of Product Innovation Management*, 29: 803–20.

Stanko, M. A., Molina-Castillo, F.-J. and Munuera-Aleman, J.-L. (2012). Speed to Market for Innovative Products: Blessing or Curse? *Journal of Product Innovation Management*, 29: 751–65.

Stock, R. M. (2014). How Should Customers Be Integrated for Effective Interorganizational NPD Teams? An Input–Process–Output Perspective. *Journal of Product Innovation Management*, 31: 535–51.

Thomas, R. J. (1995). *New Product Success Stories*. New York: John Wiley.

Zirpoli, F. and Camuffo, A. (2009). Product architecture, inter-firm vertical coordination and knowledge partitioning in the auto industry. *European Management Review*. 6(4): 250–64.

12 Expectations of entrepreneurs and patterns of growth

Introduction
The mainstream pattern of development and diffusion
The pattern reconsidered
What happens in the adaptation phase?
Implications of the pattern for entrepreneurs
Discussion
Chapter summary
Study questions
References

Introduction

This chapter focuses on entrepreneurs who have just mastered a technological principle and are about to introduce a radically new high-tech product on the basis of that principle. Although these entrepreneurs may feel as if they have completed a long journey now they have mastered a working principle and developed a radically new high-tech product, we will explain that another long and exciting journey is yet to start. The chapter discusses what these entrepreneurs can expect when introducing their product in the market.

A radically new high-tech product represents a new combination of functionality and a technological principle. It can be a finished product, material, part or component of a technological system. Examples of these products, at the time of their first introduction, were telegraphy and mobile telephony in the telecommunications market, insulin and Viagra in the medical market, nylon and Kevlar in the materials market, and the transistor and LCD screens in the electronic-equipment market. These products enabled a new functionality or were based on a new technological principle at the time of their introduction. These products typically offered unprecedented shifts in price/performance over time and, thereby, transformed existing markets. Following the typology proposed by Garcia and Calantone (2002), we therefore refer to these high-tech products as radically new.

Many radically new high-tech products were introduced in the past. At the time of invention, most entrepreneurs had no clue about what they could expect. To illustrate the point, we will describe the case of memory metal. Memory metal refers to an alloy that, after its shape has been changed, will return to its original shape when heated. The alloy seems to remember the previous shape when it is heated. Box 12.1 gives some descriptions about the invention of the alloy.

The first cited source indicates that the technological principle of memory metal was discovered in the 1930s. The next sources indicate that this discovery remained obscure

Box 12.1 The invention of memory metal

The principle of shape memory for certain alloys was first noted in the 1930s. [. . .] The shape-memory effect also known as mechanical recall was first noted by Arne Olander, a Swedish researcher, in 1932.

(Johnson, 1988, p. 17)

The discovery of shape memory in Au-Cd and Cu-Zn occurred with little fanfare in somewhat obscure technical papers with little, if any, follow-on work. However, when the shape memory effect was rediscovered in equiatomic Ni-Ti in 1962, there was suddenly a great deal of commercial interest.

(Duerig *et al.*, 1999, p. 149)

The breakthrough for engineering applications occurred with the discovery of NiTi by Buehler and coworkers while investigating materials useful for heat shielding. It was noticed that in addition to its good mechanical properties, comparable to some common engineering metals, the material also possessed a shape recovery capability. Following this observation, the term 'NiTiNOL' was coined for this NiTi material in honour of its discovery at the Naval Ordnance Laboratory (NOL). The term Shape Memory Effect (SME) was given to the associated shape recovery behaviour. The discovery of Nitinol spearheaded active research interest into SMAs. The effects of heat treatment, composition and microstructure were widely investigated and began to be understood during this period.

(Kumar and Lagoudas, 2008, p. 4)

until the principle was reinvented in the 1960s in the US Naval labs. From then on, the interest in this remarkable principle increased. At first, it was completely unclear what could be potential applications for this remarkable principle. The inventors had no idea about the pattern of development and diffusion that was yet to come, let alone about the strategies that they could adopt to commercialize their remarkable finding. Although each case of a radically new high-tech product is different, many of these cases have in common that the inventors and entrepreneurs have no idea about the pattern of development and diffusion that will unfold over time and the strategies that they can adopt to commercialize their finding.

The issue of what to expect will be discussed by looking at the pattern of development and diffusion of high-tech products. We will indicate what types of phase can be distinguished in this pattern, and how long these phases last on average. In practice, the length of these phases can vary considerably. Depending on the length of the phases, different scenarios can be distinguished. The implications for entrepreneurs will be discussed.

The next section will describe the mainstream ideas about the pattern of development and diffusion. In the third section, this pattern will be reconsidered. The fourth section will describe what happens in the adaptation phase, and the fifth will describe the implications of the pattern for entrepreneurs. The chapter ends with conclusions and a short discussion.

Box 12.2 Learning goals of the chapter

After reading this chapter, you should be able to:

- describe two models of the pattern of development and diffusion of high-tech products;
- describe three phases in the pattern and indicate the average length of these phases;
- describe different scenarios or versions of the pattern; and
- describe implications of the pattern for entrepreneurs.

The mainstream pattern of development and diffusion

The mainstream idea about development is that it can be seen as a project, a new product development project (NPD project). The typical NPD project is described by many handbooks (e.g. Wind, 1982; Crawford, 1991; Urban and Hauser, 1993; Tidd *et al.*, 2001; Trott, 2002). When development is completed, the innovation is introduced into the market, and customers start to adopt it. This gradual adoption is referred to as the diffusion of the innovation in the market. The mainstream idea about diffusion is that, when the cumulative number of customers is measured over time, this diffusion looks like an S-shaped curve. The so-called diffusion curve is described for many cases and thoroughly discussed by Rogers (2003).

The notion that the characteristics of a new product idea can be evaluated and that this evaluation can indicate later successfulness would be most useful. This notion has stimulated a lengthy scientific debate and accompanying research projects searching for success factors (Cooper and Kleinschmidt, 1995; Di Benedetto, 1999; Ernst, 2002; Panne *et al.*, 2003). If these success factors are known and are predictive of later success, and the development and introduction of new products can be managed to take these factors into account, then new product development and introduction becomes a kind of competence. Indeed, some companies seem to master this competence and are able to introduce relatively many successful new products (Galbraith *et al.*, 2006).

Another notion is that the success of product innovations can be assessed in terms of their diffusion pattern. Successful innovations diffuse in an S-shaped diffusion curve; conversely, abbreviations from this curve imply a lack of potential and success. This view is reflected in the ideas summarized in the left column of Table 12.1.

This perspective on development and diffusion, that innovation is an NDP project the success of which can be assessed in terms of the diffusion curve, is challenged by empirical findings. First, it is remarkable that NPD success rates remain constant and quite low over the decades (Crawford, 1977, 1979, 1987). That seems to imply that the overall learning rate is disappointingly low. More specific studies, investigating the antecedents of success of NPD efforts, such as the PDMA studies, indicate that success cannot simply be related to the type of development process (Griffin, 1997). Both companies adopting well-known and up-to-date NPD process practices and some with more ad hoc working processes in innovation are able to be successful. Finally, entrepreneurs mostly do not describe their development process as a structured project.

The pattern reconsidered

Let us reconsider what happens after the invention of a new principle and before the diffusion of products based on that principle. In fact, it has been shown that almost all those radically new high-tech innovations that later on successfully diffuse in an S-shaped pattern are introduced long before the large-scale diffusion starts. This period before large-scale diffusion shows an erratic diffusion pattern, and apparently that erratic process does not indicate a lack of success. So, abbreviations from the S-shaped diffusion process do not indicate a lack of success for the product innovation. Instead, this period is required to overcome all barriers that prevent large-scale diffusion and thereby paves the way for later, large-scale diffusion (Ortt and Schoormans, 2004; Ortt, 2010).

The erratic process of diffusion also indicates that development of the innovation continues next to diffusion. The product needs to be improved to compensate initial bucks for example. But the product also needs to be adapted to different customer segments and usage situations. These processes of improvement and adaptation require innovation processes after introduction. So, the idea that innovation is just one development project prior to market introduction is a simplification.

Ortt and Schoormans (2004) propose a model with three phases to describe the entire process of the development and diffusion of radically new high-tech products: the innovation phase, the market adaptation phase and the market stabilization phase. The innovation phase comprises the period from the invention of a technology up to the first market introduction of a product incorporating the technology. The second phase, referred to as the market adaptation phase, begins after the first market introduction of a product on the basis of a breakthrough technology and ends when the diffusion of this product takes off. After the first introduction, instead of a smooth S-curve, in practice an erratic process of diffusion may occur (Clark, 1985). The diffusion is often characterized by periodic introduction, decline and reintroduction of multiple products in multiple small-scale applications (Carey and Moss, 1985). The third phase, referred to as the market stabilization phase, begins when the diffusion of a product on the basis of the breakthrough technology takes off and ends when the technology is substituted. In this phase, the diffusion of a product mostly resembles an S-curve. Similar phases are distinguished by Agarwal and Bayus (2002) and Tushman and Anderson (1986). A graph showing the three phases is given in Figure 12.1.

Table 12.1 Two views on the pattern of development and diffusion contrasted

The mainstream pattern	The pattern reconsidered
Two phases can be distinguished: an innovation phase and a diffusion phase	Three phases can be distinguished: an innovation phase, an adaptation phase and a stabilization phase
In the innovation phase, a new product development project is scheduled	The innovation phase lasts from invention to first market introduction. In this phase, usually many companies work on innovations in parallel, while basic research on the technology proceeds
The diffusion phase is characterized by the gradual adoption of the innovation	The adaptation phase lasts from first introduction to the start of large-scale production and diffusion. In this phase, multiple product variants are introduced for different niches of customers
Successful innovations diffuse on a large scale in an S-shaped diffusion curve	The stabilization phase resembles the diffusion phase of the mainstream pattern

Box 12.3 The pattern for television

The pattern of development and diffusion can be illustrated by the television case. Electronic television systems were first demonstrated between 1926 and 1927 and were introduced in Germany around 1935 and in the US in 1939, both on a small scale, in a specific application. It took until late 1948 before large-scale diffusion started (Monfort, 1949; Knapp and Tebo, 1978; Van Den Ende *et al.*, 1997/1998). In this case, the Second World War may explain some of the delay in the diffusion. However, for other telecommunication appliances, materials, medicines and many breakthrough innovations, a similar succession of hallmarks such as the invention, first introduction and large-scale production and use can be seen.

Image 12.1 Old TV
Source: © Frank Edens

An overview of essential milestones in the process of development and diffusion of the photocopier, video cassette recorder, digital camera and microwave oven is given in Table 12.1.

From Table 12.1, it can be seen that the length of the early phases preceding the large-scale diffusion in a mass market took at least two decades for each of the cases. This is quite long, especially if one compares this with the period that patents remain valid (about

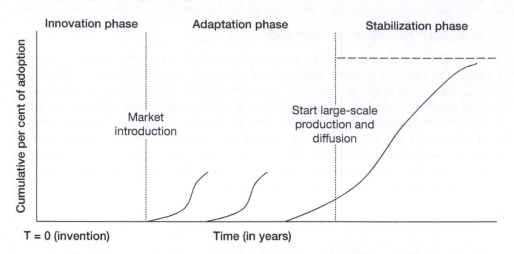

Figure 12.1 Three phases in the diffusion process

Table 12.2 Milestones in the process of development and diffusion of the products in our cases

Cases	Invention	Length of innovation phase	Market introduction	Length of market adaptation phase	Diffusion takes off	Length of innovation + market adaptation phase
Photocopier	1938	11	1949	27	1976	38
Video recorder	1951	5	1956	15	1971	20
Digital camera	1970	3	1973	17	~1990	20
Microwave oven	1945	2	1947	25	1972	27

Source: Ortt *et al.*, 2007

18 years). Similar periods have been found by other authors (Mansfield, 1968; Utterback and Brown, 1972; Agarwal and Bayus, 2002). With a larger, heterogeneous data set of fifty cases of radically new high-tech products, we found that the average length for the innovation phase is about 10 years, and the average length for the adaptation phase is about 7 years (Ortt, 2010). In Table 12.2, we contrast the two views on the pattern of development and diffusion for high-tech products.

We found large variations around these average numbers. In fact, each phase can even disappear in specific situations. These ideas are summarized in two propositions:

1   The phases can vary considerably in length. One or more phases may disappear.
2   The entire process can stop in each phase.

These propositions convey a more unpredictable process than the smooth S-shaped pattern. A description of this pattern can be found in the left column of Table 12.1. In practice, the actors involved in the commercialization of breakthrough technologies may face different scenarios. After studying the pattern of development and diffusion of fifty breakthrough

Scenario 1: Long innovation phase after invention

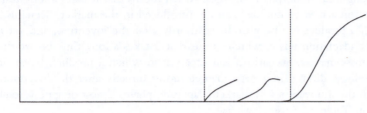

Scenario 2: Long market adaptation phase after invention

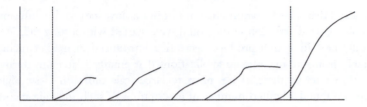

Scenario 3: Large-scale diffusion directly after invention

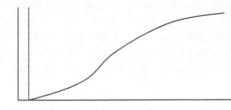

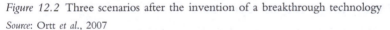

Figure 12.2 Three scenarios after the invention of a breakthrough technology
Source: Ortt *et al.*, 2007

Table 12.3 Examples of cases with a pattern that resembles one of the scenarios

Scenario	Case	Invention	Length of innovation phase	Market introduction	Length of market adaptation phase	Diffusion takes off
1	Radar technology	1904	30	1934	5	1939
	PVC	1838	93	1931	7	1938
2	Contraceptive pill	1927	1	1928	34	1962
	Laser	1960	1	1961	19	1980
3	Dynamite	1866	1	1867	0	1867
	X–ray	1895	1	1896	0	1896

Source: Ortt *et al.*, 2007

technologies, we distinguish three important scenarios (see Figure 12.2). Scenario 1 is a situation in which a long innovation phase emerges, which means that it takes a long time before a product based on a new technology can be introduced in the market. Scenario 2 is a situation in which a product can be introduced shortly after the invention, and yet it requires a long market adaptation phase, which means that it takes a long time before this product diffuses in a mass market. Scenario 3 is a situation in which a product, based on a breakthrough technology, diffuses in a mass market almost directly after the invention, which means that both the innovation and market adaptation phases almost disappear. Each scenario is illustrated in Table 12.3 using two cases.

What happens in the adaptation phase?

It is important to understand that the adaptation phase is not just a slow start to the diffusion process. In that case, the S-shaped diffusion curve could have started with a long tail. We found that many radically new high-tech products were first introduced in market niches that diverged considerably from the mainstream applications that emerged later on, during the stabilization phase. We refer to these niches prior to large-scale diffusion as strategic niches. In the literature, we found a limited number of descriptions of such strategic niches (see Table 12.4).

The cases in Table 12.4 illustrate that multiple applications appear over time for radically new high-tech products. The market for the digital camera, for example, evolved from specialized professional applications (space research, satellites, medical applications and news reporting) to the mainstream applications we know now (photography for consumers). Almost all cases show a similar transfer from specialized business or government applications towards mainstream consumer applications. Nylon, as a breakthrough material, is an outlier. It was, almost in complete secrecy, applied in toothbrushes to test the material prior to large-scale applications.

Implications of the pattern for entrepreneurs

The reconsidered pattern of development and diffusion differs considerably from the mainstream pattern. We will discuss several implications of this reconsidered pattern for entrepreneurs. These implications indicate what entrepreneurs can expect when they are about to introduce a radically new high-tech product.

First, the findings indicate that commercializing radically new high-tech products generally is a matter of long endurance. The time from the invention of such a product up to the point where diffusion takes off covers about two decades, on average. This implies that small companies that essentially focus on one product may be confronted with cash-flow problems during this period. Large companies and governmentally subsidized organizations may be in a better position to survive this period. On the other hand, these companies and organizations, because of their overheads, typically require sizeable markets and demand lower risks. These types of market are seldom available during the adaptation phase. This is why these companies and organizations have a tendency to wait and see: they monitor how the market evolves, how small entrepreneurial companies perform (or crash and burn) and how the price/performance of high-tech products develops compared with mainstream products.

Second, large-scale diffusion is an important consequence of success, but, in most cases, this diffusion is preceded by a phase in which multiple product variants diffuse in several customer segments. This phase is referred to as the adaptation phase. Large-scale diffusion is not an indicator or predictor of success but a consequence that appears quite late. Many,

Table 12.4 Historical precedents of subsequent niche applications

Author(s)	Product	Market applications
Mark *et al.* (1985)	Early computer (mainframe computer)	Complex calculation for ballistic missiles in military★ Scientific application (universities/research agencies)★ Business data processing for limited corporate customer★ General business application
Brown (1992)	Pocket calculators during 1970s	Engineers and scientists★ Accountants and other commercial users★ General public School children
	Nylon	Parachute fabric and military cloths★ Ladies' lingerie★ Low-cost carpets Fabric for consumer cloths
Levinthal (1998)	Radial tyres	High-performance sports cars★ Replacement tyres for mainstream car owners Original equipment manufacturers' market of automobile manufacturers
	Video recorder	Broadcasting industry★ Industrial and commercial users★ Mass consumer electronic market
Windrum and Birchenhall (1998)	PC	Business with low-intensity computing needs★ Designers/artists/musicians who demanded high-quality graphics and multimedia★ Individual/ordinary users
Ortt *et al.* (2007)	Photocopier	Corporate and government offices★ Catalogue publishers★ Small and medium businesses★ Individuals
	Video recorder	Broadcast industry★ Schools★ Police department★ Households
	Digital camera	Space research★ Satellite and medical applications★ News reporter★ Individual/family use
	Microwave oven	Hospitals★ Schools★ Restaurants★ Railways and ocean liners★ Households

Note: ★Strategic niches, later applications are mass-market applications
Source: Ortt and Suprapto, 2011

later successful, high-tech products were at first confronted with disappointing levels of diffusion. In this adaptation phase, entrepreneurs try to match specific product variants with the needs and demands of specific customer segments and, while doing so, have to circumvent all types of market barrier with which radically new products are typically confronted. During diffusion, the technology evolves. The new product typically has to compete with traditional products supplied by incumbent companies and, at the same time, has to compete with other new types of product also trying to gain a foothold in the market. The adaptation phase requires entrepreneurial skills. During the innovation phase, assessment of what type of product variants and applications later on will form a mainstream market is highly uncertain.

Box 12.4 A dry toothbrush

Before the invention of nylon was announced by DuPont, consumers unknowingly had a taste of the new material, literally. When preparing to produce nylon commercially, DuPont tested prototype machinery in two trial facilities, the semi-works (1936) and the pilot plant (1938), before full-scale commercial production began in 1939. The nylon polymer produced at the semi-works during equipment testing was not suitable for making yarn for hosiery. Nonetheless, DuPont found a use for the nylon polymer made at the semi-works. In 1937, before the invention of nylon was announced, the amazing new Dr. West's Miracle-Tuft toothbrush hit the market. Unbeknown to consumers, its bristles were made from nylon polymer produced at the semi-works. DuPont didn't reveal the chemical nature of the new bristles. It simply referred to the material by the name 'Exton'. The new toothbrush actually dried out in the time between uses, unlike the old boar-bristle brushes. It was the public's first experience with a polymer that would soon change their lives.

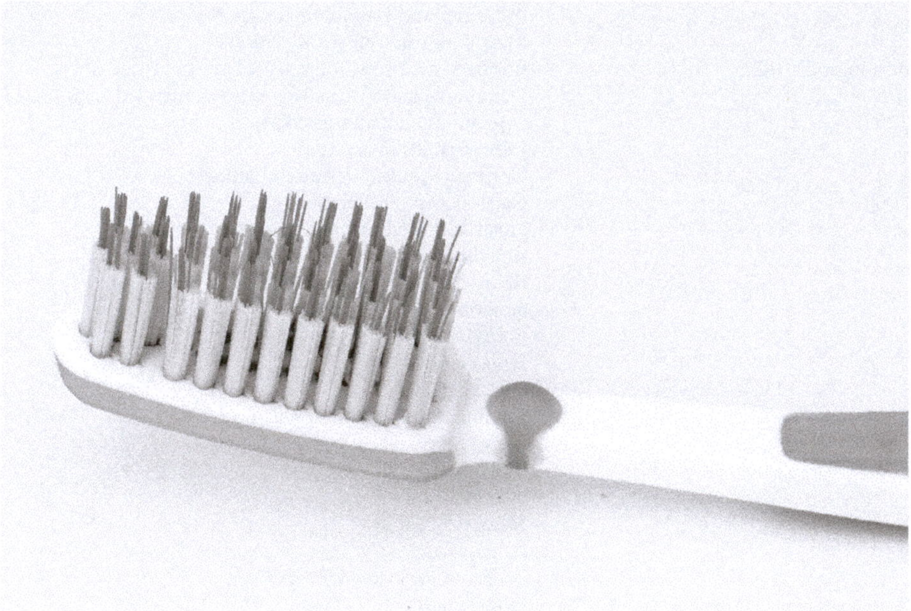

Image 12.2 Toothbrush
Source: © Marie-Lan Nguyen

Source: www.chemheritage.org/discover/media/magazine/
articles/26-3-nylon-a-revolution-in-textiles.aspx

Third, in individual cases, the exact pattern of development and diffusion is also highly uncertain. We could identify the three phases in the pattern for more than fifty cases of radically new high-tech products, but the variation in length of the phases in the pattern is considerable for individual cases. This uncertainty is reflected in the three scenarios that were distinguished. The uncertainty caused by the erratic process in the adaptation phase and by the highly uncertain length of the phases in the pattern of development and diffusion for individual cases has serious consequences. It is remarkable how many companies involved in the invention of breakthrough technologies lose out before the technology is applied on a large scale (Olleros, 1986; Pech, 2003). Projects dedicated to breakthrough technologies are risky and expensive and usually take several years to produce results (Leifer *et al.*, 2000). Technical, market and organizational uncertainties associated with these projects are much higher than those associated with projects aimed at incremental improvement (Burgelman and Sayles, 1986). Tellis and Golder (1996) show that 47 per cent of the pioneers who are first to introduce such a product in the market fail and vanish. Examples of pioneering companies that have vanished include Chux (disposable diapers), MITS (PCs) and the Stanley Brothers (automobiles; Olleros, 1986; Tellis and Golder, 1996). These findings imply that the risk for pioneering companies is much higher than the risk for companies introducing incrementally new products. Chapter 9 examined some potential strategies to deal with these risks.

Discussion

To formulate expectations, we used a model describing the pattern of development and diffusion of radically new high-tech products. This model is a considerable improvement on the mainstream life-cycle model that envisions development as a project and diffusion as an S-shaped diffusion curve. It is remarkable to see that this mainstream model in fact represents an exceptional situation rather than the standard situation. Our data indicate that direct, large-scale diffusion can be expected in no more than 20 per cent of the cases of radically new high-tech products. The adaptation phase that we distinguished, in which entrepreneurial strategies have an important role, is altogether omitted from the mainstream model. So, compared with the mainstream model, our model is far more realistic and, thereby, better reflects the uncertainties that entrepreneurs have to face.

Our model is also a simplification. In practice, technological principles do not only turn into one type of product, but may fuse (Kodama, 2014) or split into different categories of product. In reality, the pattern of development and diffusion might evolve even more chaotically than our model indicates.

Chapter summary

This chapter describes several expectations that entrepreneurs should have just after invention of a new technological principle:

- It generally takes a long time from the invention of a technological principle to large-scale diffusion of a product based on that principle. For radically new high-tech products, this takes about two decades on average.
- The mainstream diffusion theory implies that diffusion starts slowly and then proceeds as an S-shaped curve. That curve represents the cumulative number of adopters over time. We claim that the average time of two decades between invention and large-scale diffusion is not just caused by a slow start to the diffusion curve. Instead of a

smooth S-shaped diffusion curve, entrepreneurs can expect a more chaotic pattern of development and diffusion. We distinguished two phases in the time interval from invention to large-scale diffusion.

- The innovation phase (from invention to first introduction) lasts on average about 10 years. In this period, no product diffusion appears, because commercial products are not yet available.
- The adaptation phase (from introduction to large-scale diffusion) lasts on average about 8 years. After introduction, instead of a smooth S-shaped diffusion curve, usually an erratic phase of trial and error emerges, in which multiple product variants are introduced for different customer segments. Entrepreneurs can play an important role here.
- The time interval of the innovation and adaptation phase for individual cases is highly uncertain.
- To illustrate the uncertainty in the innovation and adaptation phase, we presented three scenarios.

Study questions

1   Please have a look again at the data in Table 12.3. We assume that X-ray technology and the principle of the contraceptive pill were equally radical at the time of their invention. They have in common that they seem to fulfil an obvious need, and neither needs extensive infrastructural arrangements. Both principles were introduced on the market about 1 year after their invention. How can the completely different patterns of development and diffusion for these two high-tech principles be explained, then?

- Why could the X-ray technology start diffusing on a large scale almost directly after its first introduction?
- Why was the time between first introduction and large-scale diffusion about 34 years for the contraceptive pill?
- What are the differences between the cases that can explain the difference in the pattern?

2   Suppose that we are investigating the factors that explain why, in some cases, Phase 1 (the innovation phase) is very long or, conversely, very short.

- What would be your starting list of factors explaining the length of the innovation phase? Discuss and compare these factors with the ones suggested by other students.

Suppose you are investigating the factors that explain why, in some cases, Phase 2 (the adaptation phase) is very long or, conversely, very short.

- What would be your starting list of variables explaining the length of the adaptation phase? Discuss and compare these factors with the ones suggested by other students.

3   Please look again at Figure 12.1. This figure represents a stylized version of reality: it is a model that simplifies the actual situation. In reality, the pattern of development and diffusion can have quite different forms. That is why we distinguished scenarios in Figure 12.2. We just distinguished between three scenarios. Many more scenarios can be formed.

- The basic pattern consists of three phases. Suppose that each of the first two phases can be completely omitted, relatively short, average or relatively long. How many scenarios would you get then?
- Sketch the scenarios and try to find an example for each scenario.

4   The cases presented in the chapter are historical cases of radically new high-tech products. The historic nature of the cases implies that we might suffer from a kind of hindsight bias. The cases in the chapter eventually became quite successful, meaning that they eventually diffused on a large scale. In practice, the pattern of development and diffusion of radically new high-tech products can stop before 'complete' diffusion happens.

- Suppose now that within each of the three phases the entire process of development and diffusion can stop. It can stop after invention, it can stop after the first introduction and it can stop just after the start of large-scale diffusion. How many extra scenarios would that imply?
- Do you know an example of a radically new principle that was never actually applied in practice?
- Do you know an example of a radically new product that, after its introduction, completely vanished from the market?

5   Suppose that you are an R&D manager in a company that just invented a radically new principle. Suppose also that you are able to preview the type of scenario for the pattern of development and diffusion that is likely to happen. Now have a look again at Figure 12.2.

- What would be your advice to the director about the type and size of the production capacity that needs to be built up, when you are quite sure that Scenario 3 will appear?
- Contrast that advice with the advice that you would have given in case you had expected Scenario 1 or 2!

References

Agarwal, R. and Bayus, B. L. (2002). The market evolution and sales takeoff of product innovations. *Management Science*. 48(8): 1024–41.

Brown, R. (1992). Managing the 'S' curves of innovation. *Journal of Marketing Management*. 7(2): 189–202.

Burgelman, R. and Sayles, L. R. (1986). *Inside Corporate Innovation*. New York: Free Press.

Carey, J. and Moss, M. L. (1985). The diffusion of telecommunication technologies. *Telecommunications Policy*. 6: 145–58.

Clark, K. B. (1985). The interaction of design hierarchies and market concepts in technological evolution. *Research Policy*. 14: 235–51.

Cooper, R. G. and Kleinschmidt, E. J. (1995). Benchmarking the firm's critical success factors in new product development. *Journal of Product Innovation Management*. 12(5): 374–91.

Crawford, C. M. (1977). Marketing research and the new product failure rate. *Journal of Marketing*. (April): 51–61.

Crawford, C. M. (1979). New product failure rates – Facts and fallacies. *Research Management*. (September): 9–13.

Crawford, C. M. (1987). New product failure rates: A reprise. *Research Management*. (July-August): 20–4.

Crawford, C. M. (1991). *New Products Management* (3rd edn). Homewood, IL: Irwin.

Di Benedetto, C. A. (1999). Identifying the key success factors in new product launch. *Journal of Product Innovation Management*. 16(6): 530–44.

Duerig, T., Pelton, A. and Stockel, D. (1999). An overview of nitinol medical applications. *Materials Science & Engineering*. A273–275: 149–60.

Ernst, H. (2002). Success factors of new product development: A review of the empirical literature. *International Journal of Management Reviews*. 4(1): 1–40.

Galbraith, C. S., Ehrlich, S. B. and DeNoble, A. F. (2006). Predicting technology success: Identifying key predictors and assessing expert evaluation for advanced technologies. *The Journal of Technology Transfer*. 31(6): 673–84.

Garcia, R. and Calantone, R. (2002). A critical look at technological innovation typology and innovativeness terminology: A literature review. *Journal of Product Innovation Management*. 19: 110–32.

Griffin, A. (1997). PDMA research on new product development practices: Updating trends and benchmarking best practices. *Journal of Product Innovation Management*. 14(November): 429–58.

Johnson, A. D. (1988). Shape memory metals. *IEEE Potentials*. (October): 17–19.

Knapp, J. G. and Tebo, J. D. (1978). The history of television. *IEEE Transactions on Cable Television*. CATV-3(4): 130–44.

Kodama, F. (2014). MOT in transition: From technology fusion to technology–service convergence. *Technovation*. 34(9): 505–12.

Kumar, P. K. and Lagoudas, D. C. (2008). 'Introduction to shape memory alloys', in D. C. Lagoudas (ed.), *Shape Memory Alloys; Modeling and engineering applications*. New York: Springer, pp. 1–51.

Leifer, R., McDermott, C. M., O'Connor, G. C., Peters, L. S., Rice, M. P. and Veryzer, R. W. (2000). *Radical Innovation: How mature companies can outsmart upstarts*. Boston, MA: Harvard Business School Press.

Levinthal, D. A. (1998). The slow pace of rapid technological change: Gradualism and punctuation in technological change. *Industrial and Corporate Change*, 7(2): 217–47.

Mansfield, E. (1968). *Industrial Research and Technological Innovation: An econometric analysis*. London: Longmans, Green & Co.

Mark, J., Chapman, G. M. and Gibson, T. (1985). Bioeconomics and the theory of niches. *Futures*. 17(6): 632–51.

Monfort, R. A. (1949). A brief history of television for the layman. *Hollywood Quarterly*, 4(2): 197–200.

Olleros, F. (1986). Emerging industries and the burnout of pioneers. *Journal of Product Innovation Management*. 1: 5–18.

Ortt, J. R. (2010). 'Understanding the pre-diffusion phases', in J. Tidd (ed.), *Gaining Momentum: Managing the diffusion of innovations*. London: Imperial College Press, pp. 47–80.

Ortt, J. R. and Schoormans, J. P. L. (2004). The pattern of development and diffusion of breakthrough communication technologies. *European Journal of Innovation Management*. 7(4): 292–302.

Ortt, J. R. and Suprapto, M. (2011). The role of strategic niches in creating large-scale applications for high-tech products. *Proceedings of 20th International Conference of the International Association for Management of Technology (IAMOT)*, Miami Beach, FL.

Ortt, J. R., Shah, C. M. and Zegveld, M. A. (2007). Strategies to Commercialize Breakthrough Technologies. *International Association for Management of Technology*. Miami Beach, FL.

Panne, G. van der, Beers, C. van and Kleinknecht, A. (2003). Success and failure of innovation: A literature review. *International Journal of Innovation Management*. 7(3): 309–38.

Pech, R. J. (2003). Memetics and innovation: Profit through balanced meme management. *European Journal of Innovation Management*. 6(2): 111–17.

Rogers, E. M. (2003). *Diffusion of Innovations*. New York: Free Press.

Tellis, G. J. and Golder, P. N. (1996). First to market, first to fail? Real causes of enduring market leadership. *Sloan Management Review*. (Winter): 65–75.

Tidd, J., Bessant, J. and Pavitt, K. (2001). *Managing Innovation: Integrating technological, market and organizational change*. Chichester, UK: Wiley.

Trott, P. (2002). *Innovation Management & New Product Development*. London: Prentice Hall.

Tushman, M. L. and Anderson, P. (1986). Technological discontinuities and organizational environments. *Administrative Science Quarterly*. 31(3): 439–65.

Urban, G. L. and Hauser, J. R. (1993). *Design and Marketing of New Products*. London: Prentice Hall.

Utterback, J. M. and Brown, J. W. (1972). Monitoring for technological opportunities. *Business Horizons*. 15(October): 5–15.

Van Den Ende, J., Ravesteijn, W. and De Wit, D. (1997/1998). Shaping the early development of television. *IEEE Technology & Society Magazine*. (Winter): 13–26.

Wind, Y. J. (1982). *Product Policy: Concepts, methods, and strategy*. Reading, MA: Addison Wesley.

Windrum, P. and Birchenhall, C. (1998). Is product life cycle theory a special case? Dominant designs and the emergence of market niches through coevolutionary-learning. *Structural Change and Economic Dynamics*. 9: 109–34.

Index